NEWSPAPER LIBRARIES IN THE U.S. AND CANADA

Second Edition

An SLA Directory

Elizabeth L. Anderson, Editor

Special Libraries Association
Newspaper Division
New York, New York

© Copyright 1980
Special Libraries Association
235 Park Avenue South
New York, New York 10003

Library of Congress Cataloging in Publication Data

Special Libraries Association. Newspaper Division.
　Newspaper libraries in the U.S. and Canada.

　　Includes indexes.
　1. Newspaper office libraries--United States--
Directories.　2. Newspaper office libraries--Canada--
Directories.　I. Anderson, Elizabeth L.　II. Title.
Z675.N4S63 1980　　026'.07　　80-25188
ISBN 0-87111-265-5

0-87111-265-5

TABLE OF CONTENTS

	Page
Forward	iv
Acknowledgments	v
Description of Listings	vi
Description of Responses	vii
List of Abbreviations	viii
How to Use This Directory	ix
U.S. Listings	1
Canadian Listings	277
Appendix: Washington, D.C. Bureau Libraries	298
U.S. City Index	299
Canadian City Index	305
U.S. Newspaper Group Index	306
Canadian Newspaper Group Index	311
Personnel Index	312

FORWARD

The first <u>Directory of Newspaper Libraries in the United States and Canada</u> was published in cooperation with Special Libraries Association in 1976. It included over 250 libraries in news media organizations.

Innovations in automated retrieval systems and in microfilm applications in news libraries, the expansion of library staffs, and the establishment of new libraries make a new edition necessary barely four years later.

The Directory is indispensable. It provides obviously useful information, gathered in one place, for the names and addresses of our colleagues.

It has proven itself invaluable to editors and reporters, in their quest for information, always on deadline it seems, as the telephone numbers enable the librarian to call his/her colleagues directly. This networking increases the scope of any newspaper library 350 times!

Additionally, the Directory has proven useful to artists. The Directory has been one of the few places where newspaper logos are accurately recorded.

A new feature in this new edition is the index to libraries by chain or group affiliation. This is indicative of trends in newspaper libraries, and the information will be useful in nearly every newspaper department.

The 375 member Newspaper Division of Special Libraries Association is the oldest and largest newspaper librarian organization in the world. Members like Liz Anderson, Barbara Seebers, Theresa Butcher, Sue Williams, Grace Parch and Joe Mehr, who undertook and completed this revision in just one year, testify to the efficiency and dedication of the information-oriented leadership of the Newspaper Division.

Sandy Hall
Arizona Daily Star, Tucson, Arizona

Chairman
Newspaper Division
1979-80

ACKNOWLEDGEMENTS

As with any project of this scope, this directory is the result of a great deal of group effort. Thanks go to the committee: to Grace Parch for invaluable advice, to Sue Williams for designing the questionnaire, to Theresa Butcher for compiling the mailing list, to Barbara Seebers for many patient hours machine-formatting entries, and to Joe Mehr for initial guidance and for help in gathering last-minute information.

Many thanks also go to Atef Ziko of Freelance Research Service in Houston -- his tutelage and wealth of ideas eased me over many rough spots. And thanks to Ernest Perez of the Chicago Sun-Times for his well-timed offer to help make phone calls when I needed it most. And thank you Maria Carballosa of the Houston Post staff, for your hours of help running down circulation figures and helping with indexing.

Nancy Viggiano, SLA Publications Manager, was ever helpful and supportive, and I'll always appreciate her encouragement.

This volume was composed and stored on a Lexitron VT 1303 word processor located at Freelance Research Service Inc.'s office in Houston. My thanks to Jennifer Reavis and the staff at Freelance, who put up with my odd hours working on their machine.

Elizabeth Anderson
Houston Post Library

Description of the Listings

This directory is the result of a Newspaper Division project begun in the fall of 1979. A total of 558 newspapers with daily circulations over 25,000 in the U.S. and Canada were contacted. Two follow-up mailings and telephone requests in addition to the first mailing produced a total response of 314, representing a response rate of 56%.

Out of the 117 newspapers in North America with 100,000+ daily circulation, 111 of them -- or 95% -- are listed here.

Arrangement of the listings is geographical, by state, and by city within state. Canadian listings follow the U.S. section and are arranged by province, and by city within province.

Indexes by city, newspaper group, and names of personnel follow the directory listings.

Banners of newspapers were requested, and they are included whenever they were provided by the respondents. We know of no other reference source for locating the style and exact wording of newspaper banners.

The following description of listings is given as an aid in using this directory:

Newspaper Name of newspaper is given as provided. The name may or may not include the city name, which is given at the center of the top of the page.

Letter designations following newspaper names in parentheses indicate time of issue: (m) morning, (e) evening, (S) Sunday, (all day) all day.

Address Mailing address is given, or street address if that was all that was given.

Circulation Figures are taken from the Audit Bureau of Circulation's FAS-FAX reports for March 31, 1979. Unverified figures are given in parentheses.

Telephone Numbers Complete telephone numbers are given in the center near the top of each page, underneath the newspaper banner area. When the library number was unavailable, main switchboard number is provided.

Personnel Person in charge of the library, and any assistant(s) and titles are given below the telphone number. Title such as "Mrs." are dropped whenever possible.

Public Access Many newspaper libraries are set up to serve only or primarily their own staff. Public access in person, by mail or phone is indicated by "yes" if it is available, and by "no" when it is not. "Limitations" describes the parameters of such service.

Services Available Copy machines, readers, and reader/printers available for use in the library are noted.

Hours of Operation Hours indicate the times during the week that staff is on duty in the library.

Resources   Estimates of quantities of clips, photos, etc., are given in whatever acceptable units were provided. Whether in actual numbers of items, or number of filing cabinets, or linear feet, these estimates are meant to provide some quantitative information for items which cannot be exactly counted.
   An "x" indicates simply that the library has some clips, photos, or other resources, but that no quantity was provided.

Microform Holdings   Extent of holdings of own newspaper on microfilm is given. Periodicals on fiche or film are also indicated, as are clippings on microfiche.

Indexes   Any indexes (not including clip files) of each newspaper are noted, as well as time period covered.
   "Other" indexes, such as the New York Times Index, are noted, along with time period covered.

Special Collections   Any collections of special interest.

Automation   Any mechanical filing systems used are described.
   Electronic systems, whether operational or experimental, are described, including information on software and hardware, when available.

Products for Sale   Includes a variety of responses, from photo reprints to fiche sets of special local subjects to library-produced directories.

Description of Responses

	U.S.	Canada
First mailing	151 5 - no libraries*	14
Second mailing	64 9 - no libraries	1
Third mailing	65 1 - no library	4
Total response	295	19

A response rate of 56% was obtained overall.

*Those newspapers which did respond to our questionnaire but did not indicate having at least one full time person designated "librarian" are: (Richmond CA) Independent and Gazette; Orange Coast Daily Pilot (Costa Mesa CA); Diario Las Americas (Miami FL); (Belleville IL) News-Democrat; The Herald-Palladium (St. Joseph MO); St. Cloud (MN) Times; The Gloucester County Times (Woodbury NJ); The Middletown (OH) Journal; The Tribune Chronicle (Warren OH); Youngstown (OH) Vindicator; (West Chester PA) Daily Local News; (Williamsport PA) Sun-Gazette; York (PA) Daily Record; The News (Port Arthur TX); The Wenatchee (WA) World.

LIST OF ABBREVIATIONS

Appt.................. Appointment

Asst.................. Assistant

AV.................... Audio-Visual

c .... Around

CPT................... Current Periodical Titles

Est................... Established

FTE................... Full Time Employees

Ind................... Independent

Misc.................. Miscellaneous

N/A................... Not Available

Negs.................. Negatives

w/.................... With

x .... Extension (see Description of Listings for explanation of x in Resources section of listings)

HOW TO USE THIS DIRECTORY

All alphabetization is word-by-word.

Canadian and U.S. listings are separated throughout, except in the Personnel Index.

Arrangement of the entries
Listings begin with the state of Alabama and follow alphabetically by state. Cities are arranged within states alphabetically, as are newspapers within cities.

Arrangement of the indexes
City index: Cities are listed alphabetical order. For cities with more than one newspaper, paper names follow the city name, in alphabetical order.
Group index: Papers are listed in alphabetical order, first by state, then by newspaper name within state.

For explanation of types of information contained in individual listings, see "Description of the Listings," page iii.

ALABAMA   Birmingham   ALABAMA

Birmingham News (eS)   Circulation
P.O. Box 2553   (e) 178,269
Birmingham AL 35202   (S) 212,724
                 205/325-2409

       Joan Rouse, Reference Librarian
       Betty Huff, Reference Librarian Technician

<u>Lib. est.</u> 1950   <u>Group</u>   Newhouse Newspapers   <u>FTE</u>   2

<u>Public access</u>   <u>Limitations</u>
    in person   yes   Use of microfilm only
    by mail   yes   Will mail microfilm reprints
    by phone   yes   Simple questions only

<u>Services available</u>   <u>Limitations</u>
    copy machine
    reader/printer   yes $4.00 per copy
    reader   yes

<u>Hours of operation</u>   7am-5pm, M-F

<u>Resources</u>
    clips   18 cabinets   books   100+
    photos   47 cabinets   pamphlets
    negs   5 cabinets   maps   100
    CPT   6   AV

<u>Microform holdings</u>
    own newspaper   1888-present
    periodicals
    clippings

<u>Indexes</u>
    own newspaper
    other

<u>Special collections</u>

<u>Automation</u>
  Automated files
    mechanical
    electronic
  Other automated systems

<u>Products for sale</u>

ALABAMA   Birmingham   ALABAMA

Birmingham Post-Herald

Post-Herald (meS)
2200 4th Ave. North
Birmingham AL 35202
            205/325-2492

Circulation
(m) 68,358
(e) 178,269
(S) 212,724

Nancy M. Brown, Librarian
Kay Cupp, Asst. Librarian

Lib. est. 1950   Group Scripps-Howard Newspapers   FTE

Public access
    in person   yes
    by mail   yes
    by phone   yes

Limitations
By permission of Metro Editor

Services available
    copy machine   yes
    reader/printer   yes
    reader   yes

Limitations
Staff only
$4.00 per sheet

Hours of operation   8:30am-10pm, M-F

Resources
    clips   x   books   x
    photos   x   pamphlets   x
    negs   maps   3
    CPT   7+   AV

Microform holdings
    own newspaper   1950-present
    periodicals
    clippings

Indexes
    own newspaper   none
    other   none

Special collections

Automation
   Automated files
     mechanical
     electronic
   Other automated systems

Products for sale

Huntsville Times (eS)　　　　　　　　　　　　　　　Circulation
P.O. Box 1487　　　　　　　　　　　　　　　　　　(e) 52,653
Huntsville AL 35807　　　　　　　　　　　　　　　(S) 56,885
　　　　　　　　　　　　　205/532-4000

　　　　　　　Diane Moore, Librarian

Lib. est. 1961　　　　　Group Newhouse Newspapers　　FTE 1.5

Public access　　　　　　　　Limitations
　　in person　　no
　　by mail　　　yes
　　by phone　　yes

Services available　　　　　　Limitations
　　copy machine　　yes
　　reader/printer　　yes
　　reader

Hours of operation 7am-4pm, M-F

Resources
　　clips　　　thousands　　　　books　　　hundreds
　　photos　　　　　　　　　　　pamphlets　hundreds
　　negs　　　　　　　　　　　　maps
　　CPT　　　　　　　　　　　　AV

Microform holdings
　　own newspaper　　1928-present
　　periodicals
　　clippings

Indexes
　　own newspaper　　none
　　other

Special collections

Automation
　Automated files
　　mechanical
　　electronic
　Other automated systems

Products for sale

Anchorage Times (eS)   Circulation
Box 40   (e) 46,070
Anchorage AK 99501   (S) 52,324
                                    907/279-5622

       Mary Dye, Librarian

<u>Lib. est.</u> 1956   <u>Group</u> Ind.   <u>FTE</u> 2.5

<u>Public access</u>   <u>Limitations</u>
     in person: no
     by mail   no
     by phone   no

<u>Services available</u>   <u>Limitations</u>
     copy machine
     reader/printer
     reader

<u>Hours of operation</u>

<u>Resources</u>
     clips   books
     photos   pamphlets
     negs   maps
     CPT   AV

<u>Microform holdings</u>
     own newspaper
     periodicals
     clippings

<u>Indexes</u>
     own newspaper
     other

<u>Special collections</u>

<u>Automation</u>
   Automated files
     mechanical
       electronic
   Other automated systems

<u>Products for sale</u>   We do make prints (at the discretion
                        of general manager) of photos used in the paper or
                        taken by our staff, and a fee is charged.

ARIZONA　　　　　　　　　　　　　Mesa　　　　　　　　　　　　　　　ARIZONA

Tribune (eS)　　　　　　　　　　　　　　　　　　　Circulation
120 W. 1st Ave.　　　　　　　　　　　　　　　　　(e)　23,000
Mesa AZ 85201　　　　　　　　　　　　　　　　　(S)　(22,963)
　　　　　　　　　　　602/833-1221 x211

　　　　Jeanne Sharp, Librarian/Secretary/Receptionist
　　　　Sandy Johnson

Lib. est. 1978　　　　　　　Group   Ind.　　　　　　FTE   2

Public access　　　　　　　　Limitations
　　in person　　no　　　　　Photocopies to public on request
　　by mail　　　no　　　　　(When possible)
　　by phone　　 no

Services available　　　　　Limitations
　　copy machine　　yes
　　reader/printer
　　reader

Hours of operation　　Library open to staff at all times; librarian's
　　　　　　　　　　　hours are 7:30am-4:30pm

Resources
　　clips　　　x　　　　　　　　　　books　　　　x
　　photos　　 x　　　　　　　　　　pamphlets　　x
　　negs　　　 x　　　　　　　　　　maps　　　　 x
　　CPT　　　　　　　　　　　　　　 AV

Microform holdings
　　own newspaper
　　periodicals
　　clippings

Indexes
　　own newspaper
　　other

Special collections

Automation
　Automated files
　　mechanical
　　electronic
　Other automated systems

Products for sale

THE ARIZONA REPUBLIC
The Phoenix Gazette

Arizona Republic (mS)
Phoenix Gazette (e)
120 E. Van Buren
Phoenix AZ 85004

602/271-8555

Circulation
- (m) 259,783
- (e) 110,714
- (S) 393,396

Marcy Bagley, Head Librarian
Gladys Terry, Asst. Librarian

Lib. est. 1947   Group Ind.   FTE 15

Public access   Limitations
- in person   no
- by mail   yes   Very limited; no research
- by phone   no

Services available   Limitations
- copy machine   yes
- reader/printer yes
- reader   yes

Hours of operation   7am–11:30pm, M–Sat.

Resources
- clips   5,000,000   books   500+
- photos   c. 15,000   pamphlets 200+
- negs   maps
- CPT   AV

Microform holdings
- own newspaper
- periodicals
- clippings

Indexes
- own newspaper
- other

Special collections

Automation
- Automated files
  - mechanical   Diebold
  - electronic
- Other automated systems

Products for sale

The Arizona Daily Star

Arizona Daily Star (mS)
P.O. Box 26807
Tucson AZ 85726

602/294-4433 x345

Circulation
(m) 71,794
(S) 133,640

Elizabeth Miner, Chief Librarian
Elaine Raines, Asst. Librarian
Sandy Hall, Director of Special Services

Lib. est. 1950   Group   Pulitzer Publishing Co.   FTE   13

Public access
    in person   no
    by mail   yes
    by phone   yes

Limitations
    Requests must be specific; payment in advance
    Short requests only; others by mail

Services available
    copy machine   yes
    reader/printer   yes
    reader   yes

Limitations

Hours of operation   7am-11pm, M-F; 8am-11pm, Sat., Sun. and holidays

Resources
clips	1,500,000	books	1,000
photos	160,000	pamphlets	9,000
negs	19,000	maps	400
CPT	38	AV	

Microform holdings
    own newspaper   1877-present
    clippings   12,100 jackets

Indexes
    own newspaper   1953-1979
    other   (use interlibrary loan)

Special collections   Tucson telephone directories from 1937-present; Tucson city directories 1918-present

Automation
  Automated files
    electronic

Products for sale   IRE Series, stories on American Atomics release of tritium in Tucson. On fiche for $25.00.

ARIZONA   Tucson   ARIZONA

Tucson Citizen

Tucson Citizen (e)
P.O. Box 26767
Tucson AZ 85726

602/294-4433 x257

Charlotte Nusser, Librarian
Jeannie Jett, Asst. Librarian

Circulation
(e) 66,940

<u>Lib. est.</u> 1939   <u>Group</u> Gannett Newspapers   <u>FTE</u> 7

<u>Public access</u>   <u>Limitations</u>
    in person   no
    by mail   no
    by phone   no

<u>Services available</u>   <u>Limitations</u>
    copy machine   yes   Staff only
    reader/printer   yes
    reader

<u>Hours of operation</u>   6am-7pm, M-F; 6am-Noon, Sat.

<u>Resources</u>
clips	1,500,000	books	500
photos	150,000	pamphlets	10 drawers
negs	60,000	maps	300
CPT	70	AV	

<u>Microform holdings</u>
    own newspaper   1870-present
    periodicals
    clippings   12,000 jackets

<u>Indexes</u>
    own newspaper
    other

<u>Special collections</u>

<u>Automation</u>
  Automated files
    mechanical
    electronic
  Other automated systems

<u>Products for sale</u>

ARKANSAS   Little Rock   ARKANSAS

Arkansas Democrat

Arkansas Democrat (eS)　　　　　　　　　　　　**Circulation**
Capitol & Scott　　　　　　　　　　　　　　　　(e) 54,927
Little Rock   AR 72203　　　　　　　　　　　　 (S) 99,512
　　　　　　　　　　　501/378-3489

　　　　Betty Seager, Librarian
　　　　Ruth Bergan, Librarian

<u>Lib. est.</u> 1957　　　　　<u>Group</u>   Ind.　　　　　　<u>FTE</u>   2

<u>Public access</u>　　　　　　<u>Limitations</u>
　　in person　　yes
　　by mail　　　yes
　　by phone　　 yes

<u>Services available</u>　　　<u>Limitations</u>
　　copy machine　　yes　　Fee charged
　　reader/printer　yes
　　reader

<u>Hours of operation</u>　　8am-4pm, M-F

<u>Resources</u>
　　clips　　1957-present　　　books　　　x
　　photos　 1957-present　　　pamphlets
　　negs　　　　　　　　　　　　maps
　　CPT　　　　　　　　　　　　 AV

<u>Microform holdings</u>
　　own newspaper　　1878-present
　　periodicals
　　clippings

<u>Indexes</u>
　　own newspaper
　　other

<u>Special collections</u>

<u>Automation</u>
　Automated files
　　mechanical
　　electronic
　Other automated systems

<u>Products for sale</u>

ARKANSAS   Little Rock   ARKANSAS

Arkansas Gazette (mS)
P.O. Box 1821
Little Rock AR 72203
501/371-3740

<u>Circulation</u>
(m) 134,016
(S) 160,911

Betty A. Turner, Head Librarian
Alfred M. Thomas, Asst. Librarian

<u>Lib. est.</u> 1949   <u>Group</u> Ind.   <u>FTE</u> 5.5

<u>Public access</u>
  in person   yes
  by mail   yes
  by phone   yes

<u>Limitations</u>
By appt.; no private investigators, lawyers, etc.
Will mail 10 copies.
Calls less than 5 minutes.

<u>Services available</u>
  copy machine   yes
  reader/printer
  reader   yes

<u>Limitations</u>
$.25 per article

<u>Hours of operation</u>   8am-Midnight, M-F; Noon-8pm, Sat. & Sun.

<u>Resources</u>
  clips   3,500,000   books   2000
  photos   125,000   pamphlets   500
  negs   maps   200
  CPT   10   AV

<u>Microform holdings</u>
  own newspaper   1819-present
  periodicals
  clippings

<u>Indexes</u>
  own newspaper   1819-1829, 1830-1839, 1965-present
  other   New York Times: 1863-1879, 1913-1973

<u>Special collections</u>

<u>Automation</u>
  Automated files
    mechanical   2 Lektriever 110's
    electronic   Planning index
  Other automated systems

<u>Products for sale</u>

CALIFORNIA   Chico   CALIFORNIA

Chico Enterprise-Record   (e)   Circulation
P.O. Box 9   (e) 25,183
Chico   CA 95927
                              916/891-1234

            Esther Douglas, Librarian

Lib. est. 1947   Group   Ind.   FTE

Public access   Limitations
      in person   yes   Librarian must be present
      by mail
      by phone

Services available   Limitations
      copy machine   yes   Charge for copies, small number of copies
      reader/printer   only
      reader

Hours of operation   9am-3pm, M-F

Resources
      clips   books
      photos   pamphlets
      negs   maps
      CPT   AV

Microform holdings
      own newspaper
      periodicals
      clippings

Indexes
      own newspaper
      other

Special collections

Automation
   Automated files
      mechanical
      electronic
   Other automated systems

Products for sale

11

CALIFORNIA   Long Beach   CALIFORNIA

INDEPENDENT PRESS-TELEGRAM

Independent (m)
Press-Telegram (e)
Independent Press-Telegram (S)
604 Pine Avenue
Long Beach CA 90844

Circulation
(m) 62,696
(e) 74,430
(S) 134,146

213/435-1161 x400

Violet R. Phillips, Head Librarian

<u>Lib. est.</u> January 1952   <u>Group</u> Knight-Ridder Newspapers   <u>FTE</u> 3

<u>Public access</u>
    in person   yes
    by mail   yes
    by phone   yes

<u>Limitations</u>
    9am-4pm, M-F
    Story dates checked, microprints
    Story dates checked; no research

<u>Services available</u>
    copy machine
    printer   yes
    reader

<u>Limitations</u>

    Microprints $1.00 per page

<u>Hours of operation</u> 7:30am-7:30pm, M-F; 7am-3:30pm, Sat.

<u>Resources</u>
    clips   4,415,000   books   273
    photos   88,750   pamphlets   129
    negs   maps   73
    CPT   AV

<u>Microform holdings</u>
    own newspaper   1938-present
    periodicals
    clippings

<u>Indexes</u>
    own newspaper
    other

<u>Special collections</u> Bicentennial of the U.S. - 5 volumes

<u>Automation</u>
  Automated files
    mechanical
    electronic
  Other automated systems

<u>Products for sale</u>

CALIFORNIA   Los Angeles   CALIFORNIA

Los Angeles Herald Examiner (eS)   Circulation
Box 2416 Terminal Annex   (e) 303,320
Los Angeles CA 90051   (S) 319,659
                        213/748-1212 x693

            Ann E. Sausedo, Library Director

Lib. est. late 1920's   Group   Hearst Newspapers   FTE   8

Public access   Limitations
     in person   no
     by mail   yes   Copies of articles unavailable elsewhere
     by phone   yes   Dates of articles that have run

Services available   Limitations
     copy machine
     reader/printer
     reader

Hours of operation   24 hrs. M-F; 8am-5pm Sat.

Resources
     clips   3,000,000   books   600
     photos   4,000,000   pamphlets
     negs   500,000   maps
     CPT   AV

Microform holdings
     own newspaper
     periodicals
     clippings

Indexes
     own newspaper
     other   Los Angeles Times, 1978-present

Special collections

Automation
   Automated files   none
     mechanical
     electronic
   Other automated systems

Products for sale

CALIFORNIA   Los Angeles   CALIFORNIA

Los Angeles Times (mS)   Circulation
Times Mirror Square   (m) 734,950
Los Angeles CA 90053   (S) 799,176

               213/972-7184; Reference: 972-7181

           Cecily J. Suraco, Editorial Library Director

Lib. est. 1905   Group Times Mirror Co.   FTE 50

Public access   Limitations
    in person   no   Will help other media; limited access
    by mail   no   to researchers
    by phone   no

Services available   Limitations
    copy machine   yes
    reader/printer   yes
    reader   yes

Hours of operation   8am-Midnight, Sun.-Sat.

Resources
    clips   x   books   2,500
    photos   1,000,000+   pamphlets
    negs   2,500,000+   maps
    CPT   75   AV

Microform holdings
    own newspaper   1881-present
    periodicals
    clippings

Indexes
    own newspaper   Card index Dec. 4, 1881-1897 and 1913-1935
    other

Special collections

Automation
  Automated files
    mechanical
    electronic
  Other automated systems   DIALOG, ORBIT, New York Times Information
                            Bank, Dow Jones, MARDATA, IDC

Products for sale

14

CALIFORNIA   Modesto   CALIFORNIA

Modesto Bee (mS)   Circulation
P.O. Box 3928   (m) 62,818
Modesto CA 95352   (S) 68,092
                          209/578-2370

         Lillian J. Wendt, Librarian
         Dorthea Manke, Asst. Librarian

Lib. est. 1944   Group McClatchy Newspapers   FTE 2

Public access   Limitations
     in person   yes   Discouraged
     by mail   yes
     by phone   yes

Services available   Limitations
     copy machine   yes   Staff only
     reader/printer   yes
     reader   yes

Hours of operation   10am-8:30pm, M-F

Resources
     clips   x   books   x
     photos   x   pamphlets   x
     negs   x   maps   x
     CPT   AV

Microform holdings
     own newspaper   1927-present
     periodicals
     clippings   180 fiche, 32 jackets

Indexes
     own newspaper   30 years
     other

Special collections

Automation
   Automated files
     mechanical
     electronic
   Other automated systems

Products for sale

15

CALIFORNIA   Monterey   CALIFORNIA

Monterey Peninsula Herald (eS)   Circulation
P.O. Box 271   (e) 30,948
Monterey CA 93940   (S) 32,000
                          408/372-3311 x213

            Emily Brown, Librarian
            Elayne Chanslor, Asst. Librarian

Lib. est. 1952   Group Ind.   FTE

Public access   Limitations
    in person   yes   No extensive research
    by mail   yes
    by phone   yes

Services available   Limitations
    copy machine   yes   Staff only
    reader/printer
    reader

Hours of operation 8am-5:30pm, M-F

Resources
    clips   150 drawers   books
    photos   13 drawers   pamphlets   x
    negs   maps   x
    CPT   x   AV

Microform holdings
    own newspaper   1952-present
    periodicals
    clippings

Indexes
    own newspaper
    other

Special collections Extensive historical materials

Automation
  Automated files
    mechanical
    electronic
  Other automated systems

Products for sale

16

CALIFORNIA   Oakland   CALIFORNIA

Eastbay Today (m)   Circulation
Oakland Tribune (eS)   (m) 25,639
409 13th St.   (e) 141,891
Oakland CA 94612   (S) 187,423
                            415/645-2745

            Seth Simpson, Librarian
            Yae Shinomiya, Asst. Librarian

Lib. est. 1915?   Group Gannett Newspapers   FTE 4

Public access   Limitations
    in person   no
    by mail   no
    by phone   no

Services available   Limitations
    copy machine
    reader/printer   yes
    reader   yes

Hours of operation 6am-7:30pm, M-F

Resources
    clips   x   books   x
    photos   x   pamphlets   x
    negs   maps   x
    CPT   x   AV

Microform holdings
    own newspaper
    periodicals
    clippings

Indexes
    own newspaper
    other   New York Times

Automation
  Automated files
    mechanical
    electronic
  Other automated systems

Products for sale

17

CALIFORNIA　　　　　　　　　　Palo Alto　　　　　　　　　　CALIFORNIA

Peninsula Times-Tribune (e)　　　　　　　　　　　　Circulation
P.O. Box 300　　　　　　　　　　　　　　　　　　　　(e) 45,741
Palo Alto CA 94302
　　　　　　　　　　　415/326-1200 x244

　　　　　Elizabeth R. Miller, Head Librarian
　　　　　Meg Morris, Asst.

Lib. est. 1945　　　　　　Group Tribune Co.　　　　FTE 3

Public access　　　　　　Limitations
　　in person　no
　　by mail　　yes
　　by phone　 yes

Services available　　　　Limitations
　　copy machine　yes　　$1.00 per page
　　reader/printer
　　reader　　　　yes

Hours of operation 8am-5pm, M-F

Resources
　　clips　　136 drawers　　　books　　　x
　　photos　　　　x　　　　　 pamphlets　x
　　negs　　　　　　　　　　　maps　　　 x
　　CPT　　　　　　　　　　　 AV

Microform holdings
　　own newspaper
　　periodicals
　　clippings

Indexes
　　own newspaper
　　other

Special collections

Automation
　Automated files
　　mechanical
　　electronic
　Other automated systems

Products for sale

CALIFORNIA   Redding   CALIFORNIA

Record Searchlight (e)   Circulation
1221 Placer St.   (e) 32,345
Redding CA 96001
                        916/243-2424 x26

            Karen L. Heckman, Editorial Secretary/Librarian

Lib. est.   Group   John P. Scripps Newspapers   FTE

Public access   Limitations
    in person   yes
    by mail   yes
    by phone   yes

Services available   Limitations
    copy machine   yes
    reader/printer
    reader   yes

Hours of operation   8:30am-5pm, M-F

Resources
    clips   x   books
    photos   pamphlets
    negs   maps
    CPT   AV

Microform holdings
    own newspaper   1883-present
    periodicals
    clippings

Indexes
    own newspaper
    other

Special collections

Automation
  Automated files
    mechanical
    electronic
  Other automated systems

Products for sale

CALIFORNIA   Riverside   CALIFORNIA

The Enterprise (m)   Circulation
The Press (e)   (m) 66,532
The Press Enterprise (Sat., Sun., holidays)   (e) 34,173
P.O. Box 792   (S) 106,862
Riverside CA 92502
                   714/684-1200 x396

          Joan Minesinger, Chief Librarian

Lib. est. 1968   Group   Ind.   FTE   4

Public access   Limitations
     in person   yes   6pm-8pm, T
     by mail   yes
     by phone   yes   After 3pm

Services available   Limitations
     copy machine   yes $.10 by user; $.25 by staff
     reader/printer yes $1 per copy
     reader

Hours of operation   7am-8pm, M-F

Resources
     clips   23 filing cabinets   books   c. 300
     photos   3 filing cabinets   pamphlets   c. 150
     negs   c. 5,500   maps   6 drawers
     CPT   AV

Microform holdings
     own newspaper   June 1878-present
     periodicals
     clippings   20,400 jackets

Indexes
     own newspaper   1968-present
     other

Special collections

Automation
  Automated files
    mechanical
    electronic
  Other automated systems

Products for sale   Index from 1968 in microfiche, updated annually

20

CALIFORNIA   Sacramento   CALIFORNIA

Sacramento Bee (mS)   Circulation
P.O. Box 15779   (m) 181,726
Sacramento CA 95813   (S) 209,469

                         916/446-9611

            Anna M. Michael, Librarian
            Lucille Crespo, Asst. Librarian

Lib. est.   Group   McClatchy Newspapers   FTE

Public access   Limitations
    in person   no
    by mail   no
    by phone   no

Services available   Limitations
    copy machine
    reader/printer
    reader

Hours of operation   7am-9:30pm, M-F; 1:30pm-9:30pm, Sat.& Sun.;
                        4pm-9pm, holidays

Resources
    clips   books
    photos   pamphlets
    negs   maps
    CPT   AV

Microform holdings
    own newspaper
    periodicals
    clippings

Indexes
    own newspaper
    other

Special collections

Automation
  Automated files
    mechanical
    electronic
  Other automated systems

Products for sale

Sacramento Union (mS) Circulation
301 Capitol Mall (m) 107,237
Sacramento CA 95812 (S) 110,869
        916/442-7811

  Robin Reidy, Librarian
  Alan Tomiyami, Library Asst.

Lib. est. 1965 Group Sierra Publishing Co. FTE 1.5

Public access   Limitations
 in person no
 by mail no
 by phone no

Services available Limitations
 copy machine yes
 reader/printer yes
 reader

Hours of operation 8am-5pm, M-F; 9am-3pm, Sat.

Resources
 clips 200,000   books
 photos   pamphlets
 negs 1965-present maps
 CPT 5   AV

Microform holdings
 own newspaper 1965-present
 periodicals
 clippings

Indexes
 own newspaper 1977-present
 other

Special collections

Automation
 Automated files
  mechanical
  electronic
 Other automated systems

Products for sale

CALIFORNIA   San Bernadino   CALIFORNIA

Sun (mS)   Circulation
399 North D St.   (m) 81,810
San Bernadino CA 92401   (S) 88,778
                              714/889-9666

                Blanche Lewis, Librarian
                Anita Kuschube, Asst. Librarian

Lib. est. 1950   Group Gannett Newspapers   FTE 2

Public access   Limitations
    in person   yes   With permission of Publisher or Editor;
    by mail   scholars doing research permitted. No
    by phone   attorneys, police, investigators, private
                                citizens

Services available   Limitations
    copy machine
    reader/printer
    reader   yes

Hours of operation 9am-7pm, M-F

Resources
    clips   250,000   books   500
    photos   20,000   pamphlets   500
    negs   250,000   maps   100
    CPT   150+   AV

Microform holdings
    own newspaper   1900-present
    periodicals
    clippings

Indexes
    own newspaper   none
    other

Special collections

Automation
  Automated files
    mechanical
    electronic
  Other automated systems

Products for sale

CALIFORNIA   San Diego   CALIFORNIA

San Diego Union (mS)   Circulation
Evening Tribune (e)   (m) 207,510
P.O. Box 191   (e) 134,185
San Diego CA 92112   (S) 335,943
                          714/299-3131

          Sharon Stewart Reeves, Director of Library Service
          Linda F. Ritter, Asst. Director

Lib. est. 1945   Group Copley Newspapers   FTE 15.75

Public access   Limitations
    in person   yes   9am-4pm, M-F
    by mail   yes
    by phone   yes   9am-11am & 2pm-4pm, M-F

Services available   Limitations
    copy machine   yes   not self-service
    reader/printer yes   not self-service
    reader   yes
    other   photo reprints

Hours of operation   24 hrs., M-F; 7am-10pm Sat.; 2pm-10pm Sun.

Resources
    clips   25,000,000   books   1,000
    photos   1,500,000   pamphlets   5,000
    negs   1,000,000   maps   500
    CPT   40   AV

Microform holdings
    own newspaper   1869-present
    periodicals   1,200 rolls
    clippings   2,000 jackets

Indexes
    own newspaper   1869-1903, 1929-1975 by San Diego Public Library
    other   Crime index

Special collections

Automation
  Automated files
    mechanical   Lektrievers
    electronic
  Other automated systems   DIALOG, New York Times Information Bank

Products for sale

24

CALIFORNIA   San Francisco   CALIFORNIA

San Francisco Chronicle

San Francisco Chronicle (m)
San Francisco Chronicle (with Examiner) (S)   Circulation
901 Mission St.   (m) 498,000
San Francisco CA 94119   (S) 670,100
                           415/777-1111

              Suzanne Casten, Head Librarian
              June Dellapa, Asst. Head Librarian

Lib. est. early 1900's   Group   Ind.   FTE   10

Public access   Limitations
    in person   no   Except other newspaper people
    by mail   yes
    by phone   yes   2pm-4pm, M-Th.

Services available   Limitations
    copy machine   yes   For public: $1 plus tax per page
    reader/printer
    reader   yes   Staff only

Hours of operation   9am-Midnight, Sun.-Fri.

Resources
    clips   7,000,000   books   c. 600
    photos   c. 1,000,000   pamphlets   c. 300
    negs   600,000   maps   c. 300
    CPT   4   AV

Microform holdings
    own newspaper   1865-present
    periodicals
    clippings

Indexes
    own newspaper   Jan. 1976-present (compiled by Bell & Howell,
                          local stories only)
    other   New York Times

Special collections

Automation
  Automated files
    mechanical
    electronic
  Other automated systems

Products for sale

CALIFORNIA　　　　　　　　　San Francisco　　　　　　　　　CALIFORNIA

San Francisco Examiner (e)　　　　　　　　　　Circulation
San Francisco Examiner (with Chronicle) (S)　　(e) 159,879
110 5th St.　　　　　　　　　　　　　　　　　　(S) 670,100
San Francisco CA 94103
　　　　　　　　　　　415/777-7845

　　　　Judy Gerritts, Head Librarian

Lib. est. 1907　　　　Group Hearst Newspapers　　　FTE 9

Public access　　　　　　Limitations
　　in person　　no
　　by mail　　　no
　　by phone　　no

Services available　　　　Limitations
　　copy machine　　yes
　　reader/printer　yes
　　reader

Hours of operation　　4:30am-10pm, M-Sun.

Resources
　　clips　　6,000,000　　　　books　　　4,000
　　photos　 4,000,000　　　　pamphlets　2,000
　　negs　　 4,000,000　　　　maps　　　 2,000
　　CPT　　　　　15　　　　　　AV

Microform holdings
　　own newspaper　　1865-present
　　periodicals　　　2 on fiche
　　clippings

Indexes
　　own newspaper
　　other

Special collections　　California and San Francisco history

Automation
　Automated files
　　mechanical
　　electronic
　Other automated systems

Products for sale　　In one year, after large microfilming project, will be selling microfiche copies

CALIFORNIA   San Jose   CALIFORNIA

San Jose Mercury (m)
San Jose News (e)   Circulation
San Jose Mercury News (S)   (m) 149,966
750 Ridder Park Drive   (e) 67,479
San Jose   CA 95190   (S) 261,660
                              408/289-5345

                    Richard Geiger, Chief Librarian

Lib. est. 1926   Group   Knight-Ridder Newspapers   FTE   9

Public access   Limitations
     in person   yes   View papers in binders; dates of
                                 articles; photocopying
     by mail   yes   Dates of articles; photocopying
     by phone   yes   Dates of articles

Services available   Limitations
     copy machine   yes $1 first page; $.50 each add'l
     reader/printer   yes   Same as above
     reader

Hours of operation   5am-Midnight, M-Th; 5am-11pm, F;
                        9am-11pm, Sat.; 2pm-10pm, Sun.

Resources
     clips   1,704,000   books   950
     photos   250,000   pamphlets   60 boxes
     negs   maps   85
     CPT   90   AV

Microform holdings
     own newspaper   From 1853-present
     periodicals
     clippings

Indexes
     own newspaper
     other   New York Times, Los Angeles Times

Special collections   Santa Clara County, California history

Automation
  Automated files
     mechanical   Lektrievers
     electronic
  Other automated systems

Products for sale

27

CALIFORNIA			San Mateo			CALIFORNIA

The Times (e)   Circulation
1080 S. Amphlett Blvd.   (e) 44,323
San Mateo CA 94402
                            415/348-4344

            June C. Malkemus, Librarian
            Naomi Youngdoff, Part-time Librarian
            Robert Biggs, Part-time Librarian

Lib. est. late 1930's   Group Ind.   FTE   2.5

Public access   Limitations
    in person   no   City library has microfilm with viewer-
                             printer available - librarians will look
                             up dates
    by mail   yes   If doesn't involve too much research time
    by phone   yes   Will give dates and refer to city library
                             for copies

Services available   Limitations
    copy machine
    reader/printer
    reader

Hours of operation   8am-5:30pm, M-F; 8am-1pm, Sat.

Resources
    clips   175+ drawers   books   18 3-ft. shelves
    photos   18 drawers   pamphlets
    negs   maps   2 atlases & misc.
    CPT   AV

Microform holdings
    own newspaper   1889-present with a few exceptions
    periodicals

Indexes
    own newspaper   none
    other

Special collections   San Mateo County historical volumes

Automation
  Automated files
    mechanical
    electronic
  Other automated systems

Products for sale

CALIFORNIA   Santa Ana   CALIFORNIA

Register (meS)   Circulation
625 N. Grand Ave.   (m) 105,561
Santa Ana CA 92711   (e) 107,977
                                                  (S) 243,274
                        714/835-1234

             Janice Rose, Librarian

Lib. est. 1965   Group Freedom Newspapers   FTE 3

Public access   Limitations
    in person   yes   Must be reasonable request
    by mail   yes
    by phone   yes

Services available   Limitations
    copy machine   yes   Charge varies
    reader/printer
    reader   yes

Hours of operation 8am-5pm, M-F

Resources
    clips   x   books
    photos   x   pamphlets
    negs   x   maps
    CPT   AV

Microform holdings
    own newspaper   1905-present
    periodicals
    clippings

Indexes
    own newspaper   1905-present
    other

Special collections

Automation
  Automated files
    mechanical
    electronic
  Other automated systems

Products for sale

CALIFORNIA Santa Barbara CALIFORNIA

SANTA BARBARA NEWS-PRESS

The oldest daily newspaper in Southern California, serving the entire county

Santa Barbara News-Press (eS)   Circulation
P.O. Drawer NN   (e) 46,087
Santa Barbara CA 93102   (S) 51,907
                      805/966-3911 x284

            Carol Wilson, Librarian

<u>Lib. est.</u> prior to 1951   <u>Group</u> Ind.   <u>FTE</u> 4

<u>Public access</u>   <u>Limitations</u>
    in person   yes   Will assist with dates &/or copying of
    by mail   yes   articles for reasonable (10-15 min.)
    by phone   yes   request. Will not assist with school
                               projects or research papers

<u>Services available</u>   <u>Limitations</u>
    copy machine   yes $1.00 per 3 sheets
    reader/printer yes   Mail requests only; $1.00 per sheet
    reader   yes   Mail requests only

<u>Hours of operation</u>   8am-5pm, M-F

<u>Resources</u>
    clips   500 linear feet   books   1,430
    photos   80 linear feet   pamphlets   80
    negs   for 5 years   maps   100
    CPT   AV

<u>Microform holdings</u>
    own newspaper   1869-present
    periodicals
    clippings

<u>Indexes</u>
    own newspaper
    other

Special collections

<u>Automation</u>
  Automated files
    mechanical
    electronic
  Other automated systems

<u>Products for sale</u>   Reprints of photographs

CALIFORNIA   Santa Rosa   CALIFORNIA

Press Democrat (eS)   Circulation
P.O. Box 569   (e) 61,247
Santa Rosa   CA 95402   (S) 66,349
                         707/546-2020 x232

           Elaine Barnard Cant, Librarian

Lib. est. 1950   Group Ind.   FTE 1

Public access   Limitations
    in person   no   Exceptions by appointment
    by mail   yes
    by phone   yes   9am-2pm, M-F

Services available   Limitations
    copy machine   yes
    reader/printer
    reader   yes   Staff only

Hours of operation   7:30-3:30, M-F; Noon-8pm, Sat.

Resources
    clips   254 drawers   books   x
    photos   44 drawers   pamphlets   x
    negs   15 drawers   maps
    CPT   AV

Microform holdings
    own newspaper   1857-present
    periodicals
    clippings

Indexes
    own newspaper
    other

Special collections   Microfilm of Sonoma Democrat Weekly 1857-1898
                      and Santa Rosa Daily Democrat 1883-1890

Automation
  Automated files
    mechanical   2 Lektriever 200's
    electronic
  Other automated systems

Products for sale

CALIFORNIA   Stockton   CALIFORNIA

Stockton Record (eS)   Circulation
P.O. Box 900   (e) 56,249
Stockton CA 95201   (S) 56,771
                         209/466-2652 x238

            Dorothy M. Frankhouse, Librarian
            Kathy Deluso, Asst. Librarian
            Patricia Smith, Asst. Librarian

Lib. est. 1952   Group Gannett Newspapers   FTE 3

Public access   Limitations
     in person   no
     by mail   no
     by phone   no

Services available   Limitations
     copy machine   yes   Staff only
     reader/printer
     reader   yes   Staff only

Hours of operation 7am-4pm, M-F

Resources
     clips   300 drawers   books   300
     photos   12 drawers   pamphlets
     negs   maps
     CPT   AV

Microform holdings
     own newspaper   April 1895-present
     periodicals
     clippings

Special collections

Automation
  Automated files
    mechanical
    electronic
  Other automated systems

Products for sale

CALIFORNIA　　　　　　　　　Torrance　　　　　　　　　CALIFORNIA

The Daily Breeze

Daily Breeze (eS)
5215 Torrance Blvd.
Torrance CA 90509

213/540-5511 x376

Janet Budro, Head Librarian

Circulation
(e) 81,022
(S) 95,516

<u>Lib. est.</u> 1969　　　　　<u>Group</u>　Copley Newspapers　　　　<u>FTE</u>　1

<u>Public access</u>　　　　　　<u>Limitations</u>
    in person　　yes
    by mail　　　yes
    by phone　　 yes

<u>Services available</u>　　　　<u>Limitations</u>
    copy machine　　yes　$.50 per copy
    reader/printer
    reader

<u>Hours of operation</u>　9am-5pm, M-F

<u>Resources</u>
    clips　　x　　　　　　　　books　　　　x
    photos　 x　　　　　　　　pamphlets
    negs　　 x　　　　　　　　maps
    CPT　　　　　　　　　　　 AV

<u>Microform holdings</u>
    own newspaper　　1909-present
    periodicals
    clippings

<u>Indexes</u>
    own newspaper
    other

<u>Special collections</u>

<u>Automation</u>
  Automated files
    mechanical
    electronic
  Other automated systems

<u>Products for sale</u>

CALIFORNIA   Van Nuys   CALIFORNIA

Valley News (mS) 14539 Sylvan St. Van Nuys CA 91401	Circulation (m) (235,280) (S) (240,817)

213/997-4162

Andrew Merrill, Librarian
Henri Mondachein, Asst. Librarian

Lib. est. 1968   Group Tribune Co.   FTE 2

Public access
- in person   no
- by mail   yes
- by phone   yes

Limitations
Public must have Managing Editor's approval. Will help other libraries and companies

Services available
- copy machine
- reader/printer
- reader   yes

Limitations

Public must have special permission

Hours of operation 9am-6pm, M-F

Resources
- clips   x
- photos   x
- negs
- CPT
- books   x
- pamphlets x
- maps   x
- AV

Microform holdings
- own newspaper   1911-present
- periodicals
- clippings

Indexes
- own newspaper   none
- other

Special collections

Automation
- Automated files
  - mechanical
  - electronic
- Other automated systems

Products for sale

Ventura County Star-Free Press (eS)　　　　　　　　Circulation
P.O. Box 6711　　　　　　　　　　　　　　　　　　　(e) 39,954
Ventura CA 93006　　　　　　　　　　　　　　　　　(S) 42,088
　　　　　　　　　　　　805/659-4111 x257

　　　　　　Sara J. Riley, Librarian

Lib. est. 1956　　　　Group　John P. Scripps Newspapers　　　　FTE

Public access　　　　　　　　Limitations
　　in person　　yes　　　　3-5pm, Wed. and Thurs.
　　by mail　　　yes　　　　Minimum
　　by phone　　 yes　　　　Try to refer elsewhere

Services available　　　　　Limitations
　　copy machine　yes　　　 $.50 per page
　　reader/printer
　　reader　　　　yes　　　 Staff only

Hours of operation 8am-5pm, M-F

Resources
　　clips　　350,000　　　　　books　　　100
　　photos　 mugs only　　　　pamphlets　200
　　negs　　　　　　　　　　　 maps　　　 25
　　CPT　　　　　　　　　　　　AV

Microform holdings
　　own newspaper　　1876-present
　　periodicals
　　clippings

Indexes
　　own newspaper　　1890-1910; 1940-present
　　other

Special collections　Various scrapbooks, e.g., St. Francis Dam Disaster,
　　　　　　　　　　　1968; '78 and '80 floods

Automation
　Automated files
　　mechanical
　　electronic
　Other automated systems

Products for sale

CALIFORNIA   Walnut Creek   CALIFORNIA

ContraCostaTimes

Contra Costa Times (m) (M-F, S)
P.O. Box 5088
Walnut Creek CA 94596
                    415/943-8190

<u>Circulation</u>
(m) 102,000

    Ellen D. Wood, Librarian
    Beverly Borgman, Library Asst.

<u>Lib. est.</u> 1978   <u>Group</u> East Bay Newspapers   <u>FTE</u> 2.5

<u>Public access</u>
    in person   yes
    by mail   yes
    by phone   yes

<u>Limitations</u>
    By appointment

<u>Services available</u>
    copy machine   yes
    reader/printer yes
    reader

<u>Limitations</u>
    For papers no longer available from back issues; $.25 per page
    $.50 per page

<u>Hours of operation</u>   8:30am-5:30pm, M-F

<u>Resources</u>
    clips   52 drawers   books   200
    photos   15 drawers   pamphlets 6 drawers
    negs   maps
    CPT   25   AV

<u>Microform holdings</u>
    own newspaper   1913-present
    periodicals
    clippings

<u>Indexes</u>
    own newspaper
    other   Abridged Reader's Guide, current 2 years

<u>Special collections</u>   Bay Area Rapid Transit collection

<u>Automation</u>
  Automated files
    mechanical
    electronic
  Other automated systems

<u>Products for sale</u>

COLORADO   Boulder   COLORADO

Daily Camera

Daily Camera (e)
Sunday Camera (S)
P.O. Box 591
Boulder CO 80306

Circulation
(e) 27,395
(S) 31,243

303/442-1202 x252

Edith Wood, Librarian

<u>Lib. est.</u> 1930's   <u>Group</u> Knight-Ridder Newspapers   <u>FTE</u> 1

<u>Public access</u>
- in person   no
- by mail   no
- by phone   no

<u>Limitations</u>
Some special research permitted

<u>Services available</u>
- copy machine   yes
- reader/printer   yes
- reader

<u>Limitations</u>
$.10 per page
$1.00 per print

<u>Hours of operation</u>   8am-4pm, M-F

<u>Resources</u>
- clips   x
- photos   x
- negs   x
- CPT
- books   x
- pamphlets   x
- maps   x
- AV

<u>Microform holdings</u>
- own newspaper   June-Oct. 1891, March 1892-present
- periodicals
- clippings

<u>Indexes</u>
- own newspaper   1892-1930, 1941-1943
- other

<u>Special collections</u>

<u>Automation</u>
   Automated files
     mechanical
     electronic
   Other automated systems

<u>Products for sale</u>

GAZETTE-TELEGRAPH

Colorado Springs

Colorado Springs Gazette Telegraph (meS)
1779 S. Prospect
Colorado Springs   CO 80901

303/632-5511 x287

Circulation
(m) 20,785
(e) 53,369
(S) 78,265

Linda Dougherty, Clipping Librarian
Carol Blanchard, Art Librarian

<u>Lib. est.</u> 1949   <u>Group</u>   Freedom Newspapers Inc.   <u>FTE</u>   2

<u>Public access</u>
   in person   yes
   by mail   yes
   by phone   yes

<u>Limitations</u>
No access to newspapers other than clips
No access to newspapers other than clips
No access to newspapers other than clips

<u>Services available</u>
   copy machine   yes
   reader/printer
   reader

<u>Limitations</u>
$1 per page for 15x24 copy

<u>Hours of operation</u>   8am-5pm, M-F

<u>Resources</u>
   clips   25,000 files   books   50
   photos   178,800   pamphlets
   cuts   13,200   maps   10
   CPT   AV

<u>Microform holdings</u>
   own newspaper
   periodicals
   clippings

<u>Indexes</u>
   own newspaper
   other

<u>Special collections</u>

<u>Automation</u>
  Automated files
    mechanical
    electronic
  Other automated systems

<u>Products for sale</u>

COLORADO   Colorado Springs   COLORADO

Colorado Springs Sun

Colorado Springs Sun (mS)   Circulation
P.O. Box 130   (m) 24,402
Colorado Springs   CO 80901   (S) 24,688

                      303/633-3881

           Patsy St. John, Librarian

Lib. est. 1977   Group   Ind.   FTE   1

Public access   Limitations
     in person   yes   No direct access to files
     by mail   yes
     by phone   yes

Services available   Limitations
     copy machine   yes   Charge per copy
     reader/printer   yes
     reader

Hours of operation

Resources
     clips   thousands   books   200
     photos   thousands   pamphlets   400
     negs   maps   40
     CPT   60   AV

Microform holdings
     own newspaper   x
     periodicals
     clippings

Indexes
     own newspaper
     other   New York Times

Special collections

Automation
  Automated files
    mechanical
    electronic
  Other automated systems

Products for sale

COLORADO   Denver   COLORADO

THE DENVER POST

The Denver Post (eS) 650 15th St. Denver CO 80201	Circulation (e) 267,034 (S) 357,047

303/820-1565 (Reference)
303/820-1691 (Librarian)

Kathryn D. Sweeney, Librarian
Marilyn L. Harrison, Asst. Librarian

Lib. est. c. 1900   Group   Ind.   FTE   13

Public access   Limitations
    in person   yes   By appt. only
    by mail   yes   Answer all written requests
    by phone   no

Services available   Limitations
    copy machine   yes   Charges for all copies
    reader/printer   yes   Charges for all copies
    reader

Hours of operation   7am-8pm, M-Th; 7am-10pm, F; 9am-6pm, Sat.

Resources
    clips   900,000   books   250
    photos   950,000   pamphlets
    negs   maps   included w/ photos
    CPT   3   AV

Microform holdings
    own newspaper   1895-present
    periodicals
    clippings

Indexes
    own newspaper   1903-present
    other

Special collections

Automation
  Automated files
    mechanical
    electronic
  Other automated systems

Products for sale   Denver Post Index from Jan. 1979, published
                    and sold by Bell & Howell Co.

Rocky Mountain News (mS)
400 W. Colfax
Denver CO 80204
303/892-5000

Circulation
(m) 261,079
(S) 285,109

Paula Shonkwiler, Librarian
Susan Schwellenbach, Asst. Librarian

Lib. est. 1951   Group Scripps-Howard Newspapers   FTE 5

Public access
- in person   yes
- by mail   yes
- by phone   yes

Limitations
Limited hours for public access

Services available
- copy machine   yes
- reader/printer yes
- reader   yes

Limitations

Hours of operation   8:30am-11pm, M-F; 9:30am-9pm, Sat.& Sun.

Resources
- clips   x
- photos   x
- negs
- CPT   x
- books   x
- pamphlets x
- maps   x
- AV

Microform holdings
- own newspaper   1859-99 (incomplete); 1900-present
- periodicals
- clippings

Indexes
- own newspaper
- other

Special collections

Automation
Automated files
  mechanical
  electronic
Other automated systems

Products for sale

COLORADO　　　　　　　　　Grand Junction　　　　　　　　　COLORADO

Daily Sentinel (eS)　　　　　　　　　　　　　　　　Circulation
P.O. Box 668　　　　　　　　　　　　　　　　　　　(e) 27,584
Grand Junction CO 81501　　　　　　　　　　　　(S) 30,158
　　　　　　　　　　　303/242-5050 x238

　　　　　　Sherry L. Staggs, Librarian

Lib. est.　　　　　　　　Group Ind.　　　　　　FTE 1

Public access　　　　　　Limitations
　　in person　　yes
　　by mail　　　yes
　　by phone　　 yes

Services available　　　 Limitations
　　copy machine　yes　 $.10 per page
　　reader/printer
　　reader　　　　yes

Hours of operation

Resources
　　clips　　x　　　　　　　　books　　　x
　　photos　 x　　　　　　　　pamphlets　x
　　negs　　　　　　　　　　　maps　　　 x
　　CPT　　　x　　　　　　　　AV

Microform holdings
　　own newspaper　　1894-present
　　periodicals
　　clippings

Indexes
　　own newspaper
　　other

Special collections

Automation
　Automated files
　　mechanical
　　electronic
　Other automated systems

Products for sale

42

COLORADO   Pueblo   COLORADO

Chieftain (m)
Star Journal (e)
Star Journal & Chieftain (S)
825 W. 16th St.
Pueblo CO 81002

Circulation
(m) 37,292
(e) 14,932
(S) 51,133

303/544-2035 x266

Betty M. Carnes, Librarian
Cecil Osborne, Library Consultant

Lib. est. 1950   Group Ind.   FTE 1.5

Public access
 in person yes
 by mail yes
 by phone yes

Limitations
Must be reasonable request
Must be reasonable request
Must be reasonale request

Services available
 copy machine yes
 reader/printer yes
 reader

Limitations
$.25 per page
$.50 per half page, $1.00 per full page

Hours of operation 8am-4:30pm, M-F

Resources
 clips 11,500   books 320
 photos 2,000   pamphlets 150
 negs 10,000   maps 20
 CPT none   AV

Microform holdings
 own newspaper Chieftain, 1868-present; Star Journal, 1901-present
 periodicals
 clippings 500 aperture cards

Special collections Copies of the Pueblo Leader 1911-1913; the Bessemer Indicator 1895-1913, incomplete

Automation
 Automated files
  mechanical
  electronic
 Other automated systems

Products for sale

CONNECTICUT — Danbury — CONNECTICUT

The News-Times (eS)
333 Main St.
Danbury CT 06810

203/744-5100 x168

Circulation
(e) 39,070
(S) 41,476

Helene Schmitt, Librarian

Lib. est. 1968   Group Ottaway Newspapers Inc.   FTE 1

Public access
- in person yes
- by mail
- by phone yes

Limitations
Public use very limited as library is set up for working staff

Services available
- copy machine yes
- reader/printer
- reader

Limitations
Staff only

Hours of operation 7:30am-4:30pm, M-F

Resources
- clips x
- photos x
- negs x
- CPT
- books x
- pamphlets x
- maps x
- AV

Microform holdings
- own newspaper   Jan. 1974-present (Danbury Public has 1890-present)
- periodicals
- clippings

Indexes
- own newspaper
- other

Special collections

Automation
- Automated files
  - mechanical
  - electronic
- Other automated systems

Products for sale

44

CONNECTICUT			Hartford			CONNECTICUT

The Hartford Courant

Hartford Courant (mS)
285 Broad St.
Hartford   CT 06115

                        203/249-6411 x229

Circulation
(m) 215,385
(S) 288,186

Kathleen McKula, News Librarian

Lib. est. ?	Group Ind.	FTE 4

Public access
- in person   yes
- by mail   yes
- by phone   yes

Limitations
Appt. required; answer only questions which can be researched in own files; no in-depth research or extensive photocopying.

Services available
- copy machine   yes
- reader/printer
- reader   yes

Limitations
Limited to 10 or fewer copies

Hours of operation   8:30am-11pm, M-F; 2:30pm-11pm, Sat. & Sun.

Resources
- clips   x
- photos   x
- negs   x
- CPT
- books   x
- pamphlets   x
- maps   x
- AV

Microform holdings
- own newspaper   1764-present
- periodicals
- clippings

Indexes
- own newspaper
- other   New York Times 1913-present

Special collections

Automation
- Automated files
  - mechanical
  - electronic
- Other automated systems

Products for sale

CONNECTICUT   Manchester   CONNECTICUT

Journal Inquirer (e)   Circulation
306 Progress Drive   (e) 35,641
Manchester CT 06040
                203/646-0500 x213

    Sandra Sullivan, Librarian
    Larry Linders, Editorial Asst.
    Glenn Waterman, Editorial Asst.

Lib. est. 1974   Group Ind.   FTE 3

Public access   Limitations
    in person   yes   Public allowed afternoons, after
    by mail   yes   deadlines
    by phone   yes

Services available   Limitations
    copy machine   yes   Copies made by staff; there is a charge
    reader/printer
    reader

Hours of operation   7am-5pm, M-F

Resources
    clips   c. 100,800   books   50
    photos   c. 63,000   pamphlets   many
    negs   in Photo Dept.   maps   many
    CPT   10-15   AV

Microform holdings
    own newspaper   back issues in books 1968-present
    periodicals
    clippings

Indexes
    own newspaper
    other

Special collections

Automation
  Automated files
    mechanical
    electronic
  Other automated systems

Products for sale

New Haven Journal-Courier (m)　　　　　　　　　Circulation
New Haven Register (eS)　　　　　　　　　　　　(m)　 37,581
367 Orange St.　　　　　　　　　　　　　　　　　(e)　101,897
New Haven　CT 06503　　　　　　　　　　　　　　(S)　141,180
　　　　　　　　　　203/562-1121 x581,582

　　　　　　　Wilbur Mesing, Librarian

Lib. est. 1935　　　　　　Group Ind.　　　　　　FTE 2

Public access　　　　　　Limitations
　　in person　　yes　　By appt. only
　　by mail　　　yes　　Limited
　　by phone　　 yes　　Limited

Services available　　　 Limitations
　　copy machine　　yes　$.25 per page
　　reader/printer　yes　$1.00 per page
　　reader　　　　　yes

Hours of operation 8:30am-4pm, M-F

Resources
　　clips　　3 Lektrievers　　　books　　　x
　　photos　 1 Lektriever　　　 pamphlets　x
　　negs　　　　　　　　　　　　maps　　　 x
　　CPT　　　　　　　　　　　　 AV

Microform holdings
　　own newspaper　　Register 1954-present; Courier 1964-present
　　periodicals
　　clippings

Indexes
　　own newspaper
　　other

Special collections

Automation
　Automated files
　　mechanical　　Lektrievers
　　electronic
　Other automated systems

Products for sale

The Day (e)
47 Eugene O'Neill Drive
New London CT 06320

203/443-2882 x366

Circulation
(e) 37,541

Clare Peckham, Librarian

Lib. est. 1929   Group   Ind.   FTE

Public access   Limitations
    in person   yes   Microfilm for staff only
    by mail   yes
    by phone   yes

Services available   Limitations
    copy machine   yes   Staff only
    reader/printer
    reader   yes   Staff only

Hours of operation   7am-3pm, M-F

Resources
    clips   x   books
    photos   x   pamphlets
    negs   x   maps
    CPT   AV

Microform holdings
    own newspaper   1929-1977
    periodicals
    clippings

Indexes
    own newspaper   1929-1977
    other

Special collections

Automation
  Automated files
    mechanical
    electronic
  Other automated systems

Products for sale

CONNECTICUT   Stamford   CONNECTICUT

THE ADVOCATE

The Advocate (e)   <u>Circulation</u>
258 Atlantic St.   (e) 32,000
Stamford   CT 06901
                         203/327-1600

               Anne McRae Hudock, Librarian
               Dobie Andrews, Library Asst.

<u>Lib. est.</u> 1930   <u>Group</u>   Times Mirror Co.   <u>FTE</u>   1

<u>Public access</u>   <u>Limitations</u>
    in person   yes   Appts. must be made in advance; not open
    by mail   no   to public
    by phone   no

<u>Services available</u>   <u>Limitations</u>
    copy machine   yes   Permission must be granted in advance
    reader/printer
    reader

<u>Hours of operation</u>   8am-5pm M-F

<u>Resources</u>
    clips   books   30
    photos   2,000   pamphlets   200
    negs   maps   10
    CPT   AV

<u>Microform holdings</u>
    own newspaper
    periodicals
    clippings

<u>Indexes</u>
    own newspaper
    other

<u>Special collections</u>

<u>Automation</u>
  Automated files
    mechanical
    electronic
  Other automated systems

<u>Products for sale</u>   Advocate 150th edition (contact Circulation Dept.)

CONNECTICUT   Waterbury   CONNECTICUT

WATERBURY REPUBLICAN

Waterbury Republican (mS)
Waterbury American (e)
P.O. Box 2090
Waterbury CT 06722

Circulation
(m) 35,511
(e) 37,535
(S) 69,580

203/574-3636

Clarissa D. Laukaitis, Librarian
Lorraine Boyles, Asst. Librarian

Lib. est.   Group Ind.   FTE 2

Public access   Limitations
  in person   no   Except to look up ads on microfilm
  by mail   no
  by phone   yes   Spot reference only

Services available   Limitations
  copy machine
  reader/printer
  reader   yes

Hours of operation   8:30am-4:30pm, M-F

Resources
  clips   10 double drawer 5x8   books   2,000
            cabinets
  photos   7 double drawer files   pamphlets 3 letter size files
  negs   being eliminated   maps   included w/ photos
  CPT   AV

Microform holdings
  own newspaper   1884-present
  periodicals
  clippings

Indexes
  own newspaper
  other

Special collections

Automation
  Automated files
    mechanical
    electronic
  Other automated systems

Products for sale

50

DELAWARE   Dover   DELAWARE

Delaware State News (eS)   Circulation
Maryland State News (eS)   (e) 25,587
P.O. Box 737   (S) 29,096
Dover DE 19901
                        302/674-3600 x47 or x49

          Katherine Brown
          Sharon Cannon

Lib. est.   Group   Independent Newspapers Inc.   FTE   2

Public access   Limitations
    in person   yes
    by mail
    by phone

Services available   Limitations
    copy machine   yes $.25 per copy
    reader/printer yes $.25 per copy
    reader

Hours of operation   10am-4pm, M-F

Resources
    clips   x   books   x
    photos   x   pamphlets   x
    negs   x   maps   x
    CPT   AV

Microform holdings
    own newspaper   1945-present
    periodicals
    clippings

Indexes
    own newspaper   1945-present
    other

Special collections

Automation
  Automated files
    mechanical   3M Filmac 400
    electronic
  Other automated systems

Products for sale

51

DELAWARE   Wilmington   DELAWARE

Morning News (m)   Circulation
Evening Journal (e)   (m) 47,303
News-Journal (Sat. & holidays)   (e) 83,469
Sunday News Journal (S)   (S) 103,465
831 Orange St.
Wilmington DE 19899
                         302/573-2038

             Vickie J. Houk, Librarian
             Dorothy Brown, Asst. Librarian

Lib. est. 1955   Group   Gannett Newspapers   FTE   6

Public access   Limitations
    in person   yes   By Appt. only, if we are sole source
    by mail   yes
    by phone   yes   9am-4pm, M-F

Services available   Limitations
    copy machine   yes   Copies made if papers unavailable, $25
                             per page
    reader/printer yes   Staff only
    reader   yes

Hours of operation   7am-11pm, M-F; 2pm-9pm, Sat.; Noon-9pm, Sun.

Resources
    clips   5,500,000   books   1500 titles
    photos   74 drawers   pamphlets   40 drawers
    negs   none   maps   3 drawers
    CPT   150   AV   none

Microform holdings
    own newspaper   1871-present
    periodicals   360 rolls
    clippings   250,000 jackets

Indexes
    own newspaper
    other   New York Times, 1964-present

Special collections   10 years Delaware General Assembly bills; Wilmington city directories, 1900-present; 2 drawers company archives

Automation
  Automated files
    mechanical   1 Lektreiver
    electronic
  Other automated systems

Products for sale

                               52

DISTRICT OF COLUMBIA   Washington   DISTRICT OF COLUMBIA

The Washington Post

Washington Post (mS)	Circulation
1150 15th St. N.W.	(m) 598,213
Washington DC 20071	(S) 822,133

202/334-7341

Mark Hannan, Director of Research
William Hifner, Librarian

<u>Lib. est.</u> 1933   <u>Group</u> Washington Post Co.   <u>FTE</u> 23

<u>Public access</u>   <u>Limitations</u>
   in person   no
   by mail   no
   by phone   no

<u>Services available</u>   <u>Limitations</u>
   copy machine   yes
   reader/printer   yes
   reader   yes

<u>Hours of operation</u>   8am-1:30am, M-F; 10am-1:30am, Sat.; Noon-1:30am, Sun.

<u>Resources</u>
   clips   5,000,000   books   20,000
   photos   1,000,000   pamphlets   100 drawers
   negs   maps
   CPT   85   AV

<u>Microform holdings</u>
   own newspaper   1877-present
   periodicals
   clippings

<u>Indexes</u>
   own newspaper   1972-present
   other   Wall Street Journal 1970-present; New York Times 1911-present

<u>Special collections</u>

<u>Automation</u>
  Automated files
   mechanical   Lektriever
   electronic   Nexis (full-text)
  Other automated systems

<u>Products for sale</u>

DISTRICT OF COLUMBIA Washington DISTRICT OF COLUMBIA

The Washington Star

Washington Star (eS)
225 Virginia Ave.
Washington DC 20061

202/484-4375

Circulation
(m) 340,150
(S) 316,608

Angelina O'Donnell, Director
Mary Lou White, Asst. Director

Lib. est. 1922   Group   Time Inc.   FTE   9

Public access   Limitations
   in person   no   No researching; will gives dates of
   by mail   yes   articles
   by phone   yes

Services available   Limitations
   copy machine   yes $.50 per photocopy
   reader/printer yes
   reader   yes

Hours of operation 24 hrs., M-Sat.; 1pm-9pm, Sun.

Resources
   clips   13,000,000   books   5,000
   photos   1,020,000   pamphlets   50
   negs   In Photo lab   maps   10 atlases
   CPT   10   AV

Microform holdings
   own newspaper   1852-present
   periodicals
   clippings

Indexes
   own newspaper   1901-1973
   other   Washington Post, New York Times

Special collections

Automation
  Automated files
   mechanical   12 Lektriever filing cabinets
   electronic
  Other automated systems

Products for sale

FLORIDA   Bradenton   FLORIDA

The Bradenton Herald

The Bradenton Herald (eS)   Circulation
401 13th St. W   (e) 29,872
Bradenton FL 33505   (S) 35,153
                    813/748-0411 x280

           Helen J. Milstead, Librarian
           Delores J. Rickman, Library Clerk

Lib. est. 1967   Group Knight-Ridder Newspapers   FTE 2

Public access   Limitations
    in person   yes   No research for public
    by mail   yes   Only photo orders and photocopies
    by phone   yes   Refer to public library if possible

Services available   Limitations
    copy machine yes $1.00 per photocopy
    reader/printer
    reader   yes

Hours of operation   8 hrs., M-F

Resources
    clips   500,000   books   450
    photos   5,000   pamphlets   150
    negs   15,000   maps   15
    CPT   40   AV

Microform holdings
    own newspaper
    periodicals
    clippings

Indexes
    own newspaper
    other

Special collections

Automation
  Automated files
    mechanical
    electronic
  Other automated systems

Products for sale

55

Journal (m)
News (e)
News-Journal (S)
901 Sixth St.
Daytona Beach FL 32108
904/252-1511 x266

Circulation
(m) 50,357
(e) 31,069
(S) 69,896

Joan Hulbert, Head Librarian
Sandra Mallory, Asst. Librarian

Lib. est. 1945   Group Ind.   FTE 2

Public access   Limitations
    in person   yes   Clip files, hanging files, microfilm only
    by mail   yes
    by phone   yes   Check for local items only

Services available   Limitations
    copy machine   yes   Charge
    reader/printer
    reader   yes

Hours of operation 8:30am-5pm, M-F

Resources
    clips   38 cabinets   books   30
    photos   10 cabinets   pamphlets
    negs   maps   x
    CPT   6   AV

Microform holdings
    own newspaper   1915-present
    periodicals
    clippings

Special collections

Automation
  Automated files
    mechanical
    electronic
  Other automated systems

Products for sale

FLORIDA   Fort Lauderdale   FLORIDA

Sun Sentinel (m)	Circulation
Fort Lauderdale News (e)	(m) 65,657
News and Sun Sentinel (S)	(e) 111,400
101 N. New River Dr., East	(S) 178,135
Fort Lauderdale FL 33302	

305/761-4255

Mildred America, Head Librarian
Irving Olshan, Asst. Librarian

Lib. est. 1965   Group Tribune Co.   FTE 8

Public access   Limitations
   in person   no   Special permission from Managing Editor
   by mail   no
   by phone   no   Will help other news media

Services available   Limitations
   copy machine   yes
   reader/printer
   reader   yes

Hours of operation 6am-11pm, M-F; 2pm-11pm, Sun.

Resources
clips	5,000,000+	books	120
photos	1,000,000	pamphlets	150
negs		maps	40+
CPT	10	AV	

Microform holdings
   own newspaper   1913-present
   periodicals
   clippings

Indexes
   own newspaper
   other   New York Times 1974-present

Special collections

Automation
  Automated files
    mechanical
    electronic
  Other automated systems

Products for sale

FLORIDA　　　　　　　　　Fort Myers　　　　　　　　　FLORIDA

FORT MYERS NEWS-PRESS

Fort Myers News-Press (mS)　　　　　　　　Circulation
P.O. Box 10　　　　　　　　　　　　　　　　(m) 69,277
Fort Myers FL 33902　　　　　　　　　　　　(S) 80,329
　　　　　　　　　813/334-2351 x140

　　　　Emily Richardson, Librarian
　　　　Margie Bril, Assistant Librarian

<u>Lib. est.</u> 1973　　　　<u>Group</u> Gannett Newspapers　　　<u>FTE</u> 1

<u>Public access</u>　　　　　　　<u>Limitations</u>
　　in person　　yes　　　10pm-6pm, T-F with librarian's help only
　　by mail　　　yes
　　by phone　　 yes　　　Long distance only

<u>Services available</u>　　　　<u>Limitations</u>
　　copy machine　　yes　　$1.00 per photocopy
　　reader/printer　yes　　$5.00 per 8x10 page
　　reader

<u>Hours of operation</u> 10pm-6pm, T-F

<u>Resources</u>
　　clips　　18,000 folders　　　books　　　c. 400
　　photos　 14,000 folders　　　pamphlets　c. 200
　　negs　　　　　　　　　　　　maps　　　　 10
　　CPT　　　16　　　　　　　　　AV

<u>Microform holdings</u>
　　own newspaper　　1884-present
　　periodicals
　　clippings

<u>Indexes</u>
　　own newspaper　　none
　　other

<u>Special collections</u>

<u>Automation</u>
　Automated files
　　mechanical　 Astromatic Power files, one unit
　　electronic
　Other automated systems

<u>Products for sale</u>

FLORIDA   Gainesville   FLORIDA

Gainesville Sun

Gainesville Sun (mS)   Circulation
Drawer A   (m) 36,911
Gainesville FL 32602   (S) 39,206
                        904/378-1411 x299

              Robert Ivey, Librarian

Lib. est. 1964   Group New York Times Co.   FTE 1.5

Public access   Limitations
    in person   no   Exception: some journalism classes
    by mail   no
    by phone   no

Services available   Limitations
    copy machine   yes
    reader/printer
    reader   yes

Hours of operation 9am-5:50pm, M-F

Resources
    clips   200 drawers   books   525
    photos   9,500   pamphlets   1 drawer
    negs   maps   115
    CPT   AV

Microform holdings
    own newspaper   x
    periodicals
    clippings

Indexes
    own newspaper   two years
    other

Special collections

Automation
  Automated files
    mechanical
    electronic   On-line index: Hewlett-Packard, Computek terminals
  Other automated systems New York Times Information Bank

Products for sale

59

FLORIDA   Hollywood   FLORIDA

Hollywood Sun-Tattler

Hollywood Sun-Tattler (e)   <u>Circulation</u>
2600 N. 29th Ave.   (e) 43,608
Hollywood FL 33020
                 305/922-1511 x229

        Flo Daniels, Head Librarian
        Margo Spinelli, Asst. Librarian

<u>Lib. est.</u> 1971   <u>Group</u>   Scripps Howard Newspapers   <u>FTE</u>   3

<u>Public access</u>   <u>Limitations</u>
    in person   yes
    by mail   yes
    by phone   yes

<u>Services available</u>   <u>Limitations</u>
    copy machine   yes   Only our librarians can use
    reader/printer   yes   Only our librarians can use
    reader   no

<u>Hours of operation</u>   8am-5pm, M-F

<u>Resources</u>
    clips   x   books
    photos   x   pamphlets
    negs   maps
    CPT   x   AV

<u>Microform holdings</u>
    own newspaper   1930-present
    periodicals
    clippings

<u>Indexes</u>
    own newspaper
    other

<u>Special collections</u>

<u>Automation</u>
  Automated files
    mechanical
    electronic
  Other automated systems

<u>Products for sale</u>

FLORIDA   Jacksonville   FLORIDA

Florida Times-Union (mS)
Jacksonville Journal (e)
One Riverside Ave.
Jacksonville FL 32202

Circulation
(m) 157,514
(e) 51,692
(S) 198,440

904/791-4237

Martin L. Crotts, Editorial Library Director
Pauline Sauer, Head Library Asst.

<u>Lib. est.</u> 1967   <u>Group</u> Ind.   <u>FTE</u> 7

<u>Public access</u>   <u>Limitations</u>
- in person   yes   yes
- by mail   yes   yes
- by phone   yes   yes

<u>Services available</u>   <u>Limitations</u>
- copy machine   yes $.50 per page
- reader/printer
- reader   yes

<u>Hours of operation</u>   7am-11pm, M-F

<u>Resources</u>
- clips   x   books   1,500+
- photos   x   pamphlets   x
- negs   maps
- CPT   60   AV

<u>Microform holdings</u>
- own newspaper   1882-present
- periodicals
- clippings

<u>Indexes</u>
- own newspaper   1902-present
- other   New York Times   1917-present

<u>Special collections</u>

<u>Automation</u>
Automated files
- mechanical
- electronic   under consideration

Other automated systems

<u>Products for sale</u>

FLORIDA   Lakeland   FLORIDA

The Ledger (eS)
401 S. Missouri Ave.
Lakeland FL 33802
813/687-7843

Circulation
(e) 43,277
(S) 50,558

Gail Sharp, Librarian

Lib. est.   Group   New York Times Co.   FTE   1

Public access   Limitations
- in person   yes   T-Th, mornings
- by mail   yes
- by phone   yes

Services available   Limitations
- copy machine   yes
- reader/printer   yes
- reader

Hours of operation   40 hours, M-F

Resources
- clips   x   books   x
- photos   x   pamphlets   x
- negs   maps   x
- CPT   x   AV

Microform holdings
- own newspaper   1943-present
- periodicals
- clippings

Indexes
- own newspaper
- other

Special collections

Automation
- Automated files
  - mechanical
  - electronic
- Other automated systems

Products for sale

FLORIDA   Miami   FLORIDA

Miami Herald (mS)   Circulation
No.1 Herald Plaza   (m) 447,587
Miami FL 33101   (S) 580,839
                        305/350-2419

            Luis Bueno, Librarian
            Nora Medley, Asst. Librarian

Lib. est. 1930   Group   Knight-Ridder Newspapers   FTE

Public access   Limitations
     in person   no
     by mail   yes
     by phone   no

Services available   Limitations
     copy machine
     reader/printer
     reader

Hours of operation   5am-Midnight, M-Sat.; 8am-11pm Sun.

Resources
     clips   4,170,000   books   1,000
     photos   1,007,000   pamphlets   1,000
     negs   1,000   maps   none
     CPT   AV

Microform holdings
     own newspaper   1904-present
     periodicals
     clippings

Indexes
     own newspaper
     other   New York Times

Automation
  Automated files
     mechanical
     electronic
  Other automated systems New York Times Information Bank; AP Political
                           Databank

Products for sale

63

FLORIDA   Miami   FLORIDA

The Miami News

Miami News (e)
Box 615
Miami FL 33152

Circulation
(e) 63,613

305/350-2200

Joseph Wright, Librarian
Dorothy McDermott, Asst. Librarian

Lib. est. ?   Group Cox Enterprises   FTE 6.5

Public access   Limitations
- in person   no   Working news media admitted
- by mail   yes
- by phone   no

Services available   Limitations
- copy machine   yes
- reader/printer yes
- reader   yes

Hours of operation 7am-6:30pm, M-F

Resources
clips	900,000	books	500
photos	410,000	pamphlets	12 drawers
negs		maps	
CPT	13	AV	

Microform holdings
- own newspaper   1896-present
- periodicals
- clippings   1,000 + cards

Indexes
- own newspaper
- other

Special collections Photographs of early Miami history

Automation
- Automated files
  - mechanical
  - electronic   Computer printout of subject headings for clips and photos
- Other automated systems

Products for sale

FLORIDA   Orlando   FLORIDA

Sentinel Star (mS)			Circulation
633 N. Orange Ave.			(m) 200,825
Orlando FL 32802		305/420-5510	(S) 231,243

Wendy A. Barager, Librarian
Jeannine DeLancett, Library Clerk

Lib. est. 1950's   Group Tribune Co.   FTE 6

Public access   **Limitations**
   in person   yes   Through Reader's Service Dept., with Editor's permission
   by mail   yes   Through Reader's Service Dept.
   by phone   yes   Through Reader's Service Dept.

Services available   **Limitations**
   copy machine
   reader/printer
   reader   yes

Hours of operation 8am-Midnight, M-F; Noon-9pm, Sat.; 3:30-Midnight, Sun.

Resources
clips	47,890		books	432
photos	62,400		pamphlets	300
negs	34,157		maps	
CPT	1		AV	

Microform holdings
   own newspaper   1912-present
   periodicals
   clippings   2389 jackets

Indexes
   own newspaper   1966-1970 (done by Orlando Public Library)
   other

Special collections

Automation
  Automated files
    mechanical   5 Lektrievers
    electronic   Planned for 1980
  Other automated systems

Products for sale

FLORIDA   St. Petersburg   FLORIDA

St. Petersburg Times
FLORIDA'S BEST NEWSPAPER

Evening Independent
The People Paper

Times (mS)
Evening Independent (e)
P.O. Box 1121
St. Petersburg FL 33731

813/893-8111

James S. Scofield, Chief Librarian

Circulation
(m) 216,918
(e) 39,877
(S) 270,926

Lib. est. 1923   Group Ind.   FTE 16

Public access   Limitations
    in person   no   Newspapers have established a Reader
    by mail   no   Service Unit for public information
    by phone   no   (not part of library)

Services available   Limitations
    copy machine   yes   For news staff use only
    reader/printer yes
    reader   yes

Hours of operation 6:30am-12:30am, M-Sat.; 9am-12:30am, Sun.

Resources
    clips   4,000,000   books   5,000
    photos   950,000   pamphlets 2,000
    negs   5,000   maps   7,500
    CPT   100   AV

Microform holdings
    own newspaper   Times 1901-present; Evening Independent 1907-
                      present
    periodicals   New York Times 1955-present
    clippings   4,000 jackets
Indexes
    own newspaper
    other   New York Times 1946-present

Special collections   Congressional Quarterly, 1945-present;
                         world's largest spot color map collection
                         drawn by our own newspaper map artists
Automation
  Automated files
    mechanical   Remington-Rand Lektrievers (6)
    electronic
  Other automated systems

Products for sale

Sarasota Herald-Tribune (mS)
Sarasota Journal (e)
Postal Drawer 1719
Sarasota   FL 33578

Circulation
(m) 82,928
(e) 8,219
(S) 92,542

813/953-7755 x390

Carl H. Johnson, Librarian

Lib. est. 1962   Group   Ind.   FTE   4

Public access   Limitations
    in person   yes   8am-4:30pm, M-F
    by mail   yes
    by phone   yes

Services available   Limitations
    copy machine   yes   Staff use only
    reader/printer   yes   Staff use only
    reader   yes   Public with supervision

Hours of operation   7am-9:30pm, M-F

Resources
    clips   9,000 subjects   books   240
    photos   x   pamphlets   x
    negs   maps   x
    CPT   AV

Microform holdings
    own newspaper   Oct. 4, 1925-present
    periodicals
    clippings

Indexes
    own newspaper
    other

Special collections

Automation
  Automated files
    mechanical
    electronic
  Other automated systems

Products for sale

FLORIDA   Tampa   FLORIDA

Tampa Tribune (m)
Tampa Times (e)
Tampa Tribune and Times (S)
202 S. Parker St.
Tampa FL 33602

<u>Circulation</u>
(m) 192,969
(e) 24,142
(S) 228,260

813/272-7711

Louise Leggette, Chief Librarian
Catherine Gess, Asst. Librarian

<u>Lib. est.</u> 1950's   <u>Group</u> Media General Inc.   <u>FTE</u> 14.5

<u>Public access</u>   <u>Limitations</u>
    in person   no
    by mail   yes $1.00 per article
    by phone   yes

<u>Services available</u>   <u>Limitations</u>
    copy machine   no
    reader/printer   yes
    reader   yes

<u>Hours of operation</u>   7am-11pm, M-F; 8am-5pm, Sat.

<u>Resources</u>
    clips   x   books   3,000
    photos   x   pamphlets   x
    negs   maps   x
    CPT   10   AV

<u>Microform holdings</u>
    own newspaper   Tribune, 1895-present; Times 1947-present
    periodicals
    clippings

<u>Indexes</u>
    own newspaper   no
    other

<u>Automation</u>
   Automated files
     mechanical   Lektriever
     electronic
   Other automated systems

<u>Products for sale</u>

FLORIDA   West Palm Beach   FLORIDA

Palm Beach Post (m)
Palm Beach Times (e)   Circulation
Palm Beach Post-Times (S)   (m) 88,022
2751 So. Dixie Highway   (e) 31,587
West Palm Beach FL 33405   (S) 131,820

                    305/833-7411 x394

         Richard Ploch, Chief Librarian
         Virginia Lyon

Lib. est. ?   Group Cox Enterprises   FTE 5

Public access   Limitations
    in person   yes   Microfilm viewing only - very limited
    by mail   yes   If send money and have specific request
    by phone   yes   Will give date, refer to public library

Services available   Limitations
    copy machine   yes   Limited public copying - $.50 per page
    reader/printer   yes $2.50 quarter page, $7.50 whole page
    reader   yes

Hours of operation 5:30am-6pm, M-F

Resources
    clips   c. 1,000,000   books   650
    photos   500,000   pamphlets   6 file drawers
    negs   not in library   maps   180
    CPT   AV

Microform holdings
    own newspaper   1933-present
    periodicals
    clippings   c. 20,000 clips on fiche

Indexes
    own newspaper
    other

Special collections

Automation
  Automated files
    mechanical
    electronic   Computer list of subject headings
  Other automated systems

Products for sale

GEORGIA   Atlanta   GEORGIA

Atlanta Constitution (m)   Circulation
Atlanta Journal (e)   (m) 219,153
Atlanta Journal and Constitution (S)   (e) 218,347
72 Marietta St. NW   (S) 514,561
Atlanta GA 30303
                        404/572-5420

    Julia M. Vance, Director of Library Services
    Gerald Joiner, Asst. Director of Library Services

Lib. est. 1945   Group Cox Enterprises   FTE 12.5

Public access   Limitations
    in person   no   Legitimate researchers with approval of
    by mail   no   Director, work on fee basis only
    by phone   no

Services available   Limitations
    copy machine   yes $.50 per page
    reader/printer yes $.50 per page
    reader   yes $.50 per page

Hours of operation   4am-Midnight, M-F; 8am-Midnight, Sat.; Noon-
                      Midnight, Sun.
Resources
    clips   5,000,000   books   4,000
    photos   2,500,000   pamphlets   x
    negs   maps   x
    CPT   150   AV

Microform holdings
    own newspaper   1868-present, Const.; 1883-present, Journal
    periodicals   8 titles on microfiche

Indexes
    own newspaper   Journal 1940's-June 1979; Jrnal. & Const. 1980-
    other   New York Times 1947-present
Automation
  Automated files
    electronic   Combined on-line library system with ready reference,
                  authority file, book catalog & serials control. Hard-
                  ware: 2 IBM 3330's, 3270 terminals & printers. Soft-
                  ware: Turnkey's Documaster
  Other automated systems New York Times Information Bank, SDC, DIALOG

GEORGIA   Augusta   GEORGIA

The Augusta Chronicle
The South's Oldest Newspaper – Established 1785

Augusta Chronicle (mS)
Augusta Herald (e)
News Building
725 Broad St.
Augusta GA 30903

Circulation
(m) 56,102
(e) 18,844
(S) 80,173

404/724-0851 x229

Edward S. Mitchell, Jr., Librarian
Jerry W. Brown, Asst. Librarian

Lib. est. 1965   Group Southeastern Newspapers Corp.   FTE 2

Public access
     in person   yes
     by mail   yes
     by phone   yes

Limitations
     Single files only
     Research time $7.00 per hour plus copy
     No research

Services available
     copy machine   yes
     reader/printer   yes
     reader   yes

Limitations
     Library personnel minimum charge
     Library personnel $1.00 per page

Hours of operation   9am-9pm, M-F

Resources
     clips   818 linear feet   books
     photos   pamphlets
     negs   maps
     CPT   AV

Microform holdings
     own newspaper   1786-present
     periodicals
     clippings

Indexes
     own newspaper   none
     other

Automation
  Automated files
    mechanical
    electronic
  Other automated systems

Products for sale

GEORGIA   Columbus   GEORGIA

The Columbus Enquirer (m)   Circulation
The Columbus Ledger (e)   (m) 33,527
The Sunday Ledger-Enquirer (S)   (e) 30,929
P.O. Box 711   (S) 68,992
Columbus GA 31902
                        404/324-5526 x433

              Patricia F. Hardy, Librarian
              Gladys Sandoval, Asst. Librarian

Lib. est. 1947   Group Knight-Ridder Newspapers   FTE 2

Public access   Limitations
    in person   no
    by mail   yes   Copies of clippings
    by phone   yes   Addresses of newspapers in other cities

Services available   Limitations
    copy machine   yes $2.00 per page
    reader/printer
    reader   yes $10.00 per hour

Hours of operation 8am-8pm, M-F

Resources
    clips   600,000   books   1,500
    photos   20,000   pamphlets   10,000
    negs   100,000   maps   250
    CPT   50   AV

Microform holdings
    own newspaper   May 1832-present
    periodicals
    clippings

Indexes
    own newspaper   none
    other

Automation
  Automated files
    mechanical
    electronic
  Other automated systems

Products for sale

72

HAWAII   Honolulu   HAWAII

Honolulu Advertiser (m)   Circulation
Honolulu Star Bulletin (e)   (m) 85,218
Honolulu Star Bulletin and Advertiser (S)   (e) 120,389
P.O. Box 3350   (S) 204,589
Honolulu HI 96801

                          808/525-7669

            Beatrice Kaya, Chief Librarian
            Margaret Iwamoto, Asst. Librarian

Lib. est. 1930   Group Gannett Pacific Corp. (Star & Bulletin) FTE 10
                         Ind. (Advertiser)

Public access   Limitations
    in person   yes   By appointment only
    by mail   yes   Dates of articles provided
    by phone   yes   Dates of articles provided

Services available   Limitations
    copy machine   yes $1.00 per page
    reader/printer yes $4.00 per page
    reader   yes   By appointment only

Hours of operation   7am-9:30pm, M-F; 7am-8pm, Sat.; Noon-8pm, Sun.

Resources
    clips   3,500,000   books   2,500
    photos   500,000   pamphlets   12 drawers
    negs   maps   5 drawers
    CPT   AV

Microform holdings
    own newspaper   1840-present
    periodicals
    clippings   32,900

Indexes
    own newspaper   1929-1978
    other

Special collections   Hawaiiana

Automation
  Automated files
    mechanical   Lektriever
    electronic
  Other automated systems

73

The Idaho STATESMAN

Idaho Statesman (mS)
P.O. Box 40
Boise ID 83707

208/377-6435

Circulation
(m) 55,773
(S) 70,502

Nancy Van Dinter, Librarian
A.M. Fritz, Library Asst.
Lynda Irons, Library Asst.

Lib. est. 1972   Group Gannett Newspapers   FTE 2.5

Public access
- in person   yes
- by mail   yes
- by phone   yes

Limitations
No public use of clip files. Specified articles copied only. Dates supplied by mail or phone. Microfilm users referred to other area libraries.

Services available
- copy machine   yes
- reader/printer yes
- reader   yes

Limitations
$.25 per page
$1.00 per page

Hours of operation   8am-10:30pm, M-F; 9am-1pm, Sat.

Resources
clips	220,500	books	450
photos	12,000	pamphlets	6 drawers
negs		maps	200
CPT	25	AV	

Microform holdings
- own newspaper   July 26, 1864-present
- periodicals
- clippings

Indexes
- own newspaper   none

Special collections   Idaho maps, photos, government documents

Automation
  Automated files
    mechanical
    electronic
  Other automated systems

ILLINOIS   Bloomington   ILLINOIS

The Daily Pantagraph

Daily Pantagraph (all day)	**Circulation**
Sunday Pantagraph (S)	(all day)
301 W. Washington	52,077
Bloomington IL 61701	(S) 50,612
309/829-9411	

Diane Miller, Head Librarian
Sally Vance, Asst. Librarian

Lib. est. 1930   Group Ind.   FTE 4

Public access   **Limitations**
     in person   yes
     by mail   yes
     by phone   yes

Services available   **Limitations**
     copy machine   yes   Charge for copies
     reader/printer   yes
     reader   yes

Hours of operation   8am-4:30pm, M-F

Resources
clips	1,000,000	books	500
photos	2,000	pamphlets	150
negs	10,000	maps	150
CPT		AV	

Microform holdings
     own newspaper   1947-present
     periodicals
     clippings   30,000

Indexes
     own newspaper
     other

Special collections   Adlai Stevenson II, railroad pictures

Automation
   Automated files
     mechanical
     electronic
   Other automated systems

Products for sale

ILLINOIS   Champaign   ILLINOIS

Champaign-Urbana News-Gazette (eS) 48 Main St. Champaign IL 61820 217/351-5228	Circulation (e) 41,101 (S) 44,304

Deborah Voigt, Chief Librarian
Lucille Molt, Asst. Librarian

Lib. est. 1946   Group Ind.   FTE 2

Public access   Limitations
   in person   yes   M-F, room use only
   by mail   yes
   by phone   no   Only local service by phone

Services available   Limitations
   copy machine yes   Librarian makes all copies
   reader/printer no
   reader   yes

Hours of operation   7:30am-4:30pm, M-F; 8am-Noon, Sat.

Resources
   clips   100,000   books   300
   photos   5,000   pamphlets 600
   negs   maps   100
   CPT   AV

Microform holdings
   own newspaper   1853-present (1853-present kept at University
                             of Illinois Newspaper Library; 1953-present
                             kept at News-Gazette)

Indexes
   own newspaper   none
   other

Special collections

Automation
  Automated files
    mechanical
    electronic
  Other automated systems

Products for sale

Chicago Sun-Times (mS)
401 N. Wabash Ave.
Chicago IL 60611
312/321-2593

Circulation
(m) 671,366
(S) 720,201

Ernest Perez, Head Librarian
Terri M. Golembiewski, Chief Reference Librarian

Lib. est. 1908   Group Ind.   FTE 21

Public access
- in person   no
- by mail   no
- by phone   no

Limitations
Public Service Bureau for outside requests; visiting journalists or serious researchers allowed.

Services available
- copy machine   yes
- reader/printer yes
- reader   yes

Limitations

Hours of operation 24 hrs., M-Sun.

Resources

clips	466,000 files	books	3,200 volumes
photos	315,000 files	pamphlets	1,800
negs	255,000 envelopes	maps	600
CPT	61	AV	

Microform holdings
- own newspaper   1875-present
- periodicals   2700 rolls
- clippings

Indexes
- own newspaper   Online index of Sun-Times and Daily News 1976-present
- other   New York Times, 1930-1978; Tribune 1972-1976

Special collections Books published by staff members

Automation
  Automated files
   mechanical: Remington-Rand Lektriever, Elecompakt
   electronic: IBM STAIRS index 1976-present; full text system in development
  Other automated systems: New York Times Information Bank

ILLINOIS   Chicago   ILLINOIS

Chicago Tribune

Chicago Tribune (all day,S)
435 N. Michigan Ave.
Chicago IL 60611

312/222-4416

<u>Circulation</u>
(all day)
    783,041
(S) 1,157,870

Barbara Newcombe, Manager, Editorial Information Center
Mary Huschen, Asst. Manager

<u>Lib. est.</u>   <u>Group</u> Ind.   <u>FTE</u> 20

<u>Public access</u>   <u>Limitations</u>
   in person   no   Except out-of-town working press & non-profit institutions
   by mail   yes $13 to search and copy
   by phone   no

<u>Services available</u>   <u>Limitations</u>
   copy machine   yes
   reader/printer   yes
   reader   yes

<u>Hours of operation</u> 24 hrs., 7 days

<u>Resources</u>
   clips   18,000,000   books   8,000
   photos   6,000,000   pamphlets   8 drawers
   negs   1973-present   maps   30+
   CPT   200   AV

<u>Microform holdings</u>
   own newspaper   1847-present
   periodicals   New York Times 1969-present on fiche; 22 titles on rolls since 1967

<u>Indexes</u>
   own newspaper   1972-present
   other   Reader's Guide 1935-present; Facts on File 1970-present; New York Times 1913-present; Current Biography; Biography Index; Book Review Index; Wall Street Journal 1979-present

<u>Automation</u>
  Automated files
    electronic
  Other automated systems New York Times Information Bank; Dow Jones News Retrieval

<u>Products for sale</u>

ILLINOIS · Decatur · ILLINOIS

Decatur Herald (m)
Decatur Review (e)
Decatur Herald and Review (S)
601 E. William St.
Decatur IL 62525

217/429-5151 x40 or 42

Circulation
(m) 38,167
(e) 26,893
(S) 62,179

Faye Spencer, Library Supervisor
Geraldine Hearn, Asst. Library Supervisor

Lib. est. 1910   Group Lindsay Schaub Newspapers   FTE 9

Public access
   in person   yes
   by mail   no
   by phone   yes

Limitations
Service fee charged

Limited

Services available
   copy machine   yes
   reader/printer
   reader

Limitations
Charge

Hours of operation   7am-11pm, M-Sat.; 2:30pm-11pm, Sun.

Resources
clips	300,000	envelopes	books	1,000
photos	100,000		pamphlets	1,200
negs	20,000		maps	
CPT			AV	

Microform holdings
   own newspaper   1872-present (incomplete)
   periodicals
   clippings

Indexes
   own newspaper
   other

Special collections

Automation
  Automated files
    mechanical
    electronic
  Other automated systems

Products for sale

ILLINOIS   Joliet   ILLINOIS

Herald-News (eS)   Circulation
300 Caterpillar Dr.   (e) 50,987
Joliet IL 60436   (S) 52,252
                         815/729-6065

        Dolores Gretz, Librarian
        Connie Hodge, Asst.

Lib. est. 1839   Group Copley Newspapers   FTE 2

Public access   Limitations
    in person   yes
    by mail   yes
    by phone   yes

Services available   Limitations
    copy machine
    reader/printer
    reader

Hours of operation 9:30am-6pm, M-Sat.

Resources
    clips   books
    photos   pamphlets
    negs   maps
    CPT   AV

Microform holdings
    own newspaper
    periodicals
    clippings

Indexes
    own newspaper
    other

Special collections

Automation
  Automated files
    mechanical
    electronic
  Other automated systems

Products for sale

ILLINOIS   Kankakee   ILLINOIS

Journal (eS)   Circulation
8 Dearborn Square   (e) 33,718
Kankakee IL 60901   (S) 35,523
                            815/937-3378

              Kathleen Belletete, Head Librarian

Lib. est.   Group Small Newspapers   FTE 2.5

Public access   Limitations
     in person   no   Staff only
     by mail
     by phone

Services available   Limitations
     copy machine   yes   Staff only
     reader/printer
     reader

Hours of operation 7am-5pm, M-F; 8am-Noon, Sat.

Resources
     clips   x   books
     photos   x   pamphlets
     negs   x   maps   x
     CPT   AV

Microform holdings
     own newspaper   1853-present
     periodicals
     clippings

Indexes
     own newspaper
     other

Special collections

Automation
  Automated files
     mechanical
     electronic
  Other automated systems

Products for sale

81

ILLINOIS   Moline   ILLINOIS

THE DAILY DISPATCH

The Daily Dispatch (eS)   <u>Circulation</u>
1720 5th Ave.   (e) 35,803
Moline IL 61275   (S) 37,168
                        309/764-4344

            Joanne Wiklund, Librarian

<u>Lib. est.</u> 1928   <u>Group</u> Small Newspapers   <u>FTE</u>

<u>Public access</u>   <u>Limitations</u>
    in person   yes   Afternoons
    by mail   Research done time permitting; extensive
    by phone   research by librarian, fee basis only

<u>Services available</u>   <u>Limitations</u>
    copy machine   yes $.50 per sheet
    reader/printer no
    reader   no

<u>Hours of operation</u> 7am-3pm, M-F

<u>Resources</u>
    clips   32,000+ envelopes   books
    photos   inc. with clips   pamphlets
    negs   maps   In Art Dept.
    CPT   AV

<u>Microform holdings</u>
    own newspaper   1953-present
    periodicals
    clippings

<u>Indexes</u>
    own newspaper
    other

<u>Special collections</u>

<u>Automation</u>
  Automated files
    mechanical
    electronic
  Other automated systems

<u>Products for sale</u>

ILLINOIS   Peoria   ILLINOIS

Journal Star (all day,S)   Circulation
1 News Plaza   (all day)
Peoria IL 61643   102,929
                                                       (S) 119,937
                            309/686-3108

              Judy A. Howard, Head Librarian

Lib. est. Prior to 1900   Group Ind.   FTE 4

Public access   Limitations
       in person   no   Closed to public
       by mail   yes
       by phone   yes   Public given dates and referred to
                               public library

Services available   Limitations
       copy machine
       reader/printer
       reader

Hours of operation 8am-12:30am, M-F

Resources
       clips   750,000 files   books   x
       photos   x   pamphlets   x
       negs   1970-present   maps   In Art Dept.
       CPT   AV

Microform holdings
       own newspaper   1929-present
       periodicals
       clippings

Indexes
       own newspaper   1937-present
       other

Special collections

Automation
  Automated files
     mechanical
     electronic
  Other automated systems

Products for sale

83

ILLINOIS   Quincy   ILLINOIS

Quincy Herald-Whig (eS)   Circulation
130 S. Fifth St.   (e) 30,829
Quincy IL 62301   (S) 33,599
                              217/223-5100

          Linda Reinold, Librarian

Lib. est. ?   Group Ind.   FTE

Public access   Limitations
    in person   yes   Files must remain in office
    by mail
    by phone

Services available   Limitations
    copy machine yes $.25 per page
    reader/printer
    reader   yes

Hours of operation 8am-4pm, M-Sat.

Resources
    clips   x   books
    photos   pamphlets
    negs   maps
    CPT   AV

Microform holdings
    own newspaper   1850-present
    periodicals
    clippings

Indexes
    own newspaper
    other

Special collections

Automation
  Automated files
    mechanical
    electronic
  Other automated systems

Products for sale

ILLINOIS　　　　　　　　　Rockford　　　　　　　　　ILLINOIS

Rockford Register Star (meS)　　　　　　　　　　Circulation
97 East State St.　　　　　　　　　　　　　　　　(m) 57,302
Rockford IL 61115　　　　　　　　　　　　　　　　(e) 22,951
　　　　　　　　　　　　　　　　　　　　　　　　(S) 83,086
　　　　　　　　　　　　　815/987-1349

　　　　Edith Piercy, Chief Librarian
　　　　Clarence Kamber, Librarian

Lib. est. 1958　　　　Group　Gannett Newspapers　　　FTE 2

Public access　　　　　　　Limitations
　　in person　　no　　　　Will make photocopies of clips
　　by mail　　　yes　　　　No geneaology research.
　　by phone　　 yes

Services available　　　　Limitations
　　copy machine　　　no
　　reader/printer　 no
　　reader　　　　　　no

Hours of operation　8:30am-11pm, M-F

Resources
　　clips　　c. 108,160　　　　books　　　　500
　　photos　 c. 20,000　　　　pamphlets　　250
　　negs　　 c.   1,000　　　　maps　　　 1,000
　　CPT　　　　　　　　　　　　AV

Microform holdings
　　own newspaper　　1865-present
　　periodicals
　　clippings

Indexes
　　own newspaper　　none
　　other

Special collections

Automation
　Automated files
　　mechanical
　　electronic
　Other automated systems

Products for sale

85

ILLINOIS Springfield ILLINOIS

State Journal & Register (meS)
313 South 6th St.
Springfield IL 62701

Circulation
(m) 59,551
(e) 13,734
(S) 74,263

217/788-8769

Sandra Vance, Librarian
Mary Hayes, Library Clerk

Lib. est. 1931   Group Copley Newspapers   FTE 2

Public access
- in person yes
- by mail   yes
- by phone   yes

Limitations

Services available
- copy machine yes
- reader/printer
- reader   yes

Limitations
$1.00 legal size copy

Hours of operation 7:30am-4:30pm, M-F

Resources
clips	2,264,000	books	700
photos	10,000	pamphlets	300
negs		maps	50
CPT		AV	

Microform holdings
- own newspaper   1831-present
- periodicals
- clippings

Indexes
- own newspaper
- other

Automation
- Automated files
  - mechanical
  - electronic
- Other automated systems

Products for sale

ILLINOIS   Waukegan   ILLINOIS

News-Sun (e)   Circulation
100 Madison   (e) 43,123
Waukegan IL 60085
                        312/689-6969

            Barbara Apple, Librarian
            Ruth Perry, Asst. Librarian

Lib. est. 1925   Group Keystone-Printing Service Inc.   FTE

Public access   Limitations
    in person   no   Only if information is not available
    by mail   no   at the public library.
    by phone   no

Services available   Limitations
    copy machine   yes   Not for public use. Will serve
    reader/printer   advertisers who need information.
    reader   yes

Hours of operation   7:30am-9:30pm, M-F

Resources
    clips   520,000   books   650
    photos   88,500   pamphlets   1,000
    negs   maps   100
    CPT   AV

Microform holdings
    own newspaper
    periodicals
    clippings

Indexes
    own newspaper   1975-present
    other

Special collections

Automation
  Automated files
    mechanical
    electronic
  Other automated systems

Products for sale

87

INDIANA Evansville INDIANA

The Evansville Press

Courier (m)
Press (e)
Courier & Press (S)
201 NW 2nd St.
Evansville IN 47702

812/464-7616

Lucille Loewenkamp, Librarian

Circulation
(m) 63,026
(e) 44,164
(S) 117,767

<u>Lib. est.</u>   <u>Group</u> Scripps-Howard Newspapers   <u>FTE</u> 1

<u>Public access</u>
   in person   yes
   by mail
   by phone

<u>Limitations</u>
With special permission

<u>Services available</u>
   copy machine
   reader/printer
   reader

<u>Limitations</u>

<u>Hours of operation</u>

<u>Resources</u>
   clips
   photos
   negs
   CPT

   books
   pamphlets
   maps
   AV

<u>Microform holdings</u>
   own newspaper
   periodicals
   clippings

<u>Indexes</u>
   own newspaper
   other

<u>Special collections</u>

<u>Automation</u>
  Automated files
    mechanical
    electronic
  Other automated systems

<u>Products for sale</u>

INDIANA   Fort Wayne   INDIANA

The Journal-Gazette

Journal-Gazette (mS)
600 West Main St.
Fort Wayne IN 46802
219/461-8378

Circulation
(m) 60,661
(S) 103,421

Rosalina Stier, Librarian
Shirla Eisberg, Photo Librarian
Doris Ross and Betty Spruill, Assistants

Lib. est. 1977   Group Ind.   FTE 3.5

Public access   Limitations
- in person   no
- by mail   no
- by phone   no

Services available   Limitations
- copy machine   yes   For Journal-Gazette newsmen
- reader/printer
- reader   yes   For Journal-Gazette newsmen

Hours of operation 8am-12:30am, M-F

Resources
- clips   c. 230,971   books   250
- photos   c. 22,250   pamphlets 250
- negs   67,000   maps   8
- CPT   1   AV

Microform holdings
- own newspaper   Jan. 1, 1884-present
- periodicals

Indexes
- own newspaper
- other

Special collections

Automation
- Automated files
  - mechanical
  - electronic
- Other automated systems

Products for sale

Post-Tribune (eS)
1065 Broadway
Gary IN 46402
                    219/886-5078

Circulation
(e) 82,464
(S) 85,587

Louise Tucker, Librarian
Carol Chisholm, Librarian

Lib. est.   Group Knight-Ridder Newspapers   FTE 2

Public access
		Limitations
in person	yes	By appointment, on very limited basis
by mail	yes	No extensive research
by phone	yes	8am-3pm, M-F; no extensive research

Services available
		Limitations
copy machine	yes	Small charge, on limited basis for public
reader/printer		
reader	yes	For employee use only

Hours of operation 7:30am-4:00pm, M-F

Resources
clips	100,000+	books	5 units
photos	several thousand	pamphlets	very few
negs		maps	very few
CPT		AV	

Microform holdings
- own newspaper   none
- periodicals
- clippings

Indexes
- own newspaper   none
- other

Special collections

Automation
  Automated files
    mechanical
    electronic
  Other automated systems

Products for sale

INDIANA   Indianapolis   INDIANA

Indianapolis Star (mS)
Indianapolis News (e)
307 N. Pennsylvania
Indianapolis IN 46206

317/633-9293

Circulation
(m) 213,470
(e) 148,905
(S) 355,622

James Post, Head Librarian
Sandra Fitzgerald, Asst. Head Librarian

Lib. est. 1912   Group   Central Newspapers   FTE 18

Public access
     in person   yes
     by mail   yes
     by phone   yes

Limitations
Research provided by staff at $9.00 per hour plus cost of copies

Services available
     copy machine   yes
     reader/printer   yes
     reader   yes

Limitations
Up to 3 articles at $.50 each
Up to 3 microfilm pages at $1.50 each

Hours of operation   6am-12:15am, M-F; 1pm-12:15am, Sat.

Resources
     clips   2,000,000   books   2,000
     photos   1,000,000   pamphlets   33 drawers
     negs   maps   filed with photos
     CPT   12   AV

Microform holdings
     own newspaper   1869-present
     periodicals

Indexes
     own newspaper   Indianapolis News, 1912-present; Indianapolis Star, 1927-present
     other   New York Times, 1969-present

Special collections   Indiana lore and history

Automation
  Automated files
    mechanical
    electronic
  Other automated systems

Products for sale

INDIANA   Kokomo   INDIANA

KOKOMO TRIBUNE

Kokomo Tribune (eS)
300 N. Union
Kokomo IN 46901

317/459-3121 x227

Circulation
(e) 30,167
(S) 30,306

Dawn L. North, Librarian

Lib. est. 1976   Group   Ind.   FTE

Public access   Limitations
    in person   yes   Photo reprints only
    by mail   yes   Copies of articles; date requests
    by phone   yes   No extensive research

Services available   Limitations
    copy machine   yes $.10 per page; by mail only
    reader/printer   yes   No public use
    reader

Hours of operation   8am-5pm, M-F

Resources
    clips   100 feet   books   200+
    photos   12 feet   pamphlets   10 feet
    negs   1958-present   maps   limited
    CPT   AV

Microform holdings
    own newspaper   1868-present
    periodicals
    clippings

Indexes
    own newspaper   1868-1968, not complete; 1969-1975, non-existent;
                        1976-present, in progress
    other

Special collections   Indiana, Howard County, Cass County, Tipton County,
                       and Miami County history

Automation
  Automated files
    mechanical
    electronic
  Other automated systems

Products for sale

INDIANA   Muncie   INDIANA

Muncie Star (mS)   Circulation
Muncie Evening Press (e)   (m) 29,481
125 S. High St.   (e) 18,329
Muncie In 47302   (S) 33,488
                           317/747-5767

            Breena Wysong, Head Librarian
            Lorie Lowery, Clerk-Typist

<u>Lib. est.</u> ?   <u>Group</u> Central Newspapers   <u>FTE</u> 2

<u>Public access</u>   <u>Limitations</u>
     in person   yes
     by mail   yes
     by phone   yes

<u>Services available</u>   <u>Limitations</u>
     copy machine   yes $.20 per page
     reader/printer
     reader   yes

<u>Hours of operation</u> 7am-9pm, M-F

<u>Resources</u>
     clips   1960-present   books   limited
     photos   x   pamphlets
     negs   maps
     CPT   AV

<u>Microform holdings</u>
     own newspaper
     periodicals
     clippings

<u>Indexes</u>
     own newspaper
     other

<u>Special collections</u>

<u>Automation</u>
   Automated files
     mechanical
     electronic
   Other automated systems

<u>Products for sale</u>

INDIANA   South Bend   INDIANA

South Bend Tribune (eS)   Circulation
223 W. Colfax   (e) 107,414
South Bend IN 46626   (S) 126,646
                       219/233-6161 x347

           Mrs. Ralph Grauel, Librarian
           Kathy Ginter, Asst. Librarian

Lib. est. 1929   Group Ind.   FTE 2

Public access   Limitations
      in person   yes   Do not encourage but will help
      by mail   yes
      by phone   yes

Services available   Limitations
      copy machine   no
      reader/printer no
      reader   yes

Hours of operation 7:30am-4:00pm, M-F

Resources
      clips   235 drawers   books   384
      photos   77 drawers   pamphlets   24
      negs   149 drawers   maps   3 atlases
      CPT   2   AV

Microform holdings
      own newspaper   1872-present
      periodicals
      clippings

Indexes
      own newspaper   none
      other

Special collections

Automation
   Automated files
      mechanical
      electronic
   Other automated systems

Products for sale

IOWA   Cedar Rapids   IOWA

The Gazette

Cedar Rapids Gazette (eS)
500 Third St.
Cedar Rapids IA 52406
319/398-8328

Circulation
(e) 68,858
(S) 76,856

Bridget Janus, Librarian
Jan Peacock, Library Asst.

Lib. est. ?   Group Ind.   FTE 2

Public access
     in person   yes
     by mail   yes
     by phone   yes

Limitations
No copying
No extended research
No extended research

Services available
     copy machine
     reader/printer
     reader   yes

Limitations

Hours of operation   7:30am-4pm, M-F

Resources
     clips   10 cabinets   books   50+
     photos   10,000   pamphlets   none
     negs   maps   5
     CPT   AV

Microform holdings
     own newspaper   x
     periodicals
     clippings

Indexes
     own newspaper
     other

Special collections

Automation
   Automated files
     mechanical
     electronic
   Other automated systems

Products for sale

IOWA   Davenport   IOWA

Quad-City Times

Quad-City Times (all day, S) 124 E. 2nd St. Davenport IA 52808	Circulation (all day) 63,872 (S) 81,625

319/383-2293

Elizabeth Van Lauwe, Librarian

Lib. est.   Group   Ind.   FTE   1

Public access   Limitations
     in person   no
     by mail   no
     by phone   no

Services available   Limitations
     copy machine
     reader/printer
     reader   yes

Hours of operation   9am-5pm, M-F

Resources
     clips   18,000 envelopes   books   150
     photos   755 envelopes   pamphlets   200
     negs   maps   2
     CPT   AV

Microform holdings
     own newspaper   x
     periodicals
     clippings

Indexes
     own newspaper
     other

Special collections

Automation
  Automated files
    mechanical
    electronic
  Other automated systems

Products for sale

IOWA   Des Moines   IOWA

Des Moines Register (m)   Circulation
Des Moines Tribune (e)   (m) 216,057
Des Moines Sunday Register (S)   (e) 86,623
715 Locust   (S) 406,842
Des Moines IA 50304
                        515/284-8000

        Phyllis Wolfe, Librarian

Lib. est. c. 1925   Group Ind.   FTE 7

Public access   Limitations
    in person   no
    by mail   no
    by phone   no

Services available   Limitations
    copy machine   yes   No public access; $25/hr + copy costs
    reader/printer yes   if research authorized; $.25 per copy
    reader   yes

Hours of operation   7:30am-10:30pm, M-F; irregular on Sat. & Sun.

Resources
    clips   1,000 drawers   books   500+
    photos   184 cabinets   pamphlets
    negs   maps
    CPT   1   AV

Microform holdings
    own newspaper   Register, 1871-present; Tribune, 1907-present
    periodicals

Indexes
    own newspaper   1975-present: selective, Iowa State Univ.

Special collections   World War II collection; very complete collection
of movie photos

Automation
  Automated files
    mechanical   installing Lundia Fullspace
    electronic
  Other automated systems   AP Political Database

Products for sale

IOWA   Dubuque   IOWA

Telegraph Herald

Telegraph Herald (eS)
P.O. Box 688
Dubuque IA 52001
319/588-5770

Circulation
(e) 39,610
(S) 42,197

Ruth C. Paine, Manager of Library Services
Letha Splinter, Library Asst.

Lib. est. 1970   Group Ind.   FTE 2.5

Public access   Limitations
- in person   yes   Article dates, copies for fee
- by mail   yes
- by phone   yes   Simple requests only

Services available   Limitations
- copy machine
- reader/printer yes   Employees only
- reader

Hours of operation   8am-5pm, M-F; 8am-11pm, Sat. (unstaffed)

Resources
- clips   100,000+   books   2,300
- photos   100,000+   pamphlets 11 drawers
- negs   maps
- CPT   78   AV   x

Microform holdings
- own newspaper   1837-present
- periodicals
- clippings

Indexes
- own newspaper
- other

Special collections   35mm slide collection-Dubuque historical photos; Dubuque city directories from 1856 (incomplete); Dubuque history

Automation
Automated files
- mechanical   Remington Rand Lektriever 100; 2 mechanized storage/retrieval machines

Products for sale

Waterloo Courier

Waterloo Courier (eS)
501 Commercial St.
Waterloo IA 50704

319/291-1477

Wilda Workman, Librarian
Beverly Knipp, Asst. Librarian

Circulation
(e) 53,931
(S) 56,821

Lib. est. 1941   Group Ind.   FTE 2

Public access
in person	no	Subject to editor's decision
by mail	no	Subject to editor's decision
by phone	yes	Only non-controversial, limited research

Limitations (as above)

Services available
copy machine	yes	Subject to limitations - $.50 per copy
reader/printer	yes	Subject to limitations - $1.00 per copy
reader		

Hours of operation 8am-4:30pm, M-Sun.

Resources

clips	100,000+	books	300
photos	12,000+	pamphlets	25
negs	13,000+	maps	1
CPT	25	AV	

Microform holdings
- own newspaper   1859-present
- periodicals
- clippings

Indexes
- own newspaper
- other

Special collections Historical cuts, veloxes and photos

Automation
- Automated files
  - mechanical
  - electronic
- Other automated systems

Products for sale

KANSAS		Topeka		KANSAS

Capital (m)   Circulation
State Journal (e)   (m) 60,799
Capital Journal (S)   (e) 26,964
616 Jefferson St.   (S) 74,212
Topeka KS 66607
                        913/295-1291

            Patricia Johnston, Librarian
            Michelle Beck, Asst. Librarian

<u>Lib. est.</u> 1955   <u>Group</u> Stauffer Communications Inc.   <u>FTE</u> 2

<u>Public access</u>   <u>Limitations</u>
    in person   yes
    by mail   yes
    by phone   yes

<u>Services available</u>   <u>Limitations</u>
    copy machine
    reader/printer
    reader   yes   No charge; not available 12:30pm-3pm

<u>Hours of operation</u> 8am-4pm, M-F

<u>Resources</u>
    clips   x   books   x
    photos   x   pamphlets   x
    negs   x   maps   x
    CPT   AV

<u>Microform holdings</u>
    own newspaper   x
    periodicals
    clippings

<u>Indexes</u>
    own newspaper
    other

<u>Automation</u>
  Automated files
    mechanical   Lektriever
    electronic
  Other automated systems

<u>Products for sale</u>

Kentucky Post (e)
421 Madison Ave.
Covington KY 41011

606/292-2616

Circulation
(e) (56,590)

Lisa Eckere, Librarian

<u>Lib. est.</u> 1979   <u>Group</u> Scripps-Howard Newspapers   <u>FTE</u> 1

<u>Public access</u>   <u>Limitations</u>
    in person   yes
    by mail   yes   Must know exact date
    by phone   yes   Must know exact date

<u>Services available</u>   <u>Limitations</u>
    copy machine   yes
    reader/printer
    reader

<u>Hours of operation</u>

<u>Resources</u>
    clips   x   books   x
    photos   x   pamphlets
    negs   maps   x
    CPT   x   AV

<u>Microform holdings</u>
    own newspaper   1899-present
    periodicals
    clippings

<u>Indexes</u>
    own newspaper
    other

<u>Special collections</u>

<u>Automation</u>
  Automated files
    mechanical
    electronic
  Other automated systems

<u>Products for sale</u>

KENTUCKY   Lexington   KENTUCKY

THE SATURDAY
HERALD AND LEADER

Lexington Herald (m)
Lexington Leader (e)
Lexington Herald and Leader (S)
239 West Short St.
Lexington KY 40507

606/254-6666 x260

Circulation
(m) 66,057
(e) 33,485
(S) 104,819

Linda L. Smith, Librarian
Barbara Webb, Library Clerk

Lib. est. 1970   Group Knight-Ridder Newspapers   FTE 1.5

Public access
- in person   no
- by mail   no
- by phone   no

Limitations
Public is encouraged to use Lexington Public Library

Services available
- copy machine   yes
- reader/printer   yes
- reader   yes

Limitations
Staff only - $.25 for personal copies

Hours of operation   8am-8pm, M-F

Resources
- clips   65,000
- photos   7,000
- negs
- CPT   12
- books   700
- pamphlets   500
- maps   100
- AV

Microform holdings
- own newspaper   1888-present
- periodicals

Indexes
- own newspaper
- other   Index to our photo collection

Special collections

Automation
- Automated files
- Other automated systems

Products for sale

Courier-Journal (mS)
Louisville Times (e)
525 W. Broadway
Louisville KY 40205

Circulation
(m) 197,204
(e) 153,558
(S) 335,604

502/582-4601   Reader Service: 582-4545

Doris J. Batliner, Chief Librarian
Leonard Tharp, Asst. Librarian

<u>Lib. est.</u> 1937   <u>Group</u> Ind.   <u>FTE</u>   21.5

<u>Public access</u>   <u>Limitations</u>
   in person   yes   Can look at one year file of papers; Own
                         research, $25 for 2 hrs.; Libn's online
                         research for $.84/min. plus $.25 per copy
   by mail   yes $5 minimum research charge
   by phone   no   Except for photo orders

<u>Services available</u>   <u>Limitations</u>
   copy machine   yes   Staff only
   reader/printer yes   Staff only

<u>Hours of operation</u> 7am-11pm, M-Sat.; 3pm-11pm, Sun.

<u>Resources</u>
   clips   5,000,000   books   7,000
   photos   2,500,000   pamphlets 10,000
   negs   maps
   CPT   50   AV   500 tapes

<u>Microform holdings</u>
   own newspaper   1868-present: microfiche and rolls
   periodicals   New York Times on roll

<u>Indexes</u>
   own newspaper   On computer 1976-present
   other   New York Times

<u>Automation</u>
   Automated files
      electronic   Info-Ky system; on-line, keyword + enhancement terms;
                   ISI Image Systems Viewers + ADM II CRT's; software
                   by Dissly Research Programming
   Other automated systems DIALOG, SDC, New York Times Information Bank

<u>Products for sale</u> Occasional bibliographies

KENTUCKY Owensboro KENTUCKY

Messenger-Inquirer

Messenger-Inquirer (mS)
1401 Frederica St.
Owensboro KY 42301

502/926-0123 x266

Circulation
(m) 32,457
(S) 32,201

Nancy Campbell, Chief Librarian

Lib. est. 1973   Group Ind.   FTE 3

Public access   Limitations
   in person   no   Prior written request required. Drop-ins
   by mail   yes   helped, but not allowed in library. For
   by phone   yes   substantial searches, fee is $15 per hour
                                       plus cost of copies.

Services available   Limitations
   copy machine   yes $.15 per copy
   reader/printer   yes $3.00 per copy
   reader   no   Microfilm users sent to public library

Hours of operation 9am-8pm, M-F

Resources
   clips   2,500 subj. headings   books   900
   photos   10,000   pamphlets   350
   negs   maps   35
   CPT   36   AV

Microform holdings
   own newspaper   1863-present
   periodicals
   clippings

Indexes
   own newspaper   1977-1979 (published by public library)
   other

Automation
  Automated files
   mechanical   Bruning 96 for fiche display, compatible with Info-Ky
   electronic   Info-Ky; online index, uses PDP 11/34, 2 megabyte
                  disk drives (online as of 1979)
  Other automated systems: Bibliofile, a unique online catalog of all
                        materials other than clippings

Products for sale   Have trade-off with public library: will produce
                    index as of 1980 in exchange for retrospective
                  index done by them

LOUISIANA — Baton Rouge — LOUISIANA

MORNING ADVOCATE
STATE TIMES
SUNDAY ADVOCATE

Advocate (mS)
State-Times (e)
P.O. Box 588
Baton Rouge LA 70821

504/383-1111 x328

Circulation
(m) 73,532
(e) 43,037
(S) 111,431

Lou Thomas, Head Librarian
Anne Leggett, Asst. Librarian

Lib. est. 1922   Group Ind.   FTE 7

Public access   Limitations
  in person   no   Limited research for fee; closed to
  by mail   no   public. Librarians and newsmen may
                             use with permission.
  by phone   Very limited

Services available   Limitations
  copy machine   yes   Staff only
  reader/printer yes   Staff only
  reader   yes   Staff only

Hours of operation   6am-10pm, M-F

Resources
  clips   3,000,000   books   1,000
  photos   118,000   pamphlets 30 drawers
  negs   maps
  CPT   40   AV

Microform holdings
  own newspaper   1845-present
  periodicals
  clippings   600,000 clippings (no jacket count)

Indexes
  own newspaper
  other

Special collections

Automation
  Automated files
    mechanical
    electronic
  Other automated systems

Products for sale

LOUISIANA　　　　　　　　　Lake Charles　　　　　　　　　LOUISIANA

Lake Charles American Press (eS)　　　　　　　Circulation
327 Broad St.　　　　　　　　　　　　　　　　　(e) 39,849
Lake Charles LA 70601　　　　　　　　　　　　(S) 42,831
　　　　　　　　　　318/439-2781 x202

　　　　Dorothy Harris, Librarian, Head
　　　　Rebecca Hughes, Librarian, Asst.

Lib. est. 1973　　　　Group Shearman Newspapers　　　FTE

Public access　　　　　　Limitations
　in person　yes　　　　If librarians have the time
　by mail　　yes　　　　If librarians have the time
　by phone　 yes　　　　If librarians have the time

Services available　　　Limitations
　copy machine　yes
　reader/printer
　reader　　　　yes

Hours of operation   8am-4:30pm, M-F

Resources
　clips　　x　　　　　　　books
　photos　　　　　　　　　pamphlets
　negs　　　　　　　　　　maps
　CPT　　　　　　　　　　 AV

Microform holdings
　own newspaper   c. 1900-present
　periodicals
　clippings

Indexes
　own newspaper
　other

Automation
　Automated files
　　mechanical
　　electronic
　Other automated systems

Products for sale

LOUISIANA   Shreveport   LOUISIANA

The Times

Shreveport Times (mS)   Circulation
P.O. Box 222   (m) 88,631
Shreveport LA 71130   (S) 126,214

318/424-0373 x308, 309, 310

Janis W. Greer, Librarian
Susan Burford, Asst. Librarian

Lib. est. 1970   Group Ind.   FTE 4

Public access   Limitations
    in person   yes   yes
    by mail   yes   yes
    by phone   yes   yes

Services available   Limitations
    copy machine
    reader/printer yes   yes
    reader

Hours of operation M-F

Resources
    clips   27.000+   books   750
    photos   20,000   pamphlets   1,000
    negs   maps   50
    CPT   30   AV

Microform holdings
    own newspaper   1871-present
    periodicals
    clippings

Indexes
    own newspaper
    other

Special collections Bound volumes of The Times 1871-present; misc.
                     microfilm of old newspapers of the area 1843-1984

Automation
  Automated files
    mechanical
    electronic
  Other automated systems

Bangor Daily News

Bangor Daily News (m)
491 Main St.
Bangor ME 04401

207/942-4881 x300

Circulation
(m) 80,591

Charles A. Campo, Head Librarian
Trudy McMahon, Library Asst.

<u>Lib. est.</u> 1956 <u>Group</u> Ind. <u>FTE</u> 3

<u>Public access</u>
    in person   yes
    by mail   yes
    by phone   yes

<u>Limitations</u>
No genealogical work

<u>Services available</u>
    copy machine   yes
    reader/printer   yes
    reader   yes

<u>Limitations</u>
$1.00 per copy
$1.00 per copy

<u>Hours of operation</u> 7:30am-9:30pm, M-F (7:30am-7pm, Wed.);
    9am-9pm, Sun.

<u>Resources</u>
    clips   1956-1975   books   500
    photos   10,000   pamphlets   200
    negs   31,000   maps   100
    CPT   1   AV

<u>Microform holdings</u>
    own newspaper   x
    periodicals

<u>Indexes</u>
    own newspaper
    other

<u>Automation</u>
  Automated files
    mechanical
    electronic
  Other automated systems

<u>Products for sale</u>

MARYLAND　　　　　　　　Baltimore　　　　　　　　　　MARYLAND

News-American (eS)　　　　　　　　　　　　　　　　Circulation
P.O. Box 1795　　　　　　　　　　　　　　　　　　　(e) 153,608
Baltimore MD 21203　　　　　　　　　　　　　　　　(S) 231,225
　　　　　　　　　　　　301/752-1212 x226, 268

　　　　　　　Clark Ickes, Head Librarian
　　　　　　　Cynthia Powers, Asst. Librarian

Lib. est. 1902　　　　　Group　Hearst Newspapers　　　FTE　4

Public access　　　　　　　Limitations
　　in person　　yes　　　By appointment
　　by mail　　　yes　　　Simple research
　　by phone　　 yes　　　Simple research

Services available　　　　Limitations
　　copy machine　　yes
　　reader/printer　yes　　Staff only
　　reader　　　　　yes

Hours of operation　7am-6pm, M-Sat.

Resources
　　clips　　3,000,000　　　　books　　　x
　　photos　　 750,000　　　　pamphlets
　　negs　　　　　　　　　　　maps
　　CPT　　　　　　　5　　　　AV

Microform holdings
　　own newspaper　　1902-present
　　periodicals
　　clippings

Indexes
　　own newspaper
　　other

Special collections　Special Events Index

Automation
　Automated files
　　mechanical
　　electronic
　Other automated systems

Products for sale

The Sun (mS)
The Evening Sun (e)
501 N. Calvert St.
Baltimore MD 21202

301/332-6253

Circulation
(m) 174,343
(e) 170,753
(S) 365,894

Clement G. Vitek, Chief Librarian
Mary A. Schultz, Asst. Librarian

Lib. est. 1906   Group   Ind.   FTE   18.5

Public access   Limitations
- in person   no
- by mail   no
- by phone   no

Services available   Limitations
- copy machine   yes $1.00 per clipping
- reader/printer   yes $3.00 per page reprint
- reader   yes   Staff only

Hours of operation   6:30am-Midnight, M-Sat.; 9am-Midnight, Sun.

Resources
clips	20,000,000	books	4,500
photos	1,000,000	pamphlets	12 drawers
negs		maps	x
CPT	50	AV	

Microform holdings
- own newspaper   1837-present
- periodicals

Indexes
- own newspaper   1893-1959
- other   New York Times, 1930-present; Facts on File, 1946-present; Keesing's

Special collections   Baltimoriana-Marylandia; H. L. Mencken clips

Automation
  Automated files
    mechanical   5 Lektreivers; 1 Kardveyor
    electronic
  Other automated systems

Products for sale

MASSACHUSETTS   Boston   MASSACHUSETTS

Boston Globe (meS)   Circulation
135 Morrissey Blvd.   (m) 324,739
Boston MA 02107   (e) 157,499
                                                 (S) 693,679
                   617/929-2540

            Jennifer Chao, Librarian
            David Jennings, Asst. Librarian

Lib. est. 1872   Group Ind.   FTE 25

Public access   Limitations
    in person   no
    by mail   yes
    by phone   no

Services available   Limitations
    copy machine   yes
    reader/printer yes
    reader

Hours of operation 5am-Midnight, M-F; 9am-Midnight, Sat. & Sun.

Resources
    clips   9,000,000+   books   10,000
    photos   3,000,000   pamphlets   50 drawers
    negs   1977-present   maps   x
    CPT   150   AV

Microform holdings
    own newspaper   1872-present
    periodicals

Indexes
    own newspaper
    other   New York Times 1911-present

Special collections Harvard collection of alumni yearbooks, histories,
                     directories, annuals, etc; Early Massachusetts
                     & historical books

Automation
  Automated files
    electronic Atex-Infotex Lib. System; full-text on-line with some
                enhancement; PDP-1134
  Other automated systems New York Times Information Bank

Products for sale

111

MASSACHUSETTS　　　　　　　　Boston　　　　　　　　MASSACHUSETTS

Boston Herald American

Boston Herald American (mS)
300 Harrison Ave.
Boston MA 02106

617/426-3000 x580-582

Circulation
(m) 273,301
(S) 351,692

John R. Cronin, Chief Librarian

Lib. est.	Group Hearst Newspapers		FTE 5

Public access
    in person   yes
    by mail   yes
    by phone   yes

Limitations
    Each request evaluated by the librarian

    Only newpaper-related questions, no general reference questions

Services available
    copy machine   yes
    reader/printer   yes
    reader

Limitations
    $.50 per page
    $1.00 per page

Hours of operation   10am-1am, M-F; Noon-8pm, Sat. & Sun.

Resources
    clips   7,000,000   books   1,000
    photos   2,500,000   pamphlets   300
    negs   maps   200
    CPT   45   AV

Microform holdings
    own newspaper   1881-present
    periodicals
    clippings

Indexes
    own newspaper   1935-present
    other

Special collections

Automation
  Automated files
    mechanical
    electronic
  Other automated systems

Products for sale

MASSACHUSETTS — Boston — MASSACHUSETTS

THE CHRISTIAN SCIENCE MONITOR

Christian Science Monitor (m)
1 Norway St.
Boston MA 02115
　　　　　　　　617/262-2300 x2680

Circulation
(m) 169,417

Geoffrey Fingland, Librarian
Emily Heard, Asst. Librarian

Lib. est. 1909　　　　Group Ind.　　　　FTE 11

Public access
- in person　yes
- by mail　yes
- by phone　yes

Limitations
- With special permission
- No general research
- No general research

Services available
- copy machine　yes
- reader/printer　yes
- reader　yes

Limitations

Minimum charge $2.00

Hours of operation 8am–4:15pm, Sun.–F

Resources
- clips　3,000,000+
- photos
- negs
- CPT　50
- books　10,000
- pamphlets　200
- maps　50
- AV

Microform holdings
- own newspaper　1908–present
- periodicals
- clippings

Indexes
- own newspaper　1949–present
- other　New York Times 1935–present

Special collections

Automation
　Automated files
　　mechanical　8 Lektrievers
　　electronic
　Other automated systems

Products for sale

Brockton Enterprise (e)
60 Main St.
Brockton MA 02403

617/586-6200

Circulation
(e) 60,165

Mary Kirby, Librarian
Beryl Costello, Clerk

Lib. est. 1932   Group Ind.   FTE 2

Public access   Limitations
   in person   yes   As long as it does not interfere with
   by mail   yes   routine operations
   by phone   yes

Services available   Limitations
   copy machine   yes
   reader/printer
   reader   yes

Hours of operation 7am-3pm, M-Sat.

Resources
   clips   50,000   books   300
   photos   10,000   pamphlets   300
   negs   maps   100
   CPT   AV

Microform holdings
   own newspaper
   periodicals
   clippings

Indexes
   own newspaper
   other

Special collections

Automation
  Automated files
    mechanical
    electronic
  Other automated systems

Products for sale

South Middlesex News (eS)
33 New York Ave.
Framingham MA 01701

617/872-4321 x294

Jean Pretzer, Librarian

Circulation
(e) 44,706
(S) 49,393

<u>Lib. est.</u> 1969   <u>Group</u> Harte-Hanks Communications Inc.   <u>FTE</u> 1

<u>Public access</u>   <u>Limitations</u>
   in person   yes   Photo sales only, refer to Public Library
   by mail   yes   Photo sales only
   by phone   yes   Photo sales only

<u>Services available</u>   <u>Limitations</u>
   copy machine
   reader/printer
   reader

<u>Hours of operation</u>   8am-4pm, M-F

<u>Resources</u>
   clips   x   books   x
   photos   x   pamphlets   x
   negs   maps   x
   CPT   AV

<u>Microform holdings</u>
   own newspaper   x
   periodicals
   clippings

<u>Indexes</u>
   own newspaper
   other

<u>Automation</u>
  Automated files
    mechanical
    electronic
  Other automated systems

<u>Products for sale</u>

MASSACHUSETTS　　　　　　　　　Holyoke　　　　　　　　　MASSACHUSETTS

Transcript-Telegram (e)　　　　　　　　　　　　　　Circulation
120 Whiting Farms Rd.　　　　　　　　　　　　　　(e) 29,672
Holyoke MA 01040
　　　　　　　　　　413/536-2300 x307

　　　　Kay Lynch, Librarian

Lib. est.　　　　　Group Newspapers of New England　　　FTE

Public access　　　　　　　　Limitations
　　in person　　yes　　　　With permission and under supervision
　　by mail
　　by phone

Services available　　　　　Limitations
　　copy machine　　yes
　　reader/printer　yes
　　reader

Hours of operation 9am-5pm, M-F

Resources
　　clips　　x　　　　　　　books　　　x
　　photos　　x　　　　　　pamphlets　x
　　negs　　x　　　　　　　maps　　　x
　　CPT　　　　　　　　　　AV

Microform holdings
　　own newspaper　　1906-present
　　periodicals
　　clippings

Indexes
　　own newspaper
　　other

Special collections

Automation
　Automated files
　　mechanical
　　electronic
　Other automated systems

Products for sale

116

MASSACHUSETTS   Lawrence   MASSACHUSETTS

Lawrence Eagle-Tribune

Lawrence Eagle-Tribune (e)
Sunday Eagle-Tribune (S)
Box 100
Lawrence MA 01842

617/685-1000 x219

Cheryl Lynch, Librarian
Regina Youngclaus, Part-time asst.

Circulation
(e) 52,194
(S) 50,160

<u>Lib. est.</u> ?   <u>Group</u> Ind.   <u>FTE</u>

<u>Public access</u>
    in person   yes
    by mail   yes
    by phone   yes

<u>Limitations</u>
With OK of managing editor or librarian
$1.00 per page of photocopies
Will give dates of stories and refer people to public library

<u>Services available</u>
    copy machine   yes

    reader/printer   yes

<u>Limitations</u>
Will photocopy major articles, dates given for rest; $1.00 per page
Not available for public use

<u>Hours of operation</u>   7:30am-3:30pm, M-F

<u>Resources</u>
    clips   40,000 files   books   200
    photos   10,000   pamphlets   x
    negs   maps   30
    CPT   2   AV

<u>Microform holdings</u>
    own newspaper   1868-present
    periodicals

<u>Indexes</u>
    own newspaper
    other

<u>Automation</u>
   Automated files
     mechanical
     electronic
   Other automated systems

<u>Products for sale</u>

MASSACHUSETTS　　　　　　　　　Lynn　　　　　　　　　MASSACHUSETTS

Daily Evening Item

Daily Evening Item (e)　　　　　　　　　　　　　　Circulation
38 Exchange St.　　　　　　　　　　　　　　　　　　(e) 30,231
Lynn MA 01903
　　　　　　　　　617/593-7700 x223

　　　　NancyAnn Rogers, Research Librarian

Lib. est. 1912　　　　　　Group Ind.　　　　　　　FTE

Public access　　　　　　　Limitations
　　in person　　yes　　　By appointment
　　by mail　　　yes　　　No in-depth research
　　by phone　　 yes　　　No in-depth research

Services available　　　　Limitations
　　copy machine　　yes　 Charge, by personnel only
　　reader/printer　yes　 Charge
　　reader

Hours of operation 7:30am-3pm, M-Thurs.; Fri. mornings; time by
　　　　　　　　　　appointment also

Resources
　　clips　　56 drawers　　　　books
　　photos　 11 drawers　　　　pamphlets
　　negs　　 1974+　　　　　　 maps　　　　x
　　CPT　　　　　　　　　　　　AV

Microform holdings
　　own newspaper　　Dec. 8, 1877-present
　　periodicals
　　clippings

Indexes
　　own newspaper
　　other

Special collections

Automation
　Automated files
　　mechanical
　　　electronic
　Other automated systems

Products for sale

MASSACHUSETTS   Pittsfield   MASSACHUSETTS

The Berkshire Eagle

Berkshire Eagle (e)
33 Eagle St.
Pittsfield MA 01201

413/447-7311 x141

Madeline F. Winter, Librarian
Cathy Carey, Asst. Librarian

Circulation
(e) 30,340

Lib. est.	Group Ind.	FTE 1

Public access
     in person   yes
     by mail   yes
     by phone   yes

Limitations

Services available
     copy machine   yes
     reader/printer
     reader   yes

Limitations
$.10 per copy

Hours of operation   8am-5pm, M-F

Resources
     clips   500,000   books
     photos   5,000   pamphlets
     negs   10,000   maps
     CPT   AV

Microform holdings
     own newspaper   1800-present
     periodicals
     clippings

Indexes
     own newspaper
     other

Special collections

Automation
   Automated files
     mechanical
     electronic
   Other automated systems

Products for sale

MASSACHUSETTS   Springfield   MASSACHUSETTS

The Morning Union

The Morning Union (m)
The Daily News (e)
The Sunday Republican (S)
1860 Main St.
Springfield MA 01101

413/787-2437

Judith Epstein, Librarian

Circulation
(m) 73,429
(e) 76,641
(S) 144,726

<u>Lib. est.</u> c. 1900 <u>Group</u> Newhouse Newspapers <u>FTE</u> 6

<u>Public access</u>
 in person no
 by mail no
 by phone no

<u>Limitations</u>

<u>Services available</u>
 copy machine yes
 reader/printer yes
 reader yes

<u>Limitations</u>

<u>Hours of operation</u>

<u>Resources</u>
 clips   books
 photos   pamphlets
 negs   maps
 CPT   AV

<u>Microform holdings</u>
 own newspaper
 periodicals
 clippings

<u>Indexes</u>
 own newspaper

<u>Special collections</u>

<u>Automation</u>
 Automated files
  mechanical AB Dick/Scott 200
  electronic
 Other automated systems

<u>Products for sale</u>

MASSACHUSETTS   Worcester   MASSACHUSETTS

Worcester Telegram (mS)   Circulation
The Evening Gazette (e)   (m) 53,512
20 Franklin St.   (e) 89,374
Worcester MA 01613   (S) 108,681
                    617/755-4321 x210 or 211

          Sharon C. Carter, Librarian
          James A. Robinson, Asst. Librarian

Lib. est. 1920   Group Ind.   FTE 7

Public access   Limitations
     in person   no
     by mail   yes   No in-depth research
     by phone   yes   Dates of recent T&G stories only

Services available   Limitations
     copy machine   yes   In house use only
     reader/printer yes   In house use only
     reader   yes   In house use only

Hours of operation   7am-Midnight, M-F; 8am-11pm, Sat.; 11am-11pm, Sun.

Resources
     clips   150,000 files   books   400
     photos   100,000 files   pamphlets
     negs   maps   100
     CPT   AV

Microform holdings
     own newspaper   1866-present
     periodicals
     clippings

Indexes
     own newspaper
     other

Automation
   Automated files
     mechanical
     electronic
   Other automated systems

Products for sale

Detroit Free Press (mS)
321 W. Lafayette
Detroit MI 48231
                      313/222-6823

Circulation
(m) 610,849
(S) 705,398

    Michele Ann Kapecky, Chief Librarian
    Mary Eliason, Asst. Librarian

Lib. est. 1928   Group Knight-Ridder Newspapers   FTE 12

Public access   Limitations
- in person no
- by mail   no
- by phone   no

Services available   Limitations
- copy machine
- reader/printer
- reader

Hours of operation 8am-Midnight, M-Sun.

Resources

clips	1928-1970	books	700
photos	500,000	pamphlets	
negs		maps	100
CPT	50	AV	

Microform holdings
- own newspaper   1928-present
- periodicals
- clippings

Indexes
- own newspaper   none
- other

Automation
  Automated files
    electronic   Clips 1971-present on 16MM fiche accessible by Meracode retrieval system
  Other automated systems New York Times Information Bank; AP Political Databank

Products for sale

Detroit News (eS)
615 Lafayette Blvd.
Detroit MI 48231

313/222-2110

Circulation
(e) 630,795
(S) 828,052

Betty W. Havlena, Chief Librarian
Edward C Betker, Reference Head

Lib. est. 1918   Group Evening News Assn.   FTE 10

Public access   **Limitations**
  in person   no
  by mail   yes   Citations from index only
  by phone   yes   Citations from index only

Services available   **Limitations**
  copy machine   yes   In-house use only
  reader/printer yes   In-house use only
  reader   yes   In-house use only

Hours of operation 8am-5pm, M-F

Resources
  clips   3,000,000   books   21,000
  photos   800,000   pamphlets   70 drawers
  negs   maps   x
  CPT   127   AV

Microform holdings
  own newspaper   1873-present
  periodicals
  clippings

Indexes
  own newspaper   1873-present
  other   New York Times 1941-present; Wall Street Journal
                   1968-present; National Observer 1969-1977;
                   Reader's Guide 1919-present

Special collections

Automation
  Automated files
    mechanical
    electronic
  Other automated systems

Products for sale

MICHIGAN   Flint   MICHIGAN

The Flint Journal

Flint, Michigan

Flint Journal (eS)
200 E. First St.
Flint MI 48502

313/767-0660 x192

David W. Larzelere, Chief Librarian

Circulation
(e) 105,830
(S) 105,104

Lib. est. 1935   Group Newhouse Newspapers   FTE 4

Public access
    in person   no
    by mail   yes
    by phone   yes

Limitations

Dates and limited information
Dates and limited information

Services available
    copy machine   yes
    reader/printer yes
    reader   yes

Limitations
Staff only
Staff only
Staff only

Hours of operation 7:30am-5:30pm, M-F; 8am-4:30pm, Sat.

Resources
    clips   1,500,000   books   3,000
    photos   240,000   pamphlets 12 drawers
    negs   75,000   maps   2,000
    CPT   45   AV

Microform holdings
    own newspaper   1898-present
    periodicals
    clippings   8,588 jackets

Indexes
    own newspaper   1963-present
    other   New York Times 1941-present

Special collections

Automation
  Automated files
    mechanical
    electronic
  Other automated systems

Products for sale

MICHIGAN   Grand Rapids   MICHIGAN

The Grand Rapids Press

Grand Rapids Press (eS)
Press Plaza, Vandenberg Center
Grand Rapids MI 49503
616/459-1474

Circulation
(e) 105,830
(S) 105,104

Diane Wheeler, Librarian
Alison Czlonka, Asst. Librarian

Lib. est. 1964   Group Booth Newspapers   FTE 6

Public access
   in person   yes
   by mail   yes
   by phone   yes

Limitations
8:30am-4:30pm, M-F; no copies
Dates only, refer to public library
Dates only, refer to public library

Services available
   copy machine   no
   reader/printer no
   reader   no

Limitations

Hours of operation   8am-5pm, M-F; 8:30am-2:30pm, Sat.

Resources
   clips   250,000   books   1,000
   photos   28,000   pamphlets 300
   negs   35,000   maps   150
   CPT   16   AV

Microform holdings
   own newspaper   1893-present
   periodicals
   clippings

Indexes
   own newspaper   none
   other

Special collections

Automation
  Automated files
    mechanical
    electronic
  Other automated systems

Products for sale   Picture reprints

MICHIGAN   Jackson   MICHIGAN

Jackson Citizen Patriot

Jackson Citizen Patriot (eS)
214 S. Jackson St.
Jackson MI 49204
               517/787-2300 x237

Circulation
(e) (41,444)
(S) (37,964)

Florence E. Farrar, Librarian
Linda L. Winchell, Asst. Librarian

Lib. est. 1930's   Group   Booth Newspapers   FTE 2.5

Public access   Limitations
- in person   yes
- by mail   yes
- by phone   yes

Services available   Limitations
- copy machine   yes $.10 per 8 1/2 x 11; $.15 per legal size; $.50 per whole page copy
- reader/printer
- reader   yes   Staff only, no outsiders

Hours of operation   8:30am-4pm, M-F

Resources
- clips   1,000,000   books   500
- photos   5,000   pamphlets   350
- negs   700,000   maps   100
- CPT   AV

Microform holdings
- own newspaper   1846-present
- periodicals

Indexes
- own newspaper
- other

Special collections

Automation
   Automated files
- mechanical
- electronic
   Other automated systems

Products for sale

The State Journal (eS)
120 E. Lenawee
Lansing MI 48919

                        517/487-4608

Circulation
- (e) 76,329
- (S) 82,425

Christine Wells, Head Librarian

Lib. est. 1950   **Group** Gannett Newspapers   **FTE**

Public access   **Limitations**
- in person   no
- by mail   no
- by phone   yes

Services available   **Limitations**
- copy machine
- reader/printer
- reader

Hours of operation 8am-5pm, M-F

Resources
clips	30 file cabinets	books	1,000
photos	500,000	pamphlets	2,000
negs	5 file cabinets	maps	300
CPT	30	veloxes	50,000

Microform holdings
- own newspaper   1855-present
- periodicals
- clippings

Indexes
- own newspaper
- other

Special collections

Automation
- Automated files
  - mechanical
  - electronic
- Other automated systems

Products for sale

Monroe Evening News (e)
20 W. First St.
Monroe MI 48161

313/242-1100

Marge McBee, Librarian

Circulation
(e) 26,655

Lib. est. 1935   Group Ind.   FTE .5

Public access
    in person   yes
    by mail   no
    by phone   no

Limitations
Use of microfilm only

Services available
    copy machine   yes
    reader/printer
    reader   yes

Limitations
Will copy clips if can be found easily

Hours of operation

Resources
    clips   200 drawers   books
    photos   pamphlets
    negs   5 years   maps   a few
    CPT   AV

Microform holdings
    own newspaper   June 10, 1825-present
    periodicals
    clippings

Indexes
    own newspaper
    other

Special collections

Automation
  Automated files
    mechanical
      electronic
  Other automated systems

Products for sale

Muskegon Chronicle (eS)   <u>Circulation</u>
981 Third St.   (e) 44,143
Muskegon MI 49443   (S) 46,589
                  616/722-3161 x236

           Linda Thompson, Librarian

<u>Lib. est.</u> about 1900   <u>Group</u> Newhouse Newspapers   <u>FTE</u> 1

<u>Public access</u>   <u>Limitations</u>
    in person   yes   Dates only; refer to public library
    by mail   yes   Dates only; refer to public library
    by phone   yes   Dates only; refer to public library

<u>Services available</u>   <u>Limitations</u>
    copy machine   yes $1.00 per page
    reader/printer
    reader   yes

<u>Hours of operation</u>   8am-4pm, M-F

<u>Resources</u>
    clips   72 drawers+   books   400
    photos   16 drawers   pamphlets   8 drawers
    negs   maps
    CPT   8   AV

<u>Microform holdings</u>
    own newspaper   1869-present
    periodicals
    clippings

<u>Indexes</u>
    own newspaper   none
    other

<u>Special collections</u>

<u>Automation</u>
  Automated files
    mechanical
    electronic
  Other automated systems

<u>Products for sale</u>   Photo reprints

The Times Herald (eS)
907 Sixth St.
Port Huron MI 48060

313/985-7171 x231

Joann Maxwell, Librarian

Circulation
(e) 31,300
(S) 34,724

Lib. est. 1910   Group Gannett Newspapers   FTE

Public access   Limitations
   in person   yes   Public must do own research after
                        receiving files
   by mail   yes   Very important material and legals
   by phone   yes   If information readily available

Services available   Limitations
   copy machine   yes   Librarian will copy for $.10 charge
   reader/printer
   reader

Hours of operation   7:30am-4:30pm M-F

Resources
   clips   c. 6,600 files   books
   photos   x   pamphlets
   negs   In Photo Dept.   maps
   CPT   AV

Microform holdings
   own newspaper   1910-present
   periodicals
   clippings

Indexes
   own newspaper
   other

Special collections

Automation
  Automated files
   mechanical
   electronic
  Other automated systems

Products for sale

The Saginaw News (eS)
201-203 S. Washington Ave.
Saginaw MI 48605
                517/752-7171 x172

Circulation
(e) 53,065
(S) 55,037

    Leland R. Watrous, Head Librarian
    Judith Ahearn, Asst. Librarian

<u>Lib. est.</u> 1940's   <u>Group</u> Booth Newspapers   <u>FTE</u>

<u>Public access</u>   <u>Limitations</u>
    in person   yes   Material located, screened
    by mail   no
    by phone   yes   Short inquiries

<u>Services available</u>   <u>Limitations</u>
    copy machine   no
    reader/printer no
    reader   yes   None

<u>Hours of operation</u> 8am-4:30pm, M-F

<u>Resources</u>
    clips   c. 2,000,000   books   c. 1,000
    photos   5,000   pamphlets   250
    negs   25,000   maps   50
    CPT   15   AV

<u>Microform holdings</u>
    own newspaper
    periodicals
    clippings

<u>Indexes</u>
    own newspaper
    other

<u>Special collections</u>

<u>Automation</u>
  Automated files
    mechanical
    electronic
  Other automated systems

<u>Products for sale</u>

MINNESOTA   Duluth   MINNESOTA

Duluth News-Tribune (mS)   Circulation
Duluth Herald (e)   (m) 52,408
424 West 1st St.   (e) 20,695
Duluth MN 55801   (S) 82,700
                              218/723-5309

            Laurie Hertzel, Librarian
            Barbara Ellingsen, Clerk

Lib. est. 1968   Group Knight-Ridder Newspapers   FTE 2

Public access   Limitations
    in person   no
    by mail   yes   Public referred to Public Library for
    by phone   yes   extensive research

Services available   Limitations
    copy machine   yes   Staff only; occasional public use at
    reader/printer $.50 per copy
    reader   yes   Staff only

Hours of operation 7:30am-7pm, M-F

Resources
    clips   800,000   books   300
    photos   250,000   pamphlets   150
    negs   maps   100
    CPT   1   AV

Microform holdings
    own newspaper   Duluth News-Tribune 1890-present; Duluth
                      Herald 1936-present
    periodicals

Indexes
    own newspaper

Special collections

Automation
  Automated files
    mechanical
    electronic
  Other automated systems

Products for sale   Reprints of photos that have appeared in the paper

132

MINNESOTA   Mankato   MINNESOTA

Free Press (e)   Circulation
418 S. Second St.   (e) 26,184
Mankato MN 56001
                              507/625-4451

        Cheri Hendricks, Librarian

Lib. est. 1976   Group Ottaway Newspapers   FTE 1

Public access   Limitations
    in person   yes
    by mail
    by phone

Services available   Limitations
    copy machine
    reader/printer
    reader   yes   Printouts can be obtained at city or
                                university libraries

Hours of operation 8am-4pm, M-Sat.

Resources
    clips   books   x
    photos   pamphlets
    negs   x   maps   x
    CPT   AV

Microform holdings
    own newspaper   1959-present
    periodicals
    clippings

Indexes
    own newspaper   1976-present
    other

Automation
  Automated files
    mechanical
    electronic
  Other automated systems

Products for sale

MINNESOTA　　　　　　　　　　Minneapolis　　　　　　　　　　MINNESOTA

Minneapolis Tribune (mS)　　　　　　　　　　　　Circulation
Minneapolis Star (e)　　　　　　　　　　　　　　(m) 231,380
425 Portland Ave.　　　　　　　　　　　　　　　　(e) 226,680
Minneapolis MN 55488　　　　　　　　　　　　　　(S) 608,550
　　　　　　　　　　612/372-4374 or 4375

　　　　Robert A. Lopez, Head Librarian
　　　　Robert H. Jansen, Asst. Librarian

Lib. est. 1946　　　　　Group Cowles Newspapers　　　FTE 18

Public access　　　　　　　　Limitations
　　in person　　yes　　　　Bound volumes and microfilm
　　by mail　　　yes
　　by phone　　 yes

Services available　　　　　Limitations
　　copy machine　　yes　　Staff only
　　reader/printer yes　　Staff only
　　reader

Hours of operation 6:30am-Midnight, M-Sat.; 3pm-11:30pm, Sun.

Resources
　　clips　　6,000,000　　　　books　　　2,000
　　photos　 3,000,000　　　　pamphlets　4,000
　　negs　　　　50,000　　　　maps　　　 5,000
　　CPT　　　　　　 25　　　　AV

Microform holdings
　　own newspaper　　1867-present
　　periodicals
　　clippings

Indexes
　　own newspaper
　　other

Special collections

Automation
　Automated files
　　mechanical
　　electronic
　Other automated systems

Products for sale Photo reprints

MINNESOTA   Rochester   MINNESOTA

Rochester Post-Bulletin

Rochester Post-Bulletin (e)   Circulation
18 1st Ave.   (e) 36,871
Rochester MN 55901

507/285-7730

Marcy Sawyer, News Librarian

Lib. est. 1960		Group Small Newspapers	FTE

Public access
    in person   yes
    by mail   yes
    by phone   yes

Limitations
Must look at files in library only

Services available
    copy machine   yes
    reader/printer
    reader

Limitations
$.25 per photocopy

Hours of operation   7:30am-4pm, M-F

Resources
clips	12,000	books	60+
photos	10,000	pamphlets	50
negs	x	maps	x
CPT	20	AV	

Microform holdings
    own newspaper   1859-present
    periodicals
    clippings

Indexes
    own newspaper
    other

Special collections

Automation
  Automated files
    mechanical   Remington Rand Lektriever
    electronic
  Other automated systems

Products for sale

MINNESOTA   St. Paul   MINNESOTA

St. Paul Pioneer Press
Minnesota's First Newspaper

St. Paul Pioneer Press (mS)
St. Paul Dispatch (e)
55 E. 4th St.
St. Paul MN 55101
                 612/222-5011 x275

<u>Circulation</u>
(m) 101,924
(e) 120,123
(S) 244,719

Judith Katzung, Head Librarian

<u>Lib. est.</u> ?   <u>Group</u>   Knight-Ridder Newspapers   <u>FTE</u>   5.5

<u>Public access</u>   <u>Limitations</u>
- in person   yes   8am–5pm, M-F
- by mail   yes   Charge for copies
- by phone   yes   Only for governmental agencies, libraries and universities

<u>Services available</u>   <u>Limitations</u>
- copy machine   yes   Staff only
- reader/printer   yes   Staff only
- reader

<u>Hours of operation</u>   7am-11pm, M-F; Noon-8:30pm, Sat.; 4pm-9pm, Sun.

<u>Resources</u>
clips	c. 540,000	books	500
photos	c. 1,000,000	pamphlets	150
negs		maps	300
CPT	4	AV	

<u>Microform holdings</u>
- own newspaper   1948-present
- periodicals
- clippings

<u>Indexes</u>
- own newspaper
- other

<u>Automation</u>
- Automated files
  - mechanical
  - electronic
- Other automated systems

<u>Products for sale</u>

MISSISSIPPI   Biloxi   MISSISSIPPI

The Sun (m)
The Daily Herald (e)
The Sun-Herald (S)
P.O. Box 4567
Biloxi MS 38531

601/896-2314

Circulation
(m) 8,380
(e) 33,496
(S) 40,406

Marilyn Pustay, Librarian
Lynn Brown, Asst. Librarian

Lib. est. 1969   Group Ind.   FTE 2

Public access   Limitations
    in person   yes   As we have time
    by mail   yes   As we have time
    by phone   yes   As we have time

Services available   Limitations
    copy machine   yes   As time permits; $.50 per copy
    reader/printer yes   As time permits; $2.50 per print, $3.00
                           mailing fee

Hours of operation   7:30am-5pm, M-F

Resources
    clips   16 4-drawer cabinets   books   c. 100
    photos   9 4-drawer cabinets   pamphlets   c. 100
    negs   maps   c. 50
    CPT   20   AV

Microform holdings
    own newspaper   1888-present
    periodicals
    clippings

Indexes
    own newspaper
    other

Special collections

Automation
  Automated files
    mechanical
    electronic
  Other automated systems

Products for sale

MISSISSIPPI		Jackson		MISSISSIPPI

The Clarion-Ledger

Clarion-Ledger (m)
Jackson Daily News (e)
Clarion-Ledger-News (S)
311 E. Pearl St
Jackson MS 39205

601/961-7000

Circulation
(m) 62,550
(e) 40,340
(S) 115,772

Jean Lane, Librarian

Lib. est. 1958   Group Ind.   FTE

Public access
   in person   yes
   by mail   yes
   by phone   yes

Limitations
For extensive research public does own research

Services available
   copy machine   yes
   reader/printer
   reader

Limitations
Charges range from $2.00 to $10.00

Hours of operation   8am-5pm, M-F

Resources
clips	30,000	books	600
photos	13,000	pamphlets	55
negs		maps	7
CPT		AV	

Microform holdings
   own newspaper   1909-present
   periodicals
   clippings

Indexes
   own newspaper   none
   other

Special collections   State telephone directories; Mississippi sightseeing pamphlets; University directories

Automation
  Automated files
    mechanical
    electronic
  Other automated systems

Products for sale

MISSOURI   Joplin   MISSOURI

The Joplin Globe

Joplin Globe (mS)   Circulation
P.O. Box 7   (m) 40,941
Joplin MO 64801   (S) 43,372
                     417/623-3480 x158

             David Blair, Librarian

Lib. est.   Group Ottaway Newspapers   FTE 1

Public access   Limitations
    in person   yes   8:30-Noon; 1:15-5pm, M-F
    by mail   yes
    by phone   yes

Services available   Limitations
    copy machine   yes $1 per copy in library; $1.50 by mail
    reader/printer yes
    reader   yes

Hours of operation   8:30am-5pm, M-F

Resources
    clips   c.10,000   books   x
    photos   x   pamphlets   x
    negs   maps   x
    CPT   AV

Microform holdings
    own newspaper   1896-present
    periodicals
    clippings

Indexes
    own newspaper
    other

Special collections   Local and Missouri history

Automation
  Automated files
    mechanical
    electronic
  Other automated systems

Products for sale

MISSOURI   Kansas City   MISSOURI

KANSAS CITY Times/STAR

Kansas City Times (m)	**Circulation**
Kansas City Star (eS)	(m) 321,002
1729 Grand Ave.	(e) 288,283
Kansas City MO 64108	(S) 408,007

816/234-4406

John Springer, Librarian
Patricia Smith, Asst. Librarian

Lib. est. 1901   Group   Capital Cities Communications Inc.   FTE 9

Public access   **Limitations**
    in person   no
    by mail   yes   When time allows
    by phone   yes   When time allows

Services available   **Limitations**
    copy machine   yes
    reader/printer   yes
    reader

Hours of operation   6am-1am, M-Sat.; 4:30pm-Midnight, Sun.

Resources
clips	1,250,000	books	2,700+
photos	500,000	pamphlets	1,000
negs		maps	
CPT	20	AV	

Microform holdings
    own newspaper   On aperture cards and rolls
    periodicals
    clippings   8,000 aperture cards

Indexes
    own newspaper   x
    other

Special collections   Harper's Weekly, 1857-1911 with card catalog

Automation
  Automated files
    mechanical
    electronic
  Other automated systems

Products for sale

MISSOURI St. Joseph MISSOURI

St. Joseph Gazette (m) Circulation
St. Joseph News-Press (eS) (m) 44,814
9th and Edmonds Sts. (e) 39,699
St. Joseph MO 64501 (S) 51,306
816/279-5671

Alice McVicker, Librarian/Staff writer

Lib. est. Group Ind. FTE 1

Public access Limitations
   in person yes In-house use only
   by mail yes If they have dates - no research
   by phone yes

Services available Limitations
   copy machine
   reader/printer
   reader yes

Hours of operation 7am-1:30am (library is open as long as newsroom is staffed)

Resources
   clips x books x
   photos x pamphlets
   negs maps
   CPT AV

Microform holdings
   own newspaper 1868-present
   periodicals
   clippings

Indexes
   own newspaper
   other

Special collections Missouri and Kansas materials

Automation
  Automated files
    mechanical
    electronic
  Other automated systems

Products for sale

MISSOURI   St. Louis   MISSOURI

St. Louis Globe-Democrat (m)   Circulation
12th Blvd. at Convention Plaza   (m) 271,645
St. Louis MO 63101
                         314/342-1357

          Leo F. January, Librarian
          Mary Ellen Davis, Asst. Librarian

Lib. est. 1920's   Group Newhouse Newspapers   FTE 5

Public access   Limitations
     in person   no   Refer to Public Library
     by mail   no
     by phone   no   Will sometimes make an exception

Services available   Limitations
     copy machine
     reader/printer
     reader

Hours of operation   9am-11pm, M-F; 9am-5:30pm, Sat.; 9am-11pm, Sun.

Resources
     clips   800 drawers   books
     photos   400 drawers   pamphlets
     negs   maps
     CPT   AV

Microform holdings
     own newspaper   1852-present
     periodicals
     clippings

Indexes
     own newspaper
     other

Special collections

Automation
  Automated files
     mechanical
     electronic
  Other automated systems

Products for sale

MISSOURI　　　　　　　　　　St. Louis　　　　　　　　　　MISSOURI

St. Louis Post-Dispatch (eS)　　　　　　　　　Circulation
900 N. 12th Blvd.　　　　　　　　　　　　　　　(e) 257,259
St. Louis MO 63101　　　　　　　　　　　　　　 (S) 436,930
　　　　　　　　　　　　314/621-1111

　　　　　Nancy Williams Stoddard, Chief Librarian
　　　　　Gerald R. Brown, Asst. Librarian

Lib. est. 1890's　　　　Group　Pulitzer Publishing Co.　　FTE　15

Public access　　　　　　　　　Limitations
　　in person　　yes　　　　　By appointment only
　　by mail　　　yes
　　by phone　　 yes　　　　　Restricted to one line; told to present
　　　　　　　　　　　　　　　all requests in writing

Services available　　　　　　Limitations
　　copy machine　　yes　　　 $1 per copy for outside users
　　reader/printer　yes　　　 Fees to outsiders
　　reader　　　　　yes　　　 Staff only

Hours of operation　6am-11:30pm, M-F; 6am-9:30pm, Sat.

Resources
　　clips　　10,000,000　　　　　books　　　c. 3,000
　　photos　　2,500,000　　　　　pamphlets　　 2,000
　　negs　　　x　　　　　　　　　maps　　　　　1,000
　　CPT　　　　　　10　　　　　　AV

Microform holdings
　　own newspaper　　1874-present
　　periodicals

Indexes
　　own newspaper　　1975-present

Special collections　Post-Dispatch authors' collection; 1904 World's Fair memorabilia; State Manuals, World Almanacs, Congressional Directories all back to 1880's

Automation
　Automated files
　　mechanical
　　electronic　　UNIDAS, full text system just begun
　Other automated systems

Products for sale

Springfield Daily News (m)
Springfield Leader & Press (e)
Springfield News-Leader (S)
651 Boonville
Springfield MO 65801

417/836-1100

Georgette Ellwood, Librarian

Circulation
(m) 34,749
(e) 44,753
(S) 85,553

<u>Lib. est.</u>   <u>Group</u> Gannett Newspapers   <u>FTE</u> 1

<u>Public access</u>   Limitations
    in person   yes   As time allows, or by subpoena
    by mail   no
    by phone   no

<u>Services available</u>   Limitations
    copy machine
    reader/printer yes   Staff use only
    reader

<u>Hours of operation</u>

<u>Resources</u>
    clips   books
    photos   pamphlets
    negs   maps
    CPT   AV

<u>Microform holdings</u>
    own newspaper
    periodicals
    clippings

<u>Indexes</u>
    own newspaper
    other

<u>Special collections</u>

<u>Automation</u>
  Automated files
    mechanical
    electronic
  Other automated systems

<u>Products for sale</u>

Lincoln Star (m)
Lincoln Journal (e)
Sunday Journal-Star (S)
926 P St.
Lincoln NE 68501

Circulation
(m) 30,402
(e) 44,639
(S) 70,675

402/473-7293

Debra Sullivan, Head Librarian
Pat Loos, Asst. Librarian

Lib. est. 1951   Group Lee Newspapers (Star)   FTE 4.5
                         Ind. (Journal)

Public access   Limitations
    in person   yes   Research and copying fees assessed
    by mail   yes   Request cash in advance
    by phone   no

Services available   Limitations
    copy machine   yes   Fee charged to public
    reader/printer yes   Fee charged to public for research and
                             copies

Hours of operation 7:30am-11pm, M-F; 8am-5pm, Sat.

Resources
    clips   150,000 files   books   3,000
    photos   860,000   pamphlets   30 drawers
    negs   maps
    CPT   AV

Microform holdings
    own newspaper   1867-present

Indexes
    own newspaper
    other   Nebraska Centennial editions index; Bicentennial
                     editions index

Special collections Obit indexes since 1951; Accident Fatalities since
1951; Starkweather photos and clips; extensive newspaper history

Automation
    Automated files
        mechanical   3 Remington Rand Lektrievers
        electronic
    Other automated systems

Products for sale

Omaha World-Herald (meS)
World-Herald Square
Omaha NE 68102

402/444-1000

Hub Ogden, Action Editor
Bette Shrader, Librarian

Circulation
(m) 124,113
(e) 110,700
(S) 278,541

Lib. est.   Group Ind.   FTE 7

Public access   Limitations
- in person   no
- by mail   yes
- by phone   yes

Services available   Limitations
- copy machine   yes   Staff only
- reader/printer   yes   Staff only
- reader   yes   Staff only

Hours of operation   7am-6pm, M-F; 8am-5pm, Sat.; always open to newsroom staff

Resources
- clips
- photos
- negs
- CPT
- books
- pamphlets
- maps
- AV

Microform holdings
- own newspaper
- periodicals
- clippings

Indexes
- own newspaper

Automation
- Automated files
  - mechanical
  - electronic
- Other automated systems

Products for sale

Las Vegas Review-Journal (mS)
P.O. Box 70
Las Vegas NV 89101
                      702/385-4241

Circulation
(m) 45,678
(s) 46,556

Glenda Harris, Librarian

Lib. est. 1950   Group Donrey Media   FTE

Public access
    in person   no
    by mail   no
    by phone   no

Limitations
Only members of staff or their authorized guests may use our facilities

Services available
    copy machine   yes
    reader/printer yes
    reader

Limitations

Hours of operation 8am-5pm, M-F

Resources
    clips   x   books   x
    photos   x   pamphlets x
    negs   maps   x
    CPT   AV

Microform holdings
    own newspaper   1905-present
    periodicals
    clippings

Indexes
    own newspaper
    other

Special collections

Automation
  Automated files
    mechanical
    electronic
  Other automated systems

Products for sale

Reno Evening Gazette

Nevada State Journal (mS)
Reno Evening Gazette (e)
P.O. Box 280
Reno NV 89520

702/786-8989 x233

Circulation
(m) 29,324
(e) 24,683
(S) 47,069

Florence Mazalewski, Librarian
Nan Spina, Asst. Librarian

<u>Lib. est.</u>   <u>Group</u> Gannett Newspapers   <u>FTE</u>

<u>Public access</u>   <u>Limitations</u>
- in person   no
- by mail   no
- by phone   no

<u>Services available</u>   <u>Limitations</u>
- copy machine
- reader/printer
- reader

<u>Hours of operation</u> 7am-6pm, M-F

<u>Resources</u>
clips	c. 1,055,000	books	c. 600
photos	c. 100,000	pamphlets	
negs		maps	c. 100
CPT		AV	

<u>Microform holdings</u>
- own newspaper   Nevada State Journal 1870-present; Reno Evening Gazette, 1979-present
- periodicals
- clippings

<u>Indexes</u>
- own newspaper
- other

<u>Automation</u>
- Automated files
  - mechanical
  - electronic
- Other automated systems

<u>Products for sale</u>

148

NEW HAMPSHIRE　　　　　　　　　Manchester　　　　　　　　　NEW HAMPSHIRE

Manchester Union Leader (all day)　　　　　　　Circulation
New Hampshire Sunday News (S)　　　　　　　　(all day)
35 Amherst St.　　　　　　　　　　　　　　　　　　　　64,136
Manchester NH 03105　　　　　　　　　　　　(S) 66,199
　　　　　　　　　　603/668-4321 x306

　　　　　　Claudette A. Gammon, Chief Librarian
　　　　　　Pauline R. Caron, Librarian-Stenographer

Lib. est.　　　　　　　　　　Group Ind.　　　　　　　　FTE 2

Public access　　　　　　　　Limitations
　　in person　　no
　　by mail　　　yes　　　　Yes
　　by phone　　yes　　　　Yes

Services available　　　　　Limitations
　　copy machine　　yes　　Charges for public use
　　reader/printer　yes　　Charges for public use
　　reader

Hours of operation 8am-4pm, M-F

Resources
　　clips　　x　　　　　　　　　　books　　　x
　　photos　x　　　　　　　　　　pamphlets　x
　　negs　　　　　　　　　　　　　maps　　　　x
　　CPT　　　　　　　　　　　　　 AV

Microform holdings
　　own newspaper　　1954-present
　　periodicals
　　clippings

Indexes
　　own newspaper　　1967-present
　　other

Special collections

Automation
　Automated files
　　mechanical　　none
　　electronic
　Other automated systems

Products for sale

NEW JERSEY   Asbury Park   NEW JERSEY

Asbury Park Press (eS)   Circulation
Press Plaza   (e) 104,352
Asbury Park   NJ 07712   (S) 136,174
                        201/774-7000

         Mrs. Peter Hastings, Librarian

Lib. est.   Group Ind.   FTE

Public access   Limitations
    in person   no
    by mail   no
    by phone   no

Services available   Limitations
    copy machine
    reader/printer
    reader

Hours of operation   24 hours daily

Resources
    clips   x   books   x
    photos   x   pamphlets   x
    negs   x   maps   x
    CPT   AV

Microform holdings
    own newspaper
    periodicals
    clippings

Indexes
    own newspaper
    other

Special collections

Automation
  Automated files
    mechanical   Lektrievers
    electronic
  Other automated systems

Products for sale

NEW JERSEY   Atlantic City   NEW JERSEY

The Press (m)   Circulation
The Sunday Press (S)   (m) 69,029
1900 Atlantic Ave.   (S) 67,831
Atlantic City NJ 08404
                              609/645-1234

            Linda J. Uhrmann, Head Librarian
            Henrietta Logan, Asst. Librarian

Lib. est.   Group Ind.   FTE 2

Public access   Limitations
    in person   yes
    by mail
    by phone

Services available   Limitations
    copy machine   yes
    reader/printer
    reader   yes

Hours of operation   10am-5:30pm, M-F

Resources
    clips   books
    photos   pamphlets
    negs   maps
    CPT   AV

Microform holdings
    own newspaper
    periodicals
    clippings

Indexes
    own newspaper
    other

Special collections

Automation
  Automated files
    mechanical
    electronic
  Other automated systems

Products for sale

NEW JERSEY   Bridgewater   NEW JERSEY

Courier-News

Courier-News (e) P.O. Box 6600 Bridgewater NJ 08807	<u>Circulation</u> (e) 58,779

201/722-8800 x328

Linda H. Crow, Librarian

<u>Lib. est.</u> 1930   <u>Group</u> Gannett Newspapers   <u>FTE</u> 1

<u>Public access</u>   <u>Limitations</u>
    in person   yes
    by mail   yes
    by phone   yes

<u>Services available</u>   <u>Limitations</u>
    copy machine   yes
    reader/printer
    reader   yes

<u>Hours of operation</u> 7:30am-3:30pm, M-F

<u>Resources</u>
    clips   240 drawers   books   c. 200
    photos   10 drawers   pamphlets
    negs   maps   c. 100
    CPT   AV

<u>Microform holdings</u>
    own newspaper   1837-present
    periodicals
    clippings

<u>Indexes</u>
    own newspaper
    other

<u>Special collections</u> Central New Jersey history

<u>Automation</u>
  Automated files
    mechanical
    electronic
  Other automated systems

<u>Products for sale</u>

NEW JERSEY   Camden   NEW JERSEY

Courier-Post (e)   Circulation
Southern NJ Newspapers Inc. (Gannett)   (e) 124,701
Camden NJ 08101
                        609/663-6000 x305

            Elizabeth Saplee, Librarian
            Jaqueline Rurk, Asst. Librarian

Lib. est. 1920   Group Gannett Newspapers   FTE 2

Public access   Limitations
    in person   yes
    by mail   yes
    by phone   yes

Services available   Limitations
    copy machine   yes
    reader/printer
    reader   yes

Hours of operation 8am-11pm, M-F

Resources
    clips   150,000   books
    photos   60,000   pamphlets
    negs   maps
    CPT   AV

Microform holdings
    own newspaper   1947-present
    periodicals
    clippings

Indexes
    own newspaper
    other

Special collections

Automation
  Automated files
    mechanical   3 Lektrievers
    electronic
  Other automated systems

Products for sale

153

NEW JERSEY　　　　　　　　Elizabeth　　　　　　　　NEW JERSEY

The Daily Journal (e)　　　　　　　　　　　　　Circulation
295-299 No. Broad St.　　　　　　　　　　　　　(e) (45,000)
Elizabeth NJ 07207
　　　　　　　　201/354-5000 x292

　　　　Theresa Pirkowski, Librarian

Lib. est.　　　　　　Group Hagadone Newspapers　　FTE 1

Public access　　　　　　Limitations
　　in person　yes
　　by mail　　yes
　　by phone　 yes

Services available　　　　Limitations
　　copy machine　yes
　　reader/printer
　　reader　　　　yes

Hours of operation

Resources
　　clips　　x　　　　　　　books
　　photos　 x　　　　　　　pamphlets
　　negs　　　　　　　　　　maps　　　x
　　CPT　　　　　　　　　　 AV

Microform holdings
　　own newspaper　　1782-present
　　periodicals
　　clippings

Indexes
　　own newspaper
　　other

Special collections History of Daily Journal

Automation
　Automated files
　　mechanical
　　electronic
　Other automated systems

Products for sale

154

NEW JERSEY Hackensack NEW JERSEY

The Record

The Record (e)
The Sunday Record (S)
150 River St.
Hackensack NJ 07602

Circulation
(e) 151,242
(S) 212,531

201/646-4090

Homer E. Martin, Jr., Chief Librarian
Adelaide Kirchner, Librarian

Lib. est. 1930   Group Ind.   FTE 13

Public access   Limitations
    in person   no
    by mail   yes
    by phone   yes   1pm-5pm, M-F

Services available   Limitations
    copy machine   yes
    reader/printer   yes
    reader   yes

Hours of operation 4pm-2am, Sun.; 7am-2am, M-Th; 7am-7pm, F; 10am-6pm, Sat.

Resources
    clips   c. 3,250,000   books   2,000
    photos   c. 250,000   pamphlets   90 drawers
    negs   maps
    CPT   110   AV

Microform holdings
    own newspaper   1901-present
    periodicals
    clippings   5,300 jackets

Indexes
    own newspaper   1959-present (published by local public library; limited to local, regional and state)

Automation
  Automated files
    mechanical   9 Remington Rand Lektrievers
    electronic   Computerized list of subject headings
  Other automated systems

Products for sale

NEW JERSEY   New Brunswick   NEW JERSEY

Home News (eS)   Circulation
123 How Lane   (e) 58,648
New Brunswick NJ 08903   (S) 73,050
                        201/246-5529

          Joan Dobrowolski, Librarian
          Carolyn Middleton, Library Clerk

Lib. est.   Group Ind.   FTE 2.5

Public access   Limitations
    in person   yes   Must know date to use microfilm
    by mail   yes   Will send one article, otherwise payment
                           first
    by phone   yes

Services available   Limitations
    copy machine   yes $.50 per page
    reader/printer yes $1.00 per page
    reader   yes

Hours of operation 8:30am-5:30pm, M-F; 7:30pm-11:30pm, M-F

Resources
    clips   500,000   books   100
    photos   10,000   pamphlets   500
    negs   none   maps   40
    CPT   6   AV

Microform holdings
    own newspaper   1903-present
    periodicals
    clippings   —

Indexes
    own newspaper
    other

Special collections

Automation
  Automated files
    mechanical
    electronic
  Other automated systems

Products for sale

156

NEW JERSEY　　　　　　　　　　Newark　　　　　　　　　　NEW JERSEY

Star-Ledger (mS)　　　　　　　　　　　　　　　　　Circulation
Ledger Plaza　　　　　　　　　　　　　　　　　　　　(m) 406,252
Newark NJ 07101　　　　　　　　　　　　　　　　　　(S) 571,665
　　　　　　　　　　　　　201/877-4141

　　　　Betty Davis, Librarian

Lib. est. 1935　　　　Group Newhouse Newspapers　　　FTE 2

Public access　　　　　　　Limitations
　　in person　　yes　　　By appointment
　　by mail　　　yes
　　by phone　　 yes

Services available　　　　Limitations
　　copy machine　　yes
　　reader/printer
　　reader　　　　　yes

Hours of operation 8:30am-4pm, M-F

Resources
　　clips　　x　　　　　　　　books　　　x
　　photos　 x　　　　　　　　pamphlets
　　negs　　　　　　　　　　　maps
　　CPT　　　　　　　　　　　 AV

Microform holdings
　　own newspaper　　1945-present
　　periodicals
　　clippings

Indexes
　　own newspaper
　　other

Special collections

Automation
　Automated files
　　mechanical
　　electronic
　Other automated systems

Products for sale

157

NEW JERSEY   Parsippany   NEW JERSEY

Daily Record (eS)   Circulation
800 Jefferson Rd.   (e) 57,894
Parsippany NJ 07054   (S) 64,869
                         201/386-0200

         Tomie Galbreath, Librarian
         Mary Conroy, Library Asst.

Lib. est. 1965   Group Ind.   FTE 2

Public access   Limitations
     in person   yes   Questions regarding information older
     by mail   yes   than 1965 referred to public or
     by phone   yes   county libraries

Services available   Limitations
     copy machine
     reader/printer yes   Usually staff only, exceptions $.25 per
     reader   page

Hours of operation   9am-Midnight, M-F

Resources
     clips   x   books   x
     photos   x   pamphlets   x
     negs   maps   x
     CPT   AV

Microform holdings
     own newspaper   x
     periodicals
     clippings

Indexes
     own newspaper
     other

Special collections

Automation
  Automated files
     mechanical
     electronic
  Other automated systems

Products for sale

158

NEW JERSEY　　　　　　　　　Passaic　　　　　　　　　NEW JERSEY

The Herald News

Herald News (eS)　　　　　　　　　　　　　　　　Circulation
988 Main Ave.　　　　　　　　　　　　　　　　　　(e) 76,407
Passaic NJ 07055　　　　　　　　　　　　　　　　(S) 62,477
　　　　　　　　　　　　201/365-3155

　　　　　　　Bernice Martino, Librarian

Lib. est. 1932　　　Group Drukker Communications Inc.　　FTE 3

Public access　　　　　　　　Limitations
　　in person　　yes　　　　Use of reader/printer and clip files
　　by mail　　　yes
　　by phone　　 yes

Services available　　　　　Limitations
　　copy machine　　yes　　$.25 per page
　　reader/printer　yes　　$.25 per page
　　reader

Hours of operation　8:30am-4:30pm, M-F

Resources
　　clips　　　x　　　　　　　　　books　　　300
　　photos　　 x　　　　　　　　　pamphlets
　　negs　　　　　　　　　　　　　maps　　　 x
　　CPT　　　　50　　　　　　　　 AV

Microform holdings
　　own newspaper　　1870-present
　　periodicals
　　clippings

Indexes
　　own newspaper
　　other

Special collections

Automation
　Automated files
　　mechanical　　Lektriever
　　electronic
　Other automated systems

Products for sale

NEW JERSEY   Paterson   NEW JERSEY

News

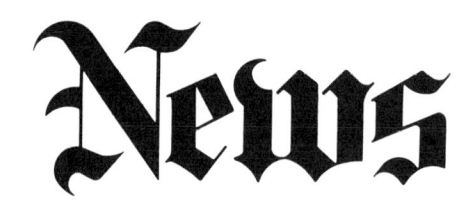

The Paterson News (me) P.O. Box 2117 Paterson NJ 07509	Circulation (m) 25,983 (e) 29,266

201/274-2000 x272

Nancy Sabino, Editorial Librarian

<u>Lib. est.</u>   <u>Group</u> Allbritton Newspapers   <u>FTE</u>

<u>Public access</u>
    in person   yes   <u>Limitations</u>
    by mail   no   With editor's permission
    by phone   yes

<u>Services available</u>   <u>Limitations</u>
    copy machine
    reader/printer
    reader   yes

<u>Hours of operation</u> 7am-3pm, M-F

<u>Resources</u>
    clips   x   books   x
    photos   x   pamphlets x
    negs   maps   x
    CPT   AV

<u>Microform holdings</u>
    own newspaper   1896-present
    periodicals
    clippings

<u>Indexes</u>
    own newspaper
    other

<u>Special collections</u>

<u>Automation</u>
  Automated files
    mechanical
    electronic
  Other automated systems

<u>Products for sale</u>

NEW JERSEY Shrewsbury NEW JERSEY

Daily Register (eS) Circulation
One Register Plaza (e) 31,688
Shrewsbury NJ 07701 (S) 30,683
 201/542-4000 x206

 Olga Boeckel, Head Librarian
 Carol Marino, Asst. Librarian

Lib. est. 1940 Group Block Newspapers FTE

Public access Limitations
 in person no
 by mail yes
 by phone yes

Services available Limitations
 copy machine
 reader/printer
 reader

Hours of operation 9am-5pm, M-F

Resources
 clips 1,000,000+ books 100
 photos 5,000 pamphlets
 negs 5,000 maps 50
 CPT 5 AV

Microform holdings
 own newspaper
 periodicals
 clippings

Indexes
 own newspaper
 other

Special collections

Automation
 Automated files
  mechanical
  electronic
 Other automated systems

Products for sale

161

NEW JERSEY   Trenton   NEW JERSEY

Trenton Times

Trenton Times (e)
Sunday Times Advertiser (S)
500 Perry St.
Trenton NJ 08605

Circulation
(e) 71,688
(S) 87,290

609/396-3232 x368

Susan Connery, Director of Research
Debra Deamer, Librarian

<u>Lib. est.</u> 1952   <u>Group</u> Washington Post Co.   <u>FTE</u> 3

<u>Public access</u>
    in person   no
    by mail   yes
    by phone   yes

<u>Limitations</u>
Police and media allowed

<u>Services available</u>
    copy machine   yes
    reader/printer   yes
    reader   yes

<u>Limitations</u>
Police and media - no charge

<u>Hours of operation</u>   7am-7pm, M-Thurs.; 7am-10pm, F; 1pm-9pm, Sat.

<u>Resources</u>

clips	x		books	500
photos	x		pamphlets	20
negs			maps	
CPT	15		AV	

<u>Microform holdings</u>
    own newspaper   1883-present
    periodicals
    clippings

<u>Indexes</u>
    own newspaper
    other

<u>Automation</u>
  Automated files
    mechanical   3 Lektrievers
    electronic
  Other automated systems

<u>Products for sale</u>

NEW JERSEY   Woodbridge   NEW JERSEY

News Tribune (e)   Circulation
1 Hoover Way   (e) 52,538
Woodbridge NJ 07095
                      201/442-0400 x234

            Flora Madsen, Librarian

Lib. est. ?   Group Ind.   FTE

Public access   Limitations
      in person   yes
      by mail
      by phone   yes

Services available   Limitations
      copy machine
      reader/printer yes
      reader

Hours of operation   8am-4pm, M-F

Resources
      clips   x   books   x
      photos   x   pamphlets   x
      negs   x   maps   x
      CPT   AV

Microform holdings
      own newspaper   1925-present
      periodicals
      clippings

Indexes
      own newspaper
      other

Special collections

Automation
   Automated files
      mechanical
      electronic
   Other automated systems

Products for sale

163

Journal (mS)
717 Silver SW
Albuquerque NM 87103

505/842-2352

Circulation
(m) 81,296
(S) 123,528

Mary R. Badghery, Librarian
Margo Saunders, Asst. Librarian

Lib. est. 1960   Group Ind.   FTE 3.5

Public access   Limitations
    in person   no
    by mail   no
    by phone   no

Services available   Limitations
    copy machine   yes $1.00 per page + $4.00 service charge
    reader/printer
    reader   yes

Hours of operation

Resources
clips	1,440,000	books	440
photos	26,480	pamphlets	750
negs	131,400	maps	300
CPT	25	AV	

Microform holdings
    own newspaper   1964-present
    periodicals
    clippings

Indexes
    own newspaper   x
    other

Special collections History of New Mexico

Automation
  Automated files
    mechanical
    electronic
  Other automated systems

Products for sale

NEW YORK   Binghamton   NEW YORK

The Evening Press

Evening Press (e)
Sun Bulletin (m)
Sunday Press (S)
Vestal Parkway East
Binghampton NY 13902

607/798-1159

Circulation
(m) 27,473
(e) 68,120
(S) 82,985

Gloria E. Keenan, Head Librarian
Kathy Semo, Asst. Librarian

Lib. est. 1942   Group   Gannett Newspapers   FTE   4

Public access
   in person   yes
   by mail   yes
   by phone   yes

Limitations
   Research done in library; 8am-4pm, M-F
   Copies of articles

Services available
   copy machine   yes
   reader/printer   yes
   reader   yes

Limitations
   $.50 per page
   $.50 per page

Hours of operation   7:30am-12:30am, M-F; Noon-8pm, Sat.; 4:30pm-12:30am, Sun.

Resources
   clips   30 cabinets   books   150
   photos   15 cabinets   pamphlets   100
   negs   maps   1 cabinet
   CPT   1   AV

Microform holdings
   own newspaper   1904-present
   periodicals

Indexes
   own newspaper   1904-present
   other   New York Times, 1947-present

Special collections   Old pictures of Broome County area

Automation
  Automated files
    mechanical
    electronic
  Other automated systems

Products for sale

Buffalo Courier-Express (mS)
795 Main St.
Buffalo NY 14240

716/847-5380

Circulation
(m) 125,163
(S) 257,219

Cynthia Hayes, Library Supervisor

Lib. est. 1930   Group Ind.   FTE 5

Public access   Limitations
   in person   yes   10am-6pm, M-F; ID required
   by mail   yes   Up to judgement of staff
   by phone   yes

Services available   Limitations
   copy machine   yes   20 copies per person, $.25 each
   reader/printer yes   20 copies per person, $.25 each
   reader

Hours of operation 9:30am-11:30pm, M-F; 11:30am-11:30pm, Sat.; 3:30pm-11:30pm, Sun.

Resources
   clips   525,000   books   400
   photos   25,000   pamphlets 800
   negs   maps   75
   CPT   1   AV

Microform holdings
   own newspaper   1813-present
   periodicals
   clippings

Indexes
   own newspaper   1890-1956
   other   Buffalo Daily Courier 1842-1926; Buffalo Express 1847-1926; Buffalo Times no dates; New York Times 1945-present

Automation
  Automated files
   mechanical
   electronic
  Other automated systems

Products for sale

NEW YORK   Buffalo   NEW YORK

Buffalo Evening News (eS)   Circulation
1 News Plaza   (e) 226,135
Buffalo NY 14240   (S) 156,600
                              716/849-4423

              Sally Schlaerth, Librarian

Lib. est. 1920   Group Ind.   FTE 7

Public access   Limitations
    in person   yes   By appointment
    by mail   yes   Simple research only
    by phone   no

Services available   Limitations
    copy machine   yes
    reader/printer yes
    reader   yes

Hours of operation 8am-4pm, M-Sat.

Resources
    clips   x   books   600
    photos   x   pamphlets x
    negs   maps   x
    CPT   AV

Microform holdings
    own newspaper   1880-present
    periodicals
    clippings

Indexes
    own newspaper   1920-1971
    other

Special collections

Automation
  Automated files
    mechanical   7 Lektrievers
    electronic
  Other automated systems

Products for sale

NEW YORK Elmira NEW YORK

Star Gazette (all day)   Circulation
Sunday Telegram (S)   (all day)
201 Baldwin St.   41,109
Elmira NY 14902   (S) 49,119
                     607/734-5151 x272

     Jean Strong, Librarian

<u>Lib. est.</u>   <u>Group</u> Gannett Newspapers   <u>FTE</u>

<u>Public access</u>   <u>Limitations</u>
    in person   yes
    by mail   yes
    by phone   yes

<u>Services available</u>   <u>Limitations</u>
    copy machine
    reader/printer
    reader   yes

<u>Hours of operation</u>   M-F

<u>Resources</u>
    clips   x   books
    photos   x   pamphlets
    negs   maps
    CPT   AV

<u>Microform holdings</u>
    own newspaper   1837-present
    periodicals
    clippings

<u>Indexes</u>
    own newspaper
    other

<u>Special collections</u>

<u>Automation</u>
  Automated files
    mechanical
    electronic
  Other automated systems

<u>Products for sale</u>

NEW YORK   Jamestown   NEW YORK

Post-Journal (e)   Circulation
11-21 W. Second St.   (e) 30,000
Jamestown NY 14701
                         716/487-1111 x255

              Norma Carlson, Librarian

Lib. est.   Group Ogden Newspapers   FTE

Public access   Limitations
    in person   yes   Legitimate study or research only
    by mail   yes   Charge for services
    by phone   yes   Charge for services

Services available   Limitations
    copy machine   yes   Per copy charge
    reader/printer yes   Study or research
    reader

Hours of operation   9am-3:30pm, M-F

Resources
    clips   x   books   x
    photos   x   pamphlets
    negs   x   maps   x
    CPT   AV

Microform holdings
    own newspaper   1826-present
    periodicals
    clippings

Indexes
    own newspaper
    other

Special collections

Automation
  Automated files
    mechanical
    electronic
  Other automated systems

Products for sale

169

Newsday (eS)
235 Pinelawn Rd., Melville
Long Island NY 11747

Circulation
(e) 513,714
(S) 563,916

516/454-2335

Andrew Ippolito, Director, Libraries/Research
Dave Hoffman, Chief Librarian

Lib. est. 1940   Group Times Mirror Co.   FTE 24

Public access   Limitations
    in person   no
    by mail   yes   Date and page numbers given, photocopies
    by phone   yes   Date and page numbers given

Services available   Limitations
    copy machine   yes $1.00 per page
    reader/printer   yes
    reader

Hours of operation 24 hours per day, M-Sat.; 1am-8am, Sun.

Resources
    clips   1,000,000   books   5,000
    photos   300,000   pamphlets   1,000
    negs   175,000   maps   200
    CPT   100+   AV

Microform holdings
    own newspaper   1940-present
    periodicals

Indexes
    own newspaper
    other   New York Times; Wall Street Journal

Special collections

Automation
  Automated files
    mechanical   Remington Rand Lektrievers, Supreme Conservatrieve
    electronic
  Other automated systems   New York Times Information Bank, DIALOG,
                            Brodart Book Express

Products for sale

Daily World (m)
239 W. 23rd St.
New York NY 10011

212/924-2523 x123

Circulation
(m) (40,000)

Saul Schulman, Librarian

Lib. est. 1924　　　　　　　Group Ind.　　　　　　　FTE 1

Public access　　　　　　　Limitations
    in person　　yes　　Staff discretion, charges at cost and
    by mail　　　yes　　service
    by phone　　 yes

Services available　　　　　Limitations
    copy machine　　yes
    reader/printer
    reader　　　　　yes

Hours of operation 9am-4pm, M-F

Resources
    clips　　x　　　　　　　　books
    photos　 x　　　　　　　　pamphlets
    negs　　　　　　　　　　　maps
    CPT　　　　　　　　　　　 AV

Microform holdings
    own newspaper　　1924-present
    periodicals
    clippings

Indexes
    own newspaper
    other

Special collections

Automation
  Automated files
    mechanical
    electronic
  Other automated systems

Products for sale

New York Daily News (mS)
220 E. 42nd St.
New York NY 10017
212/949-3569

Circulation
(m) 1,636,254
(S) 2,328,479

Joe McCarthy, Librarian

<u>Lib. est.</u> 1919   <u>Group</u> Tribune Co.   <u>FTE</u> 18

<u>Public access</u>   <u>Limitations</u>
- in person   no
- by mail   no
- by phone   no

<u>Services available</u>   <u>Limitations</u>
- copy machine   yes
- reader/printer yes
- reader   yes

<u>Hours of operation</u> 24 hrs., M-Sun.

<u>Resources</u>
clips	15,000,000	books	10,000
photos	10,000,000	pamphlets	
negs	4,000,000	maps	
CPT		AV	

<u>Microform holdings</u>
- own newspaper   1919-present
- periodicals
- clippings

<u>Indexes</u>
- own newspaper
- other

<u>Special collections</u>

<u>Automation</u>
  Automated files
    mechanical
    electronic
  Other automated systems

<u>Products for sale</u>

New York Post (eS)
210 South St.
New York NY 10002
212/349-5000 x200

Circulation
(e) 624,287
(S) 741,854

Merrill F. Sherr, Head Librarian
Faigi Rosenthal, Asst. Head Librarian

Lib. est. 1925   Group Ind.   FTE 11

Public access   Limitations
    in person   no
    by mail   yes
    by phone   yes

Services available   Limitations
    copy machine
    reader/printer
    reader

Hours of operation   24 hrs., M-F

Resources
    clips   5,000,000   books   500
    photos   pamphlets   350
    negs   maps
    CPT   20   AV

Microform holdings
    own newspaper   1801-present
    periodicals
    clippings

Indexes
    own newspaper
    other

Special collections

Automation
  Automated files
    mechanical
    electronic
  Other automated systems

Products for sale

New York Times (mS)
229 W. 43rd St.
New York NY 10036

212/556-7428

Circulation
(m) 863,532
(S) 1,435,330

Paul Greenfeder, Head of the Reference Library

<u>Lib. est.</u>   <u>Group</u> Ind.   <u>FTE</u> 4

<u>Public access</u>   <u>Limitations</u>
   in person   no
   by mail   no
   by phone   no

<u>Services available</u>   <u>Limitations</u>
   copy machine   yes   Staff only
   reader/printer yes   Staff only
   reader

<u>Hours of operation</u>   9:30am-9:30pm, M-F; 9:30am-5:30pm, Sat.

<u>Resources</u>
   clips   books   50,000+
   photos   pamphlets   68 drawers
   negs   maps   2 drawers
   CPT   500   AV

<u>Microform holdings</u>
   own newspaper
   periodicals   50 titles on roll film
   clippings

<u>Indexes</u>
   own newspaper   1851-present
   other

<u>Special collections</u>

<u>Automation</u>
  Automated files
   mechanical
   electronic   New York Times Information Bank
  Other automated systems

<u>Products for sale</u>

Wall Street Journal (m)
22 Cortlandt St.
New York NY 10007

212/285-5075

Circulation
(m) 1,632,155

Lottie Lindberg, Librarian
Dorothy Vera, Library Asst.

Lib. est. 1930's   Group Ind.   FTE 10

Public access   Limitations
    in person   no
    by mail   yes
    by phone   yes

Services available   Limitations
    copy machine   yes $1.00 per article
    reader/printer   yes
    reader   yes

Hours of operation   5am-9pm, M-F

Resources
    clips   x   books   x
    photos   pamphlets   x
    negs   maps
    CPT   56   AV

Microform holdings
    own newspaper   July 1889-present
    periodicals
    clippings

Indexes
    own newspaper   1955-present
    other   New York Times, 1958-present; National Observer, 1969-1976

Special collections   American Guide Series-45 volumes; Federal Writers Project on the states

Automation
  Automated files
    electronic   System 7: full-text of broad tape story (not newspaper story)

Products for sale

NEW YORK Niagara Falls NEW YORK

Niagara Gazette (eS) Circulation
310 LaSalle Arterial (e) 30,644
Niagara Falls NY 14302 (S) 32,460
716/282-2311 x48

Teresa Lasher, Librarian

Lib. est. 1854 Group Gannett Newspapers FTE 1

Public access Limitations
   in person yes
   by mail yes
   by phone yes

Services available Limitations
   copy machine
   reader/printer
   reader yes

Hours of operation 9am-4pm, M-F

Resources
   clips 56 drawers books 100
   photos 24 drawers pamphlets 50
   negs 1 year maps 10
   CPT 15 AV

Microform holdings
   own newspaper 1854-present
   periodicals
   clippings

Indexes
   own newspaper 1854-present
   other

Special collections Niagara Falls photos

Automation
  Automated files
    mechanical
    electronic
  Other automated systems

Products for sale

NEW YORK   Rochester   NEW YORK

Times-Union (e)   Circulation
Democrat & Republican (mS)   (m) 125,561
55 Exchange St.   (e) 124,274
Rochester NY 14614   (S) 231,684

             716/232-7100 x3211,3212

        Rex Schaeffer, Library Director
        Joy Hill, Asst. Librarian

Lib. est. 1929   Group Gannett Newspapers   FTE 6

Public access   Limitations
    in person   no   Scholars and other newspapers only
    by mail   yes
    by phone   yes

Services available   Limitations
    copy machine   yes $.25 per page
    reader/printer yes $1.00 per page
    reader   yes   Staff only

Hours of operation 8am-Midnight, M-Sat.; 4pm-Midnight, Sun.

Resources
    clips   1,000,000   books   1,500
    photos   650,000   pamphlets   20
    negs   50,000   maps   500
    CPT   80   AV

Microform holdings
    own newspaper   1914-present
    periodicals

Indexes
    own newspaper
    other

Special collections

Automation
  Automated files
    mechanical   3 Lektrievers
    electronic
  Other automated systems

Products for sale

177

Schenectady Gazette (e)
332 State St.
Schenectady NY 12301
                  518/374-4141 x237

Circulation
(e) 67,817

Collen J. Daze, Librarian

Lib. est. 1976   Group Ind.   FTE 3

Public access   Limitations
- in person   no   Not encouraged; by appointment
- by mail   yes   Quick answer only
- by phone   yes   Quick answer only

Services available   Limitations
- copy machine   yes   Only if not busy; $.25 per page
- reader/printer   yes   Only if not busy; $.25 per page
- reader
- other   yes   Will research for $8.00 per hour plus copying costs

Hours of operation   9am-11pm, M-F

Resources
- clips   x   books
- photos   x   pamphlets
- negs   maps
- CPT   AV

Microform holdings
- own newspaper   1899-present
- periodicals
- clippings

Indexes
- own newspaper   March 1978-present
- other

Automation
  Automated files
    mechanical
    electronic   Composition Systems Inc., own index going online
  Other automated systems

Products for sale   Index should be for sale in 1980

NEW YORK   Troy   NEW YORK

Times Record (e)   Circulation
Sunday Record (S)   (e) 46,296
501 Broadway   (S) 44,915
Troy NY 12181
                        518/272-2000 x535

            Ingrid Sharke, Librarian
            Lelia Follett, Asst. Librarian

Lib. est. 1974   Group Horvitz Newspapers   FTE 1

Public access   Limitations
    in person   no   Some exceptions
    by mail   yes
    by phone   yes   No extensive research

Services available   Limitations
    copy machine   yes   There is a charge
    reader/printer
    reader   yes

Hours of operation 8am-5pm, M-F

Resources
    clips   x   books   x
    photos   x   pamphlets   x
    negs   maps   x
    CPT   1   AV

Microform holdings
    own newspaper   May 1935-present
    periodicals   Troy Record 1898-1972, incomplete, on microfilm
    clippings

Indexes
    own newspaper
    other

Automation
  Automated files
    mechanical
    electronic
  Other automated systems

Products for sale

179

NEW YORK   Watertown   NEW YORK

Watertown Daily Times (e)   Circulation
260 Washington St.   (e) 41,295
Watertown NY 13601
                      315/782-1000

          Donna Belchen, Librarian

Lib. est. 1900   Group   Ind.   FTE 3

Public access   Limitations
    in person   yes   9am-Noon, M-F with Managing Editor's
    by mail   yes   approval
    by phone   yes

Services available   Limitations
    copy machine   yes $.60 per copy
    reader/printer
    reader   yes

Hours of operation 7am-3pm, M-F; 7am-Noon, Sat.

Resources
    clips   x   books   x
    photos   x   pamphlets   x
    negs   maps   x
    CPT   x   AV

Microform holdings
    own newspaper   1861-present
    periodicals
    clippings

Indexes
    own newspaper   none
    other

Special collections All newspapers ever printed in Jefferson county

Automation
  Automated files
    mechanical
    electronic
  Other automated systems

Products for sale

NEW YORK White Plains NEW YORK

The Reporter-Dispatch (eS)   Circulation
One Gannett Dr.   (e) (46,625)
White Plains NY 10604   (S) (39,379)
                       914/694-5086

         Norma Seldon, Asst. Librarian

Lib. est.   **Group** Gannett Newspapers   **FTE**

Public access   **Limitations**
     in person   no
     by mail   no
     by phone   no

Services available   **Limitations**
     copy machine   yes   Staff only
     reader/printer   yes   Staff only
     reader   yes   Staff only

Hours of operation 8am-5pm, M-F

Resources
     clips   x   books   x
     photos   x   pamphlets   x
     negs   x   maps   x
     CPT   AV

Microform holdings
     own newspaper   1949-present
     periodicals

Indexes
     own newspaper
     other

Automation
  Automated files
    mechanical
    electronic   Field testing QL system
  Other automated systems

Products for sale

NORTH CAROLINA   Charlotte   NORTH CAROLINA

The Charlotte Observer

Charlotte Observer (mS)
Charlotte News (e)
P.O. Box 32166
Charlotte NC 28232

704/374-7307

Circulation
(m) 171,219
(e) 52,979
(S) 238,621

Joy Walker, Head Librarian

Lib. est. 1956   Group Knight-Ridder Newspapers   FTE 6.5

Public access
- in person   no
- by mail   yes
- by phone   yes

Limitations

Services available
- copy machine   yes   Staff only
- reader/printer   yes   Staff only
- reader   yes   Staff only

Limitations

Hours of operation   M-Sat.

Resources
- clips   3,500,000   books   2,100
- photos   850,000   pamphlets
- negs   x   maps
- CPT   AV

Microform holdings
- own newspaper   1883-present (incomplete)
- periodicals
- clippings

Indexes
- own newspaper   none
- other

Special collections

Automation
- Automated files
  - mechanical
  - electronic
- Other automated systems

Products for sale

182

NORTH CAROLINA — Durham — NORTH CAROLINA

Durham Morning Herald
THE DURHAM SUN

Durham Morning Herald (mS)
Durham Sun (e)
115-119 Market St.
Durham NC 27702

919/682-8181

Circulation
(m) 43,876
(e) 22,355
(S) 58,049

Barbara P. Semonche, Chief Librarian
Marie Thrower, Library Asst.

Lib. est. Oct. 1976 Group Ind. FTE 2

Public access
		Limitations
in person	no	
by mail	yes	Dates only
by phone	yes	Dates only

Services available
		Limitations
copy machine		
reader/printer	yes	Staff only
reader		

Hours of operation 9am-10pm, M-F; 9am-5:30pm, Sat.; 5pm-10pm, Sun.

Resources
clips	300,000	books	3,000
photos	50,000	pamphlets	56 drawers
negs	50,000	maps	1,000
CPT	50	AV	

Microform holdings
own newspaper   1900-present

Indexes
own newspaper   1929-1969, bound; 1970-1977, microfilm
other   Law and Press Index

Special collections   Durham history

Automation
Automated files
  mechanical   3 White 7300 Power Files
  electronic   Computerized subject authority file in planning stage
Other automated systems

Products for sale Sale of local news index planned by 1980

NORTH CAROLINA   Fayetteville   NORTH CAROLINA

Fayetteville Times (m)　　　　　　　　　　　　　　　Circulation
Fayetteville Observer (e)　　　　　　　　　　　　　　(m) 20,134
Fayetteville Observer-Times (S)　　　　　　　　　　　(e) 42,037
P.O. Box 849　　　　　　　　　　　　　　　　　　　　(S) 59,204
Fayetteville NC 28302
　　　　　　　　　　919/323-4848 x279

　　　　Daisy Dockery Maxwell, Librarian
　　　　Murlene Tew, Library Asst.

Lib. est. 1969　　　　　　Group Ind.　　　　　FTE 2.5

Public access　　　　　　　　Limitations
　　in person　　yes　　　　Extensive research must be done by
　　by mail　　　yes　　　　individual
　　by phone　　 yes

Services available　　　　　Limitations
　　copy machine　　yes　　$.25 per page, reporters have priority
　　reader/printer　yes　　$.50 per page
　　reader　　　　　no

Hours of operation 8am-9pm, M-F

Resources
　　clips　　x　　　　　　　　　books　　　x
　　photos　 x　　　　　　　　　pamphlets　x
　　negs　　　　　　　　　　　　maps　　　 x
　　CPT　　　45　　　　　　　　AV

Microform holdings
　　own newspaper　　Times 1973-present; Observer 1849-present
　　periodicals
　　clippings

Indexes
　　own newspaper　　1969-1971 in progress
　　other

Special collections

Automation
　Automated files
　　mechanical
　　electronic
　Other automated systems

Products for sale

Greensboro Daily News (mS)
Greensboro Record (e)
200 E. Market St.
Greensboro NC 27420

919/373-1000 x393

Circulation
(m) 80,562
(e) 31,072
(S) 111,905

Bobby D. Isaacs, Library Director
Elizabeth D. Kelso, Asst. Librarian

Lib. est. 1969   Group Landmark Communications Inc.   FTE 3

Public access
- in person   no
- by mail   yes
- by phone   yes

Limitations

Services available
- copy machine   yes
- reader/printer yes
- reader

Limitations
$1.00 per page

Hours of operation   7:30am-8pm, M-F

Resources
clips	28 cabinets	books	1,000
photos	20 cabinets	pamphlets	800
negs	5 cabinets	maps	x
CPT	3	AV	

Microform holdings
- own newspaper   1906-present
- periodicals

Indexes
- own newspaper   none
- other

Special collections

Automation
- Automated files
  - mechanical   2 Diebold 7300 power files
  - electronic
- Other automated systems

Products for sale

NORTH CAROLINA	Raleigh	NORTH CAROLINA

The News and Observer ♦ THE RALEIGH TIMES

News and Observer (mS)
Raleigh Times (e)
215 S. McDowell St.
Raleigh NC 27602

901/821-1234 x326

Celia Wall, Librarian

Circulation
(m) 129,776
(e) 34,893
(S) 161,536

Lib. est. 1935   Group   Ind.   FTE   5

Public access   Limitations
- in person   no
- by mail   no
- by phone   no

Services available   Limitations
- copy machine   yes   Staff only
- reader/printer yes   Staff only
- reader   yes   Staff only

Hours of operation   7am-9:30pm, M-F; 2:30pm-9:30pm, Sat. & Sun.

Resources
- clips
- photos
- negs
- CPT
- books
- pamphlets
- maps
- AV

Microform holdings
- own newspaper   1877-present
- periodicals
- clippings

Indexes
- own newspaper
- other

Special collections

Automation
- Automated files
  - mechanical
  - electronic
- Other automated systems

Products for sale

186

NORTH CAROLINA Winston-Salem NORTH CAROLINA

WINSTON-SALEM JOURNAL

The Sentinel

Winston-Salem Journal (mS)
Sentinel (e)
P.O. Box 3159
Winston-Salem NC 27102

919/727-7275

Circulation
(m) 72,504
(e) 39,202
(S) 94,902

Marilyn H. Rollins, Manager, Reference Dept.

Lib. est. 1947   Group Media General Inc.   FTE 5.25

Public access   Limitations
  in person   no
  by mail   no
  by phone   no

Services available   Limitations
  copy machine   yes $.25 per pages 1-4, $1.00 per pages 5-
  reader/printer   10, $2.00 per page thereafter, $.25 per
  reader   duplicate page

Hours of operation 8am-11pm, M-F; 9am-11pm, Sat.; 2:30pm-11pm, Sun.

Resources
  clips   1,500,000   books   1,050
  photos   168,000   pamphlets   976
  negs   10,500   maps
  CPT   67   AV

Microform holdings
  own newspaper   1898-present
  periodicals
  clippings

Indexes
  own newspaper
  other

Special collections

Automation
  Automated files
    mechanical
    electronic
  Other automated systems

Products for sale

The Bismarck Tribune (e)　　　　　　　　　　　　　　Circulation
P. O. Box 1498　　　　　　　　　　　　　　　　　　　(e) 29,596
Bismarck　ND 58501
　　　　　　　　　　701/223-2500

　　　　　Kelli Herman, Librarian
　　　　　Donna Hoffman, Library Clerk

Lib. est.　　　　　　　　Group　Lee Newspapers　　　FTE

Public access　　　　　　Limitations
　　in person　　no
　　by mail　　　yes　　$10 minimum charge for library search
　　by phone　　 yes　　at librarian's discretion

Services available　　　 Limitations
　　copy machine　　yes　$.25 per copy
　　reader/printer　yes　$1 per copy
　　reader

Hours of operation　8am-5pm, M-F

Resources
　　clips　　　　　　　　　books
　　photos　　　　　　　　 pamphlets
　　negs　　　　　　　　　 maps
　　CPT　　　　　　　　　　AV

Microform holdings
　　own newspaper
　　periodicals
　　clippings

Indexes
　　own newspaper
　　other

Special collections

Automation
　Automated files
　　mechanical
　　electronic
　Other automated systems

Products for sale

NORTH DAKOTA Fargo NORTH DAKOTA

The Forum (all day,S)
P.O. Box 2020
Fargo ND 58102

Circulation
(all day)
  58,241
(S) 61,905

701/235-7311 x229

Andrea H. Halgrimson, Head Librarian
Leslie Rose, Asst. Librarian

Lib. est. 1922   Group Ind.   FTE 3

Public access   Limitations
    in person   no
    by mail   yes   Some - with charge
    by phone   yes   Some - with charge

Services available   Limitations
    copy machine   yes   None by public
    reader/printer   yes   None by public
    reader   yes   None by public

Hours of operation 7:30am-6pm, M-F; 8am-Noon, Sat.

Resources
    clips   75,000 files   books   300
    photos   17,000 mugs   pamphlets
    negs   maps
    CPT   AV

Microform holdings
    own newspaper   1879-present
    periodicals
    clippings

Indexes
    own newspaper
    other

Automation
  Automated files
    mechanical   1 Diebold unit
    electronic
  Other automated systems

Products for sale

189

Akron Beacon Journal

Akron Beacon Journal (eS)
44 East Exchange St.
Akron OH 44328

216/375-8515

Catherine M. Tierney, Chief Librarian
Vickie Victoria, Asst. Librarian

Circulation
(e) 165,223
(S) 217,991

<u>Lib. est.</u> 1939   <u>Group</u> Knight-Ridder Newspapers   <u>FTE</u> 8

<u>Public access</u>   <u>Limitations</u>
    in person   no
    by mail   no
    by phone   no

<u>Services available</u>   <u>Limitations</u>
    copy machine
    reader/printer   yes   For Editorial use
    reader

<u>Hours of operation</u>   24 hrs., M-F; 8am-10pm, Sat.

<u>Resources</u>
    clips   x   books   1,500
    photos   x   pamphlets
    negs   maps
    CPT   AV

<u>Microform holdings</u>
    own newspaper   1839-present
    periodicals

<u>Indexes</u>
    own newspaper
    other

<u>Special collections</u>   KSU riot (May 4, 1970-present); Airships; Rubber Industry

<u>Automation</u>
   Automated files
     mechanical
     electronic
   Other automated systems

<u>Products for sale</u>

OHIO Cincinnati OHIO

THE CINCINNATI ENQUIRER

Cincinnati Enquirer (mS) Circulation
617 Vine St. (m) 189,862
Cincinnati OH 45202 (S) 289,575

513/721-2700

Fred D. Morgener, Head Librarian
Marvin Harmon, Asst. Librarian
Raymond Zwick, Asst. Librarian

Lib. est. 1902 Group Combined Communications Corp. FTE 7

Public access Limitations
   in person no
   by mail yes
   by phone yes After 11am

Services available Limitations
   copy machine yes $2.40 for first 10 copies; $.15 for each additional copy
   reader/printer yes $1.00 per page

Hours of operation 8:30am-1:30am, M-F; 8:30am-1am, Sat.; 1pm-Midnight Sun.

Resources
   clips 7,000,000 books 1,000
   photos 1,000,000+ pamphlets 500
   negs maps 250
   CPT 125 AV

Microform holdings
   own newspaper x
   periodicals
   clippings Microfilm and fiche

Indexes
   own newspaper none
   other

Special collections

Automation
  Automated files
    mechanical CONSERV-A-TRIEVE
    electronic
  Other automated systems

Products for sale

The Cincinnati Post (e)   Circulation
800 Broadway   (e) 179,193
Cincinnati OH 45202
                         513/352-2785 or 2786

         Elmer L. Geers, Librarian
         Eric Davis, Asst. Librarian

<u>Lib. est.</u> 1930's   <u>Group</u>   Scripps-Howard Newspapers   <u>FTE</u> 2

<u>Public access</u>   <u>Limitations</u>
     in person   no
     by mail   no
     by phone   no

<u>Services available</u>   <u>Limitations</u>
     copy machine   yes   Editorial Dept. use only
     reader/printer   yes   Editorial Dept. use only
     reader   yes   Editorial Dept. use only

<u>Hours of operation</u>   7am-4:30pm, M-F

<u>Resources</u>
     clips   100,000 files   books
     photos   86,000 files   pamphlets
     negs   maps
     CPT   AV

<u>Microform holdings</u>
     own newspaper   1882-present
     periodicals
     clippings

<u>Indexes</u>
     own newspaper
     other

<u>Special collections</u>

<u>Automation</u>
   Automated files
     mechanical
       electronic
   Other automated systems

<u>Products for sale</u>

OHIO Cleveland OHIO

THE PLAIN DEALER

The Plain Dealer (mS)
1801 Superior Ave.
Cleveland OH 44114

Circulation
(m) 382,940
(s) 452,808

216/344-4195 (Library)
216/344-4230 (Pictures and Public Info.)

Grace D. Parch, Library Director
Patti Graziano, Asst. Librarian

Lib. est. 1908   Group Newhouse Newspapers   FTE 7

Public access
   in person no
   by mail yes
   by phone no

Limitations
  By mail only to Back Issues Dept.
  Newspaper has Public Service Dept.
  Research limited

Services available
   copy machine yes
   reader/printer yes
   reader yes

Limitations
  For news staff only

Hours of operation   8am-2am, M-F; Noon-2am, Sat.; 5pm-2am, Sun.

Resources
   clips 3,000,000   books 4,000
   photos 1,500,000   pamphlets 40 drawers
   negs   maps 500
   CPT 197   AV

Microform holdings
   own newspaper 1842-present

Indexes
   own newspaper   Case-WRU Index, April-Nov. 1971; Subj. Authority Thesaurus Index, 1974-present; partial index 1931, 1933-38 at CPL; Cleveland Public Library Index 1976-present

Special collections   Cleveland and Ohio history; photos from 1858-present; Cleveland Necrology file, 1855-1955

Automation
  Automated files
    mechanical
    electronic Computerized subject authority file only
  Other automated systems

Products for sale

OHIO   Cleveland   OHIO

Cleveland Press (e)   Circulation
901 Lakeside Ave.   (e) 303,175
Cleveland OH 44114
                   216/623-6740

         Thomas Barensfeld, Librarian
         Robert E. Noyes, Asst. Librarian

<u>Lib. est.</u> 1920   <u>Group</u> Scripps-Howard Newspapers   <u>FTE</u> 7

<u>Public access</u>   <u>Limitations</u>
    in person   yes   Very limited, screened by Public Service
    by mail   Dept.
    by phone

<u>Services available</u>   <u>Limitations</u>
    copy machine
    reader/printer
    reader   yes

<u>Hours of operation</u>   6am-4pm, M-F; 5am-1pm, Sat.

<u>Resources</u>
clips	1,000,000	books	2,000
photos	1,000,000	pamphlets	5,000
negs		maps	1,000
CPT	10	AV	

<u>Microform holdings</u>
    own newspaper   1878-present
    periodicals
    clippings

<u>Indexes</u>
    own newspaper   yes
    other

<u>Special collections</u>

<u>Automation</u>
   Automated files
     mechanical   4 Lektrievers
     electronic
   Other automated systems

<u>Products for sale</u>

Columbus Citizen-Journal (meS)
34 S. Third St.
Columbus OH 43203

614/461-5534

Doris E. Duren, Librarian

Circulation
(m) 110,981
(e) 202,097
(s) 343,589

Lib. est. 1901   Group Ind.   FTE

Public access   Limitations
   in person   yes   Partially limited
   by mail   yes   Partially limited
   by phone   yes   Partially limited

Services available   Limitations
   copy machine   yes   Staff only
   reader/printer
   reader   yes

Hours of operation M-F, Sun.

Resources
   clips   x   books
   photos   x   pamphlets
   negs   x   maps
   CPT   AV

Microform holdings
   own newspaper
   periodicals
   clippings

Indexes
   own newspaper   none
   other

Special collections

Automation
  Automated files
   mechanical
   electronic
  Other automated systems

Products for sale

OHIO   Columbus   OHIO

The Columbus Dispatch
OHIO'S GREATEST HOME NEWSPAPER

Columbus Dispatch (eS)   Circulation
34 S. Third St.   (e) 202,097
Columbus   OH 43216   (S) 343,589
                      614/461-5016

         James Hunter, Librarian

Lib. est. 1890   Group Ind.   FTE 4

Public access   Limitations
    in person   no   Will help other news organizations
    by mail   no
    by phone   no

Services available   Limitations
    copy machine   yes
    reader/printer   yes
    reader

Hours of operation   7am-5pm, M-F; 7am-3pm, Sat.

Resources
    clips   1,000,000   books   1,000
    photos   500,000   pamphlets   16 drawers
    negs   maps   200
    CPT   20   AV

Microform holdings
    own newspaper   1811-present
    periodicals
    clippings   500 jackets

Indexes
    own newspaper   1871-1937
    other

Special collections

Automation
  Automated files
    mechanical
    electronic   Online index Jan. 1980-present   (also printed)
  Other automated systems   Access to New York Times Information Bank

Products for sale

Journal Herald (m)
Dayton Daily News (eS)
4th and Ludlow Sts.
Dayton OH 45402

513/225-2430

Circulation
(m) 100,703
(e) 144,104
(S) 219,702

Harish Trivedi, Director of Libraries

Lib. est.   Group Cox Newspapers   FTE 9

Public access   Limitations
  in person   Public access very limited and at
  by mail   discretion of Director
  by phone

Services available   Limitations
  copy machine   yes   For newspaper employees only
  reader/printer   yes
  reader   yes

Hours of operation   6:30am-Midnight, M-Sat.; 1pm-Midnight, Sun.

Resources
  clips   330,000 files   books   3,000+
  photos   180,000 files   pamphlets   6,500
  negs   maps   200
  CPT   15   AV

Microform holdings
  own newspaper   1830-present
  periodicals
  clippings   90,000 jackets

Indexes
  own newspaper
  other   New York Times 1955-present

Special collections

Automation
  Automated files
    mechanical
    electronic
  Other automated systems

Products for sale

The Chronicle Telegram (eS)
225 East Ave.
Elyria OH 44035
                  216/323-3321 x219

Circulation
(e) 41,434
(S) 42,177

    Jeanne Meredith, Librarian
    Nellie Bierek, Asst. Librarian

<u>Lib. est.</u> 1955   <u>Group</u> Lorain County Printing and Publishing Co.   <u>FTE</u> 4

<u>Public access</u>
    in person
    by mail
    by phone

<u>Limitations</u>
Files are for the use of our staff, although we do try to answer questions for the general public

<u>Services available</u>
    copy machine   yes
    reader/printer
    reader

<u>Limitations</u>
Metro editor decides on public copies

<u>Hours of operation</u>   6am-3pm, M-Sat.

<u>Resources</u>
    clips   16,000+ subject files   books
    photos   pamphlets
    negs   maps
    CPT   AV

<u>Microform holdings</u>
    own newspaper   1840-present
    periodicals
    clippings

<u>Indexes</u>
    own newspaper
    other

<u>Special collections</u>

<u>Automation</u>
  Automated files
    mechanical
    electronic
  Other automated systems

<u>Products for sale</u>

Record-Courier (e)　　　　　　　　　　　　　　　　　Circulation
206 E. Erie St.　　　　　　　　　　　　　　　　　　　(e) 27,000
Kent OH 44240
　　　　　　　　　　216/673-3491

　　　　　Kathleen Mosher, News Librarian

Lib. est. 1966　　　　　　Group Ind.　　　　　　FTE .5

Public access　　　　　　　Limitations
　　in person　　yes　　　　No files may leave office
　　by mail　　　yes　　　　Photocopies $.10 each
　　by phone　　 yes

Services available　　　　Limitations
　　copy machine　　yes
　　reader/printer yes　　 Use of reader is free; prints cost
　　reader　　　　　　　　　$12 per page

Hours of operation　8am-5pm, M-F; 8am-Noon, Sat. (Reporters can aid
　　　　　　　　　　　public when librarian is not in)

Resources
　　clips　　27 drawers　　　　books　　　　75
　　photos　 back 1 year　　　pamphlets　 40
　　negs　　 back 20 years　　 maps　　　　 5
　　CPT　　　　　　　　　　　　AV

Microform holdings
　　own newspaper　　1889-present
　　periodicals
　　clippings

Indexes
　　own newspaper
　　other

Special collections May 4, 1970 shootings at Kent State and following
　　　　　　　　　　　　civil suits, investigations, and gym annex dispute
Automation
　Automated files
　　mechanical
　　electronic
　Other automated systems

Products for sale

OHIO   Lima   OHIO

The Lima News (eS)   Circulation
121 E. High St.   (e) 40,644
Lima OH 45802   (S) 47,574
                        419/223-1010 x217

                    Sarah Macpherson, Librarian

<u>Lib. est.</u> 1966   <u>Group</u> Freedom Newspapers   <u>FTE</u> 1

<u>Public access</u>   <u>Limitations</u>
    in person   yes
    by mail   yes
    by phone   yes

<u>Services available</u>   <u>Limitations</u>
    copy machine
    reader/printer
    reader   yes

<u>Hours of operation</u> 8am-5pm, M-F

<u>Resources</u>
    clips   books
    photos   pamphlets
    negs   maps
    CPT   AV

<u>Microform holdings</u>
    own newspaper
    periodicals
    clippings

<u>Indexes</u>
    own newspaper
    other

<u>Special collections</u>

<u>Automation</u>
  Automated files
    mechanical
    electronic
  Other automated systems

<u>Products for sale</u>

OHIO   Mansfield   OHIO

NEWS JOURNAL

News Journal (eS)
70 W. Fourth St.
Mansfield OH 44901

419/522-3311 x206

Circulation
(e) 40,751
(S) 50,025

Katherine Corby, Librarian

<u>Lib. est.</u> ?   <u>Group</u> Horvitz Newspapers   <u>FTE</u> .5

<u>Public access</u>   <u>Limitations</u>
     in person   yes   Must be supervised
     by mail   yes   No searches - ready reference only
     by phone   yes   No searches - ready reference only

<u>Services available</u>   <u>Limitations</u>
     copy machine   yes $.15 per copy; extensive copying by prearrangment only
     reader/printer
     reader   yes   Employees have priority for use

<u>Hours of operation</u>   8am-5pm, M-F

<u>Resources</u>
     clips   x   books   c. 350
     photos   x   pamphlets   x
     negs   x   maps   x
     CPT   x   AV

<u>Microform holdings</u>
     own newspaper
     periodicals
     clippings

<u>Indexes</u>
     own newspaper

<u>Special collections</u>

<u>Automation</u>
   Automated files
     mechanical
     electronic
   Other automated systems

<u>Products for sale</u>

OHIO   Sandusky   OHIO

Sandusky Register

Sandusky Register (eS)
314 W. Market St.
Sandusky OH 44870
419/625-5500 x251

Circulation
(e) 26,411
(S) 27,466

Elaine Barker, Head Librarian
Victoria Beatty, Asst.

Lib. est. 1973   Group   Ind.   FTE

Public access   Limitations
- in person   no
- by mail   yes
- by phone   yes

Services available   Limitations
- copy machine
- reader/printer
- reader

Hours of operation   8am-5pm, M-F

Resources
- clips   1,500 files   books   50
- photos   pamphlets
- negs   1969-present   maps
- CPT   AV

Microform holdings
- own newspaper   1827-present
- periodicals
- clippings

Indexes
- own newspaper
- other

Special collections

Automation
- Automated files
  - mechanical
  - electronic
- Other automated systems

Products for sale   Glossies of pictures that ran in paper

OHIO   Toledo   OHIO

THE BLADE

Blade (eS)   Circulation
541 Superior St.   (e) 169,766
Toledo OH 43660   (S) 208,867
                        419/259-7265

            Kathleen Trimble, Head Librarian

Lib. est. 1927   Group Block Newspapers   FTE 5

Public access   Limitations
    in person   no
    by mail   yes   Dates only
    by phone   yes   Dates only

Services available   Limitations
    copy machine   yes
    reader/printer yes
    reader

Hours of operation 7:30am-9:30pm, M-F

Resources
    clips   21,000 inches   books   2,100
    photos   21,000 inches   pamphlets
    negs   maps
    CPT   21   AV

Microform holdings
    own newspaper   1835-present
    periodicals   1970-75 Toledo Times
    clippings   1,000 microfiche of clippings

Indexes
    own newspaper   1936-38
    other   New York Times 1930-present

Special collections

Automation
  Automated files
    mechanical
    electronic
  Other automated systems

Products for sale

OKLAHOMA   Midwest City   OKLAHOMA

The Journal (meS)   Circulation
7430 SE 15th
Midwest City OK 73110
                         405/737-8811 x342

            Judy Hampton, Head Librarian

Lib. est. 1964   Group Ind.   FTE 1

Public access   Limitations
    in person   no
    by mail   yes   Photo orders only
    by phone   no

Services available   Limitations
    copy machine
    reader/printer
    reader

Hours of operation   8am-6pm, M-F

Resources
    clips   x   books   x
    photos   x   pamphlets   x
    negs   x   maps   x
    CPT   AV

Microform holdings
    own newspaper   1964-present
    periodicals
    clippings

Indexes
    own newspaper
    other

Special collections

Automation
  Automated files
    mechanical
    electronic
  Other automated systems

Products for sale

OKLAHOMA   Oklahoma City   OKLAHOMA

THE DAILY OKLAHOMAN

Daily Oklahoman (mS)	**Circulation**
Oklahoman City Times (e)	(m) 189,847
P.O. Box 25125	(e) 99,536
Oklahoma City OK 73125	(S) 289,126

405/231-3388

(Jewell) Monteray Nelson, Chief Librarian

Lib. est. ?   **Group** Ind.   **FTE** 7.25

Public access
- in person   no
- by mail   yes
- by phone   no

Limitations
Other media, libraries and researchers by appointment only
Photo orders and limited research
Referred to public library

Services available
- copy machine   yes
- reader/printer   no
- reader   yes

Limitations
Ten clippings only

In file room, not in library

Hours of operation   7:30am-10pm, M-F; 1:30pm-10pm Sat.; 3:30pm-10pm Sun.

Resources
clips	2,130,000	books	3,000
photos	1,425,000	pamphlets	10,000
negs	In Photo Dept.	maps	1,500
CPT	10	AV	

Microform holdings
- own newspaper   1903-present
- periodicals
- clippings

Indexes
- own newspaper
- other   New York Times, 1926-present

Special collections

Automation
   Automated files
     mechanical
     electronic
   Other automated systems

Products for sale

Tulsa Daily World (mS)　　　　　　　　　　　　Circulation
Tulsa Tribune (e)　　　　　　　　　　　　　　　(m) 121,127
P.O. Box 1770　　　　　　　　　　　　　　　　　(e) 78,367
Tulsa OK 74012　　　　　　　　　　　　　　　　(S) 208,808
　　　　　　　　　　918/583-2161 x342

　　　　　　　Lucy Towry, Head Librarian
　　　　　　　Charles Cunningham, Asst. Librarian

<u>Lib. est.</u> 1943　　　　　　<u>Group</u> Ind.　　　　　　<u>FTE</u> 8

<u>Public access</u>　　　　　　　<u>Limitations</u>
　　in person　　yes　　　　By appt. only, 10am-4:30pm M-F
　　by mail　　　yes
　　by phone　　 yes

<u>Services available</u>　　　　<u>Limitations</u>
　　copy machine　yes　　　$.50 per copy
　　reader/printer
　　reader　　　　yes　　　If not in use by reporters

<u>Hours of operation</u>

<u>Resources</u>
　　clips　　45-8 drawer files　　books　　　c. 400
　　photos　　x　　　　　　　　　　pamphlets
　　negs　　　x　　　　　　　　　　maps　　　　50
　　CPT　　　　　　　　　　　　　　 AV

<u>Microform holdings</u>
　　own newspaper　　1900-present, both papers
　　periodicals

<u>Indexes</u>
　　own newspaper
　　other

<u>Special collections</u>

<u>Automation</u>
　Automated files
　　mechanical
　　electronic
　Other automated systems

<u>Products for sale</u>

Eugene Register-Guard (eS)
P.O. Box 10188
Eugene OR 97440

503/485-1234

Marijoy Rubaloff, Librarian
Karen Stevens, Library Aide

Circulation
(e) 61,015
(S) 67,148

Lib. est. c. 1950   Group Ind.   FTE 2

Public access   Limitations
- in person   yes
- by mail   yes $15 research fee outside circulation area
- by phone   yes   Provide dates only

Services available   Limitations
- copy machine   yes $.25 per page
- reader/printer   yes $.25 per page
- reader   yes

Hours of operation   6:30am-5:30pm, M-F; public hours, 1-3pm, M-F

Resources
- clips   20,000   books   2,000
- photos   5,000   pamphlets   500
- negs   maps   500
- CPT   30   AV

Microform holdings
- own newspaper   1868-present
- periodicals
- clippings   20,000 fiche

Indexes
- own newspaper   7 years
- other   5 years of photo negatives

Special collections

Automation
   Automated files
     mechanical
     electronic
   Other automated systems

Products for sale

OREGON   Portland   OREGON

The Oregonian

The Oregonian (mS)
Oregon Journal (e)
1320 SW Broadway
Portland OR 97201

Circulation
(m) 242,328
(e) 104,411
(S) 415,358

503/221-8132

Doris N. Smith, Chief Librarian
Sandra Macomber, Asst. Librarian

Lib. est. Early 1930's		Group Newhouse Newspapers	FTE 10

Public access
- in person   no
- by mail   yes
- by phone   yes

Limitations

Will provide dates and send public to our Circulation Dept. or public library

Services available
- copy machine
- reader/printer

Limitations

Hours of operation   7am-7pm, 365 days a year

Resources

clips	x		books	x
photos	x		pamphlets	no
negs	no		maps	x
CPT	none		AV	no

Microform holdings
- own newspaper   1850-present
- periodicals
- clippings

Indexes
- own newspaper   1850-present with some interruptions
- other

Automation
Automated files
- mechanical   5 Remington Rand Lektrievers, 5 Diebold Power files
- electronic

Other automated systems

Products for sale

PENNSYLVANIA   Allentown   PENNSYLVANIA

SUNDAY CALL-CHRONICLE

The Morning Call (m)
The Evening Chronicle (e)
The Sunday Call-Chronicle (S)
P.O. Box 1260
Allentown PA 18105

215/820-6523 x6521

Circulation
(m) 103,421
(e) 23,968
(S) 158,711

Lois A. Doncevir, Senior Librarian

Lib. est. 1932   Group Ind.   FTE 7

Public access   Limitations
    in person   yes   By appt. only; $15 per hour service
    by mail   charge plus cost of copies
    by phone

Services available   Limitations
    copy machine   yes $.32 per copy
    reader/printer yes Microfilm, $1 per copy; fiche, $.50
    reader   per copy

Hours of operation   8am-Midnight

Resources
    clips   x   books   x
    photos   x   pamphlets   x
    negs   Photo. Dept.   maps   x
    CPT   x   AV   x

Microform holdings
    own newspaper   1870-present
    periodicals
    clippings

Indexes
    own newspaper
    other   New York Times, Washington Post

Special collections

Automation
  Automated files
    mechanical
    electronic   Info-Ky News Retrieval System; online index
  Other automated systems   New York Times Information Bank

Products for sale

PENNSYLVANIA   Beaver   PENNSYLVANIA

Beaver County Times (eS)   Circulation
P.O. Box 400   (e) 43,737
Beaver PA 15009   (S) 45,350
                         412/775-3200 x153,154,230

              Dorothy L. Basar, Head Librarian
              Zola Mae Chysh, Asst. Librarian

Lib. est. 1957   Group Calkins Newspapers   FTE 2.5

Public access   Limitations
      in person   yes
      by mail   yes
      by phone   yes

Services available   Limitations
      copy machine   yes $.25 per copy
      reader/printer yes $1.00 per copy
      reader   yes   No charge for research by customer

Hours of operation   8am-4pm, M-F

Resources
      clips   1,000,000+   books   300+
      photos   100,000+   pamphlets   300+
      negs   maps   50
      CPT   30   AV

Microform holdings
      own newspaper   1900-present
      periodicals
      clippings

Indexes
      own newspaper
      other

Special collections

Automation
   Automated files
      mechanical
      electronic
   Other automated systems

Products for sale

210

PENNSYLVANIA   Easton   PENNSYLVANIA

THE EXPRESS

The Express (e)
40 N. Fourth St.
Easton PA 18042

Circulation
(e) 52,612

215/258-7171 x601

Carol Kowitz, Librarian
Grayce O. Maley, Asst. Librarian

Lib. est. 1940   Group   Ind.   FTE   2

Public access   Limitations
- in person   yes
- by mail   yes
- by phone   yes

Services available   Limitations
- copy machine   yes $.10 per copy
- reader/printer
- reader   yes

Hours of operation

Resources
- clips   41 filing cabinets   books   x
- photos   41 filing cabinets   pamphlets   1 filing cabinet
- negs   4 filing cabinets   maps   1 filing cabinet
- CPT   6   AV

Microform holdings
- own newspaper   1855-present
- periodicals
- clippings

Indexes
- own newspaper
- other

Special collections

Automation
- Automated files
  - mechanical
  - electronic
- Other automated systems

Products for sale

Tribune Review (all day,S)
Cabin Hill Dr.
Greensburg PA 15601

412/834-1151 x203

Chriss Swaney

Circulation
(all day)
 40,248
(S) 57,675

Lib. est. 1890   Group   Ind.   FTE

Public access   Limitations
    in person   yes
    by mail   yes
    by phone   yes

Services available   Limitations
    copy machine
    reader/printer yes   Per copy charge
    reader

Hours of operation   9am-5pm, M-F

Resources
    clips   books
    photos   pamphlets
    negs   maps
    CPT   AV

Microform holdings
    own newspaper
    periodicals
    clippings

Indexes
    own newspaper
    other

Special collections

Automation
  Automated files
    mechanical
    electronic
  Other automated systems

Products for sale

PENNSYLVANIA　　　　　　　　　Lancaster　　　　　　　　　PENNSYLVANIA

Intelligencer Journal.

Intelligencer Journal (m)
Lancaster New Era (e)
Sunday News (S)
8 West King St.
Lancaster PA 17604

Circulation
(m) 40,402
(e) 60,041
(S) 131,927

717/291-8773

Helen L. Everts, Head Librarian
Jessie M. Bullock, Asst. Librarian

Lib. est. 1952　　　　　　　Group Ind.　　　　　　　FTE 5

Public access
   in person   yes
   by mail   yes
   by phone   yes

Limitations
Closed to public on Sunday
No files may be removed from library

Services available
   copy machine   yes
   reader/printer yes
   reader

Limitations
Librarians operate, $.50 per page
$.50 per page

Hours of operation   7:30am-11:30pm, M-Sat.; 3:30-11:30pm, Sun.

Resources
   clips   16,000 subject clips   books   500
   photos   x   pamphlets 500
   negs   no   maps   x
   CPT   x   AV

Microform holdings
    own newspaper   1795-present
    periodicals

Indexes
    own newspaper
    other

Automation
  Automated files
    mechanical   2 Remington Rand Lektrievers
    electronic
  Other automated systems

Products for sale

PENNSYLVANIA   Levittown   PENNSYLVANIA

Bucks County Courier Times (eS)   Circulation
8400 Rte. 13   (e) 62,349
Levittown PA 19058   (S) 64,560
                         215/752-6877

           Denise Mazeika, Head Librarian
           Sue Ditterlines

Lib. est. 1963   Group Calkins Newspapers   FTE

Public access   Limitations
    in person   no
    by mail   yes   Only quick answers, no research
    by phone   yes   Only quick answers, no research

Services available   Limitations
    copy machine   yes $.50 per copy
    reader/printer yes $2.00 for half page copy
    reader

Hours of operation 8am-4pm, M-F

Resources
    clips   x   books
    photos   x   pamphlets
    negs   maps
    CPT   AV

Microform holdings
    own newspaper   1910-present
    periodicals
    clippings

Indexes
    own newspaper
    other

Special collections

Automation
  Automated files
    mechanical   Sperry/Rand Lektriever
    electronic
  Other automated systems

Products for sale

The Bulletin (eS)
30th & Market Sts.
Philadelphia PA 19101
                      215/662-7630

Circulation
  (e) 472,509
  (S) 560,188

Raymond G. Mecca, Director of the Library

Lib. est. 1880   Group Ind.   FTE 8

Public access
  in person   no
  by mail   yes
  by phone   no

Limitations
Not open to public
Limited to searches for Back Date Dept.
Only other access by special permission in exceptional cases

Services available
  copy machine
  reader/printer
  reader

Limitations

Hours of operation 8am-Midnight, M-Sat.

Resources
  clips   15,000,000   books   15,000
  photos   1,250,000   pamphlets   2,500
  negs   maps
  CPT   7   AV

Microform holdings
  own newspaper   1847-present
  periodicals
  clippings   archival (selected pre-1950)

Indexes
  own newspaper
  other   New York Times 1913-present

Special collections

Automation
  Automated files
    mechanical
    electronic
  Other automated systems

Products for sale

Philadelphia Inquirer (mS)
Philadelphia Daily News (e)
400 N. Broad St.
Philadelphia PA 19101
                    215/854-2823

Circulation
(m) 417,066
(e) 224,091
(S) 848,592

Joseph D. DiMarino, Jr., Library Manager

<u>Lib. est.</u> 1928   <u>Group</u> Knight-Ridder Newspapers   <u>FTE</u> 10

<u>Public access</u>   <u>Limitations</u>
- in person no
- by mail   yes
- by phone   no

<u>Services available</u>   <u>Limitations</u>
- copy machine   yes
- reader/printer yes
- reader   yes

<u>Hours of operation</u> 24 hours a day, M-F; 9am-5pm, Sat.; 3pm-11pm, Sun.

<u>Resources</u>
- clips   8,000,000   books   3,000
- photos   1,000,000   pamphlets
- negs   maps
- CPT   50   AV

<u>Microform holdings</u>
- own newspaper   Inquirer 1926-present; Daily News 1960-present
- periodicals
- clippings

<u>Indexes</u>
- own newspaper   1933-1971; 1978-present
- other   New York Times

<u>Special collections</u>

<u>Automation</u>
  Automated files
    mechanical
    electronic   QL, full text system
  Other automated systems   New York Times Information Bank

<u>Products for sale</u>

Pittsburgh Post-Gazette (mS)
50 Blvd. of the Allies
Pittsburgh PA 15222
                    412/263-1100

Circulation
(m) 190,093
(S) 176,137

Angelika Kane, Librarian

Lib. est. 1930   Group Block Newspapers   FTE 3

Public access   Limitations
   in person   yes
   by mail   yes
   by phone   yes

Services available   Limitations
   copy machine
   reader/printer yes Staff only
   reader   yes

Hours of operation 7:30am-8pm, Sun.-Fri.

Resources
   clips   21 cabinets   books   x
   photos   x   pamphlets x
   negs   x   maps   x
   CPT   25   AV

Microform holdings
   own newspaper   1860-present
   periodicals
   clippings

Indexes
   own newspaper
   other

Special collections

Automation
  Automated files
    mechanical   3 Lektrievers
    electronic
  Other automated systems

Products for sale

PENNSYLVANIA   Pittsburgh   PENNSYLVANIA

The Pittsburgh Press (eS)   Circulation
Blvd. of the Allies   (e) 265,379
Pittsburgh PA 15230   (S) 666,907
                              412/263-1480

            Eileen Finster, Head Librarian

Lib. est. 1884   Group Scripps-Howard Newspapers   FTE 6

Public access   Limitations
    in person   no
    by mail   yes   Dates only
    by phone   yes   Dates only

Services available   Limitations
    copy machine   yes   Staff only
    reader/printer
    reader   yes   Staff only

Hours of operation 8:30am-5:30pm, M-Sat.

Resources
    clips   5,000,000   books   500
    photos   4,000,000   pamphlets x
    negs   x   maps   x
    CPT   AV

Microform holdings
    own newspaper   1884-present
    periodicals
    clippings

Indexes
    own newspaper   Index to photographs kept for 10 years
    other

Special collections

Automation
  Automated files
    mechanical
    electronic
  Other automated systems

Products for sale

218

Delaware County Daily Times (e) Circulation
500 Mildred Ave. (e) 42,330
Primos PA 19018
                        215/284-7200

            Peggy J. Chance, Librarian

Lib. est. 1952   Group Ingersoll Publications Inc.   FTE 1

Public access   Limitations
    in person   yes
    by mail   yes
    by phone   yes   No extensive research

Services available   Limitations
    copy machine   yes Will make limited number, $.50-$1.00
    reader/printer
    reader   yes

Hours of operation 8:30am-4:30pm, M-F

Resources
    clips   24+ file drawers   books   x
    photos   x   pamphlets   x
    negs   x   maps   x
    CPT   AV

Microform holdings
    own newspaper   Sept. 7, 1876-present
    periodicals
    clippings

Indexes
    own newspaper   none
    other

Special collections

Automation
  Automated files
    mechanical
    electronic
  Other automated systems

Products for sale

Reading Times (m)
Reading Eagle (eS)
340 Court St.
Reading PA 19601
                        215/373-4221

Circulation
(m) 42,170
(e) 44,099
(S) 100,394

Eugene R. Arnold, Head Librarian
George Homcha, Asst.
Frank Schartel, Asst.

Lib. est. 1910   Group Ind.   FTE 3

Public access   Limitations
   in person   yes   By discretion of editors
   by mail   yes
   by phone   yes

Services available   Limitations
   copy machine yes   Fee charged
   reader/printer
   reader   yes   Fee charged

Hours of operation 8am-9pm, M-F; 8am-Noon, Sat.

Resources
   clips   50,000+   books
   photos   pamphlets
   negs   maps
   CPT   AV

Microform holdings
   own newspaper   1868-present
   periodicals
   clippings

Indexes
   own newspaper   none
   other

Special collections

Automation
  Automated files
    mechanical
    electronic
  Other automated systems

Products for sale

PENNSYLVANIA   Scranton   PENNSYLVANIA

The Scranton Times

Scranton Times (e)
Sunday Times (S)
Penn. Ave. & Spruce St.
Scranton PA 18501

717/342-9151

Frank Fox, Librarian
Gerald Moon, Asst.

<u>Circulation</u>
(e) 55,927
(S) 49,834

<u>Lib. est.</u> 1920   <u>Group</u> Ind.   <u>FTE</u> 3

<u>Public access</u>   <u>Limitations</u>
- in person   yes
- by mail   yes
- by phone   yes

<u>Services available</u>   <u>Limitations</u>
- copy machine   yes
- reader/printer
- reader   yes

<u>Hours of operation</u> M-Sat.

<u>Resources</u>
- clips   x   books   x
- photos   pamphlets
- negs   maps
- CPT   AV

<u>Microform holdings</u>
- own newspaper   1895-present
- periodicals
- clippings

<u>Indexes</u>
- own newspaper
- other

<u>Automation</u>
Automated files
- mechanical
- electronic

Other automated systems

<u>Products for sale</u>

PENNSYLVANIA Scranton PENNSYLVANIA

Scranton Tribune (m)
Scrantonian (S)
336 N. Washington Ave.
Scranton PA 18501
               717/344-7221 x57

Circulation
(m) 39,383
(S) 50,336

Hal Lewis, Librarian

Lib. est. 1920   Group Ind.   FTE

Public access
- in person   yes
- by mail   yes
- by phone   yes

Limitations
No in-depth research

Services available
- copy machine   yes
- reader/printer
- reader   yes

Limitations
Fee charged

Hours of operation   3pm-11pm, M-F

Resources
- clips   x
- photos   x
- negs
- CPT
- books
- pamphlets
- maps
- AV

Microform holdings
- own newspaper   1886-present
- periodicals
- clippings

Indexes
- own newspaper
- other

Special collections

Automation
- Automated files
  - mechanical
  - electronic
- Other automated systems

Products for sale

The Daily Item (e)　　　　　　　　　　　　　　　　　　　　Circulation
P.O. Box 607　　　　　　　　　　　　　　　　　　　　　　　(e) 26,267
Sunbury PA 17801
　　　　　　　　　　　　717/286-5671

　　　　　　　　Carol Kehler, Librarian-Clerk

Lib. est. ?　　　　　　Group Ottaway Newspapers　　　　FTE

Public access　　　　　　Limitations
　　in person　yes　　　8am-5pm
　　by mail　　no
　　by phone　 no

Services available　　　Limitations
　　copy machine
　　reader/printer
　　reader

Hours of operation M-Sat.

Resources
　　clips　　thousands　　　　books　　　100
　　photos　 hundreds　　　　 pamphlets　100
　　negs　　 hundreds　　　　 maps　　　　25
　　CPT　　　20　　　　　　　 AV

Microform holdings
　　own newspaper　　1951-present
　　periodicals
　　clippings

Indexes
　　own newspaper
　　other

Special collections

Automation
　Automated files
　　mechanical
　　electronic
　Other automated systems

Products for sale

Valley News Dispatch (e)
210 Fourth Ave.
Tarentum PA 15084
412/224-4321

Circulation
(e) 42,422

Audrey H. Land, Librarian

Lib. est. 1978   Group Gannett Newspapers   FTE 1

Public access
   in person no
   by mail no
   by phone no

Limitations
   Staff only

Services available
   copy machine
   reader/printer yes
   reader

Limitations
   Fee charged

Hours of operation   8am-Noon, M-F

Resources
   clips   24,000+   books   650
   photos 6,600   pamphlets
   negs   79,000+   maps
   CPT   AV

Microform holdings
   own newspaper   1892-present
   periodicals
   clippings

Indexes
   own newspaper
   other

Special collections

Automation
  Automated files
    mechanical
    electronic
  Other automated systems

Products for sale

RHODE ISLAND　　　　　　　　Pawtucket　　　　　　　　RHODE ISLAND

Evening Times (e)　　　　　　　　　　　　　　　　　<u>Circulation</u>
23 Exchange St.　　　　　　　　　　　　　　　　　　(e) 31,218
Pawtucket RI 02862
　　　　　　　　　401/722-4000 x322

　　　　Doris Hearn, Librarian

<u>Lib. est.</u> 1950　　　　　<u>Group</u> Ind.　　　　　　<u>FTE</u>

<u>Public access</u>　　　　　　<u>Limitations</u>
　　in person   yes
　　by mail   yes
　　by phone   yes

<u>Services available</u>　　　<u>Limitations</u>
　　copy machine
　　reader/printer yes　　Staff use mostly; $.20 per copy for public
　　reader

<u>Hours of operation</u> 8am-4pm, M-F

<u>Resources</u>
　　clips   x　　　　　　　books   x
　　photos   x　　　　　　　pamphlets   x
　　negs   x　　　　　　　maps   x
　　CPT　　　　　　　　　　　　AV

<u>Microform holdings</u>
　　own newspaper   1920-present
　　periodicals
　　clippings

<u>Indexes</u>
　　own newspaper
　　other

<u>Special collections</u> Historic books

<u>Automation</u>
　Automated files
　　mechanical
　　electronic
　Other automated systems

<u>Products for sale</u>

RHODE ISLAND   Providence   RHODE ISLAND

The Evening Bulletin
The Providence Journal

Providence Journal (m)	Circulation
Evening Bulletin (e)	(m) 72,412
Providence Sunday Journal (S)	(e) 142,692
75 Fountain St.	(S) 224,305
Providence RI 02902	

401/277-7393

Joseph O. Mehr, Librarian

Lib. est. 1919   Group Ind.   FTE 11

Public access
- in person   yes
- by mail   yes
- by phone   yes

Limitations
- By appointment
- No in-depth research
- Simple research

Services available
- copy machine   yes
- reader/printer yes
- reader   yes

Limitations
- $.25 per copy
- $6.00 per 18x24 print
- Staff only

Hours of operation   7am-1am, M-F; 3pm-11pm, Sat. & Sun.

Resources

clips	4,000,000+	books	2,500
photos	600,000	pamphlets	30 drawers
negs		maps	10 drawers
CPT	19	AV	

Microform holdings
- own newspaper   1820-present
- periodicals

Indexes
- own newspaper
- other   New York Times, 1911-present

Special collections   Journal-Bulletin Almanac, 1892-present; Rhode Island General Assembly Index, last 5 years

Automation
- Automated files
  - mechanical   Elecompack mobile storage units
  - electronic
- Other automated systems

Products for sale   Providence Journal-Bulletin Alamanac

SOUTH CAROLINA   Charleston   SOUTH CAROLINA

The News and Courier

The South's Oldest Daily Newspaper

News and Courier (m)
Evening Post (e)
News and Courier/Evening Post (S)
134 Columbus St.
Charleston SC 29402

<u>Circulation</u>
(m) 67,182
(e) 36,395
(S) 97,215

803/577-7111 x290

Louise N. Mazorol, Chief Librarian

<u>Lib. est.</u> 1946   <u>Group</u> Ind.   <u>FTE</u> 3

<u>Public access</u>   <u>Limitations</u>
   in person   yes   By appointment
   by mail   no
   by phone   no

<u>Services available</u>   <u>Limitations</u>
   copy machine
   reader/printer yes   By appointment; $.50 per copy
   reader

<u>Hours of operation</u>   8am-6pm, M-Sat.

<u>Resources</u>
clips	168 drawers	books	1,868
photos	13 drawers	pamphlets	3,000
negs		maps	75
CPT	300	AV	

<u>Microform holdings</u>
   own newspaper   1803-present
   periodicals
   clippings

<u>Special collections</u> 100 rolls of 35mm microfilm of local 19th century newspapers

<u>Automation</u>
  Automated files
    mechanical   Lektriever
    electronic
  Other automated systems

<u>Products for sale</u>

SOUTH CAROLINA Columbia SOUTH CAROLINA

State (mS)   Circulation
Columbia Record (e)   (m) 103,935
P.O. Box 1333   (e) 33,228
Columbia SC 29202   (S) 122,233
              803/771-8493 or 771-8340

         Dargan A. Richards, News Librarian
         L. Dee McCurry, Reference Librarian

Lib. est. 1955   Group Ind.   FTE 5.5

Public access   Limitations
    in person   yes   By appointment
    by mail   yes
    by phone   yes

Services available   Limitations
    copy machine   yes   10 clippings; $.50 each, $.25 students
    reader/printer yes   10 clippings; $.50 each, $.25 students
    reader   yes

Hours of operation 8am-10pm, M-F; 3pm-10pm, Sat. & Sun.

Resources
    clips   300,000   books   600
    photos   8,000   pamphlets   300
    negs   maps   150
    CPT   25   AV

Microform holdings
    own newspaper   1891-present
    periodicals
    clippings   1400 jackets

Indexes
    own newspaper   none
    other

Special collections

Automation
  Automated files
    mechanical   Remington-Rand Lektrievers
    electronic
  Other automated systems

Products for sale

SOUTH CAROLINA · Greenville · SOUTH CAROLINA

𝕮𝖍𝖊 𝕲𝖗𝖊𝖊𝖓𝖛𝖎𝖑𝖑𝖊 𝕹𝖊𝖜𝖘
— and —
GREENVILLE PIEDMONT

Greenville News (m)
Greenville Piedmont (e)
Greenville News-Piedmont (S)
305 S. Main St.
Greenville SC 29602

Circulation
(m) 84,639
(e) 23,297
(S) 94,623

803/298-4323

Helen B. Tedards, Head Librarian
Susan Shabkie, Librarian

Lib. est. 1956   Group Multimedia Newspapers   FTE 3

Public access   Limitations
    in person   no   Staff only
    by mail   no
    by phone   no

Services available   Limitations
    copy machine   yes $.10 per page
    reader/printer
    reader   yes

Hours of operation 8am-10pm, M-F

Resources
    clips   2,000,000   books   700
    photos   110,000   pamphlets   500
    negs   maps   x
    CPT   3,000   AV

Microform holdings
    own newspaper   1900-present
    periodicals
    clippings

Indexes
    own newspaper   none
    other

Special collections   South Carolina news and photos

Automation
  Automated files
    mechanical
    electronic
  Other automated systems

Products for sale

TENNESSEE   Chattanooga   TENNESSEE

The Chattanooga Times

Chattanooga Times (mS)   Circulation
117 E. 10th St.   (m) 53,946
Chattanooga TN 37402   (S) 57,680
                        615/756-1234 x342

                Trina McLeod, Librarian
                Valerie Austin, Asst. Librarian

<u>Lib. est.</u> 1963   <u>Group</u> Ind.   FTE 1.5

<u>Public access</u>   <u>Limitations</u>
    in person   yes
    by mail   yes
    by phone   yes

<u>Services available</u>   <u>Limitations</u>
    copy machine   yes $.10 per copy
    reader/printer
    reader

<u>Hours of operation</u>   24 hrs., 7 days a week for staff; open to public
                        when librarian is working

<u>Resources</u>
    clips   x   books   x
    photos   x   pamphlets   x
    negs   maps   x
    CPT   2   AV

<u>Microform holdings</u>
    own newspaper   1838-present
    periodicals
    clippings

<u>Indexes</u>
    own newspaper
    other   New York Times

<u>Special collections</u>

<u>Automation</u>
  Automated files
    mechanical
    electronic
  Other automated systems

<u>Products for sale</u>

230

Jackson Sun (eS)
P.O. Box 1059
Jackson TN 38301
                901/427-3333 x157

Circulation
(e) 32,170
(S) 32,830

Danny Walker, News Librarian

Lib. est. 1974   Group Des Moines Register & Tribune Co.   FTE

Public access
    in person   yes
    by mail   yes
    by phone   yes

Limitations
If time; $2.00 service charge per hour
if more than 15 minutes required

Services available
    copy machine   yes
    reader/printer
    reader   yes

Limitations
$.25 per copy

By appointment; staff has priority

Hours of operation   7am-4pm, M-F

Resources
    clips   10,000+   books
    photos   4 drawers   pamphlets
    negs   maps
    CPT   AV

Microform holdings
    own newspaper   1936-present
    periodicals
    clippings

Indexes
    own newspaper   none
    other

Special collections

Automation
  Automated files
    mechanical
    electronic
  Other automated systems

Products for sale

TENNESSEE Johnson City TENNESSEE

	Circulation
Johnson City Press-Chronicle (meS)	(m) 4,721
P.O. Box 1717	(e) 22,014
Johnson City TN 37601	(S) 28,435
615/929-3111	

Edith Bridger, Librarian

Lib. est. 1950   Group Ind.   FTE 1

Public access   Limitations
   in person   yes
   by mail   yes
   by phone   yes

Services available   Limitations
   copy machine
   reader/printer
   reader   yes

Hours of operation   8am-5pm, M-F; available to staff members 24 hours per day, six days a week

Resources
   clips   x   books   2,000
   photos   pamphlets x
   negs   maps
   CPT   AV

Microform holdings
   own newspaper   1948-present
   periodicals
   clippings

Indexes
   own newspaper
   other

Special collections Newspaper/journalism textbooks and biographies

Automation
  Automated files
    mechanical   Soon will install 3M in-house aperture card processing with text editing capabilities
  Other automated systems

Products for sale

The Knoxville Journal

Knoxville Journal (m)
208 Church Ave.
Knoxville   TN 37902

615/522-4141 x428

Christie Gentry, Librarian

Circulation
(m) 59,636

Lib. est. 1940	Group Ind.	FTE

Public access
    in person   yes
    by mail   yes

Limitations
    No extensive research

Services available
    copy machine   yes
    reader/printer
    reader   yes

Limitations

Hours of operation   9am-6pm, M-F

Resources
    clips   65,000   books
    photos   x   pamphlets
    negs   about 20 years maps
    CPT   AV

Microform holdings
    own newspaper   1940-present
    periodicals
    clippings

Indexes
    own newspaper   none
    other

Special collections

Automation
  Automated files
    mechanical
    electronic
  Other automated systems

Products for sale

Knoxville News-Sentinel (eS) Circulation
300 Church (e) 103,069
Knoxville TN 37901 (S) 158,740
                          615/523-3131

     Shirley L. Carter, Librarian

Lib. est. 1945   Group Scripps-Howard Newspapers   FTE 2

Public access   Limitations
    in person   yes   By appointment
    by mail   yes
    by phone   yes

Services available   Limitations
    copy machine   yes
    reader/printer
    reader   yes

Hours of operation 6am-5pm, M-F

Resources
    clips   x   books   x
    photos   x   pamphlets x
    negs   x   maps
    CPT   AV

Microform holdings
    own newspaper   1922-present
    periodicals
    clippings

Indexes
    own newspaper
    other

Special collections

Automation
  Automated files
    mechanical
    electronic
  Other automated systems

Products for sale

THE COMMERCIAL APPEAL

Commercial Appeal (eS)
495 Union Ave.
Memphis   TN 38101

901/529-2211

Circulation
- (e) 103,072
- (S) 287,999

Eugene G. Brady, Jr., Librarian

Lib. est. 1922   Group Scripps-Howard Newspapers   FTE 3.5

Public access   Limitations
   in person   no
   by mail   yes   Simple research only
   by phone   yes

Services available   Limitations
   copy machine   yes
   reader/printer
   reader   yes

Hours of operation   10am-4pm, M-F

Resources
   clips   50,000   books   x
   photos   3,000   pamphlets
   negs   2,500   maps
   CPT   AV

Microform holdings
   own newspaper   1945-present
   periodicals
   clippings

Indexes
   own newspaper   1922-present
   other

Special collections

Automation
  Automated files
    mechanical
    electronic
  Other automated systems

Products for sale

Memphis Press-Scimitar (e)   <u>Circulation</u>
495 Union Ave.   (e) 103,072
Memphis TN 38101
                           901/529-2535

                David Tankerly, Librarian

<u>Lib. est.</u> c. 1900   <u>Group</u> Scripps-Howard Newspapers   <u>FTE</u> 3

<u>Public access</u>   <u>Limitations</u>
    in person   no   No material available except pictures,
    by mail   no   which are for sale at $5 per print
    by phone   no

<u>Services available</u>   <u>Limitations</u>
    copy machine
    reader/printer
    reader

<u>Hours of operation</u> 6am-6pm, M-F; 6am-Noon, Sat.

<u>Resources</u>
    clips   c. 300,000   books
    photos   c. 12,000   pamphlets
    negs   maps
    CPT   AV

<u>Microform holdings</u>
    own newspaper
    periodicals
    clippings

<u>Indexes</u>
    own newspaper   1900-present
    other

<u>Special collections</u>

<u>Automation</u>
  Automated files
    mechanical
    electronic
  Other automated systems

<u>Products for sale</u>

TENNESSEE   Nashville   TENNESSEE

Nashville Banner (e)   Circulation
1100 Broadway   (e) 84,728
Nashville TN 37202
                             615/255-5401

             Sally Moran, Librarian
             Avita Maples, Asst. Librarian

Lib. est. 1940   Group Gannett Newspapers   FTE 4

Public access   Limitations
     in person   no   Exceptions with permission of editor
     by mail   no
     by phone   no

Services available   Limitations
     copy machine   yes
     reader/printer
     reader   yes

Hours of operation   7am-4pm, M-F; 7am-1pm, Sat.

Resources
     clips   x   books   200
     photos   pamphlets   x
     negs   x   maps
     CPT   6   AV

Microform holdings
     own newspaper   1880-present
     periodicals
     clippings

Indexes
     own newspaper
     other

Special collections

Automation
   Automated files
     mechanical
     electronic
   Other automated systems

Products for sale

TENNESSEE   Nashville   TENNESSEE

The Tennessean (mS)   Circulation
1100 Broadway   (m) 129,408
Nashville TN 37202   (S) 229,022
                         615/255-1221 x327

             Sandra Roberts, Head Librarian
             Leslie Pomeroy, Asst. Librarian

Lib. est. 1948   Group Gannett Newspapers   FTE 5

Public access   Limitations
    in person   no
    by mail   yes   Only scholarly requests accepted
    by phone   yes   Short answer only

Services available   Limitations
    copy machine   yes $.25 per page
    reader/printer   yes   Staff or journalists only
    reader   yes

Hours of operation 8am-Midnight, M-Sat.; 2pm-10pm, Sun.

Resources
    clips   30 file cabinets   books   250
    photos   25 file cabinets   pamphlets   200
    negs   maps   200
    CPT   30   AV

Microform holdings
    own newspaper   1907-present
    periodicals
    clippings

Indexes
    own newspaper
    other   New York Times 1960-1966

Special collections

Automation
  Automated files
    mechanical
    electronic
  Other automated systems

Products for sale

Amarillo Daily News (m)
Amarillo Globe-Times (e)
Amarillo Sunday News-Globe (S)
P.O. Box 2091
Amarillo TX 79166

806/376-4488 x330 or 331

Circulation
(m) 44,394
(e) 30,877
(S) 72,959

Bobbie Fortenberry, Librarian
Sammie Parr, Asst. Librarian

Lib. est. 1950   Group Morris Communications Corp.   FTE 4

Public access
   in person   yes
   by mail   yes
   by phone   yes

Limitations
No extensive research

Services available
   copy machine   yes
   reader/printer yes
   reader   yes

Limitations
$.25 per copy
$.50 per copy

Hours of operation   8am-5pm, M-F

Resources
   clips   x   books   x
   photos   x   pamphlets x
   negs   maps   x
   CPT   AV

Microform holdings
   own newspaper   1912-present
   periodicals
   clippings

Special collections

Automation
  Automated files
    mechanical
     electronic
  Other automated systems

Products for sale

Austin American-Statesman

Austin American Statesman (meS)
P.O. Box 670
Austin TX 78767

512/397-1212

Kay Smith Guleke, Librarian
Karen Anderson, Asst. Librarian

Circulation
(m) 88,763
(e) 36,543
(S) 136,474

Lib. est. 1975   Group Cox Enterprises   FTE 3

Public access   Limitations
- in person   yes
- by mail   yes
- by phone   yes

Services available   Limitations
- copy machine   yes $.25 per copy
- reader/printer yes $.25 per copy
- reader   yes

Hours of operation 8am-5pm, M-F

Resources
clips	25,000	books	300
photos	35,000	pamphlets	
negs		maps	250
CPT	15	AV	

Microform holdings
- own newspaper   x
- periodicals
- clippings

Indexes
- own newspaper   Sept. 1977-present
- other

Automation
  Automated files
    mechanical
    electronic
  Other automated systems

Products for sale

TEXAS   Corpus Christi   TEXAS

Corpus Christi Caller (m)
Corpus Christi Times (e)
Corpus Christi Caller-Times (S)
P.O. Box 9136
Corpus Christi TX 78408

Circulation
(m) 63,341
(e) 26,385
(S) 88,643

512/884-2011 x242

Linda James, Librarian
Susan Wiggs, Library Clerk

Lib. est. 1954   Group Harte-Hanks Communications Inc.   FTE 3

Public access
    in person   no
    by mail   yes
    by phone   no

Limitations
Refer to public library
Limited
Refer to public library

Services available
    copy machine   yes
    reader/printer
    reader   yes

Limitations
$1.00 per page

Hours of operation   7am-6pm, M-F

Resources
    clips   x   books   300
    photos   x   pamphlets   600
    negs   maps
    CPT   8   AV

Microform holdings
    own newspaper   1874-present
    periodicals
    clippings

Special collections

Automation
    Automated files
       mechanical
       electronic
    Other automated systems

Products for sale

The Dallas Morning News

The Dallas Morning News (mS)
Communications Center
Dallas TX 75265
214/745-8302

Circulation
(m) 280,124
(S) 345,618

Barbara C. May, Reference Editor
Judy Metcalf, Asst. Reference Editor

Lib. est. 1917   Group Ind.   FTE 11

Public access   Limitations
   in person   no   Service provided for other libraries
   by mail   no
   by phone   no

Services available   Limitations
   copy machine   yes $.50 per page
   reader/printer   yes
   reader   yes

Hours of operation   8am-Midnight, M-Sat.; 2pm-10pm, Sun.

Resources
   clips   8,000,000   books   5,000
   photos   150,000   pamphlets   2 drawers
   negs   none   maps   100
   CPT   112   AV

Microform holdings
   own newspaper   1885-present
   periodicals   7 titles

Indexes
   own newspaper   1917-present
   other

Special collections   Texas history collection

Automation
  Automated files
   mechanical   4 Diebold Power Files
   electronic
  Other automated systems   DIALOG, New York Times Information Bank,
                              Dow Jones News Retrieval, SDC Orbit

Products for sale

TEXAS   Dallas   TEXAS

Dallas Times Herald (eS)   Circulation
P.O. Box 5445   (e) 242,515
Dallas TX 75234   (S) 339,787
                              214/744-6240

                    Elaine Walden, Librarian

Lib. est.   Group Times Mirror Co.   FTE 4

Public access   Limitations
    in person   no
    by mail   no
    by phone   no   Refer to Dallas Public Library

Services available   Limitations
    copy machine   yes
    reader/printer   yes
    reader   yes

Hours of operation   7am-11pm, M-F; Noon-9pm, Sat. & Sun.

Resources
    clips   9,000+   books   x
    photos   x   pamphlets   none
    negs   maps   x
    CPT   9   AV

Microform holdings
    own newspaper   1886-present
    periodicals
    clippings

Indexes
    own newspaper   none
    other

Special collections

Automation
  Automated files
    mechanical   3 Lektrievers
    electronic
  Other automated systems   New York Times Information Bank

Products for sale

243

TEXAS   Fort Worth   TEXAS

Fort Worth Star-Telegram

Fort Worth Star-Telegram (meS)
400 W. 7th St.
Fort Worth TX 76102

817/336-9271

Hettie Arleth, Librarian

<u>Circulation</u>
(m)   93,633
(e) 147,485
(s) 249,852

<u>Lib. est.</u> 1906   <u>Group</u> Capital Cities Communications Inc.   <u>FTE</u> 3

<u>Public access</u>
    in person   yes
    by mail   yes
    by phone   yes

<u>Limitations</u>

<u>Services available</u>
    copy machine   yes
    reader/printer
    reader

<u>Limitations</u>
$.20 per sheet

<u>Hours of operation</u>   8am-4:30pm, M-F

<u>Resources</u>
    clips   2,000,000+   books   250
    photos   c. 275,000   pamphlets   500
    negs   290,960   maps   x
    CPT   AV

<u>Microform holdings</u>
    own newspaper   1876-present
    periodicals
    clippings

<u>Indexes</u>
    own newspaper
    other

<u>Special collections</u>

<u>Automation</u>
  Automated files
    mechanical   Lektriever III
    electronic
  Other automated systems

<u>Products for sale</u>

TEXAS   Houston   TEXAS

Houston Chronicle

Houston's Family Newspaper

Houston Chronicle (eS)
P.O. Box 4260
Houston TX 77210
713/220-7313

Circulation
(e) 330,639
(S) 426,685

Sherry Ray, Librarian
Barbara Seebers, Asst. Librarian

Lib. est. 1960   Group   Ind.   FTE   11.5

Public access   Limitations
- in person   no   Except for librarians and non-local media
- by mail   yes
- by phone   no   Except for librarians and non-local media

Services available   Limitations
- copy machine   yes $.15 per legal size copy
- reader/printer
- reader   yes

Hours of operation   7:30am–10:45pm, M-F

Resources
clips	2,792,000	books	2,100
photos	311,000	pamphlets	1,500
negs	keep five years	maps	100
CPT	21	AV	

Microform holdings
- own newspaper   film from 1901-present
- periodicals   3 titles on fiche
- clippings   on fiche

Indexes
- own newspaper   none
- other   New York Times 1961-present

Special collections

Automation
   Automated files
     mechanical   Diebold Power Files
     electronic
   Other automated systems   Access to New York Times Information Bank

Products for sale   Photos taken by staff photographers

TEXAS   Houston   TEXAS

The Houston Post

Houston Post (mS)
4747 Southwest Freeway
Houston   TX 77001
713/840-5833

Circulation
(m) 320,683
(S) 380,159

Kathy Foley, Chief Librarian
Elizabeth Anderson, Asst. Librarian

Lib. est. c. 1950   Group Ind.   FTE 12.5

Public access
   in person   no
   by mail   no
   by phone   no

Limitations
PhD level students and authors only; no local media.

Services available
   copy machine   yes
   reader/printer   yes
   reader   yes

Limitations
$.15 per page
$.15 per page

Hours of operation   8am-Midnight, M-Thurs.; 8am-10pm, Fri.; 10am-10pm, Sat.; 2pm-10pm, Sun.

Resources
   clips   750 linear feet   books   3,000
   photos   602.5 linear feet   pamphlets   800
   negs   maps   300
   CPT   90   AV

Microform holdings
   own newspaper   1880-present
   periodicals   6 titles on fiche
   clippings   on fiche

Indexes
   own newspaper   1976-present (produced by Bell & Howell)
   other   New York Times 1946-present; Washington Post 1976-present

Special collections   Houston City Directories 1887-present

Automation
  Automated files
  Other automated systems

Products for sale

TEXAS   San Angelo   TEXAS

Standard (m)   Circulation
Times (e)   (m) 38,166
Standard Times (S)   (e) 7,220
P.O. Box 5111   (S) 42,503
San Angelo TX 76902
                         915/653-1221

            Naomi James, Librarian

Lib. est. 1930's   Group Harte Hanks Communications Inc.   FTE

Public access   Limitations
    in person   yes   With Librarian's help
    by mail   yes   No extensive research
    by phone   yes   No extensive research

Services available   Limitations
    copy machine   yes $.10 per page
    reader/printer
    reader   yes
    other   yes $5.00 per print

Hours of operation   8am-5pm, M-F

Resources
    clips   x   books   x
    photos   x   pamphlets   x
    negs   maps   x
    CPT   AV

Microform holdings
    own newspaper   1886-present
    periodicals
    clippings

Indexes
    own newspaper
    other

Special collections

Automation
  Automated files
    mechanical
    electronic
  Other automated systems

Products for sale

247

TEXAS   San Antonio   TEXAS

THE SUNDAY
EXPRESS-NEWS

San Antonio Express (mS)
San Antonio News (e)
P.O. Box 2171
San Antonio TX 78297
512/225-7411 x381

<u>Circulation</u>
(m) 82,122
(e) 74,846
(S) 183,865

Judy Robinson, Head Librarian
Gina Sullivan, Clerk

<u>Lib. est.</u> 1950?   <u>Group</u> News America Publishing Inc.   <u>FTE</u> 1.5

<u>Public access</u>
- in person   yes
- by mail   yes
- by phone   no

<u>Limitations</u>
By appointment

<u>Services available</u>
- copy machine   yes $1.00 per sheet
- reader/printer   yes $1.00 per sheet
- reader   yes

<u>Limitations</u>

<u>Hours of operation</u>   8:30am-4:30pm, M-F

<u>Resources</u>
- clips   20 4-drawer cabinets   books
- photos   30 8-tier shelves   pamphlets
- negs   maps
- CPT   20   AV

<u>Microform holdings</u>
- own newspaper   1865-present
- clippings   (A-C)

<u>Indexes</u>
- own newspaper   Beginning index of A-C filmed clips

<u>Special collections</u>   Photo collection of San Antonio dates back to 1800's

<u>Automation</u>
   Automated files
     mechanical
     electronic
   Other automated systems

<u>Products for sale</u>

TEXAS   San Antonio   TEXAS

San Antonio Light (eS)   Circulation
P.O. Box 161   (e) 123,171
San Antonio TX 78291   (S) 186,129
                         512/226-4271

       Willie Alonso, Librarian

Lib. est. ?   Group   Hearst Newspapers   FTE   1

Public access   Limitations
    in person   no
    by mail   no
    by phone   no

Services available   Limitations
    copy machine
    reader/printer
    reader   yes

Hours of operation

Resources
    clips   x   books   x
    photos   x   pamphlets   x
    negs   x   maps   x
    CPT   AV

Microform holdings
    own newspaper   1881-present
    periodicals
    clippings

Indexes
    own newspaper   none
    other

Special collections

Automation
  Automated files
    mechanical
    electronic
  Other automated systems

Products for sale

Deseret News (e) P.O. Box 1257 Salt Lake City UT 84110

801/237-2155

Circulation
(e) 72,603

Connie Christensen, Librarian
Pat Carrigan, Asst. Librarian

Lib. est. 1955   Group Ind.   FTE 5

Public access
   in person   no
   by mail   no
   by phone   no

Limitations

Services available
   copy machine   yes
   reader/printer
   reader   yes

Limitations
$.50 per page

Hours of operation 6am-6pm, M-Sat.

Resources
   clips   114 drawers   books   c. 1900
   photos   47 drawers   pamphlets   included with clips
   negs   100 drawers   maps
   CPT   5   AV

Microform holdings
   own newspaper   1850-present
   periodicals
   clippings

Indexes
   own newspaper
   other

Special collections

Automation
  Automated files
    mechanical
    electronic
  Other automated systems

Products for sale

UTAH   Salt Lake City   UTAH

The Salt Lake Tribune

The Salt Lake Tribune (mS)
143 South Main
Salt Lake City UT 84110
                801/237-2001

Circulation
  (m) 104,934
  (S) 179,549

Laurene Sowby, Department Head

Lib. est. 1942   Group Ind.   FTE 4

Public access
- in person yes
- by mail yes
- by phone yes

Limitations
Restricted use of clip files

Won't look up ads or answer legal, medical or homework questions

Services available
- copy machine yes
- reader/printer yes
- reader yes

Limitations
$1.00 per page
$2.00 per page

Hours of operation   9am-Midnight, Sun.-Sat.

Resources
clips	c. 670,000 files	books	1,500
photos	c. 95,000 files	pamphlets	200
negs	x	maps	60
CPT		AV	

Microform holdings
- own newspaper   1871-present
- periodicals   Salt Lake Herald 1870-1920; Salt Lake Telegram 1902-1952; New York Times 1958-present

Indexes
- own newspaper   1940-present
- other

Special collections   Utah history books and documents, mining pictures, historic pcitures of events and people of Western region

Automation
  Automated files
    mechanical
    electronic
  Other automated systems

Products for sale

The Burlington Free Press (mS)　　　　　　　　　　　Circulation
191 College St.　　　　　　　　　　　　　　　　　　　(m) 48,052
Burlington VT 05401　　　　　　　　　　　　　　　　(S) 41,463
　　　　　　　　　　　802/863-3441

　　　　Barbara R. VonBruns, Librarian
　　　　Jane Milizia, Asst. Librarian

<u>Lib. est.</u> 1955　　　　　<u>Group</u>　Gannett Newspapers　<u>FTE</u>　1.75

<u>Public access</u>　　　　　　　<u>Limitations</u>
　　in person　　yes　　　　Used in presence of librarian
　　by mail　　　yes　　　　Photocopying done for $10 per hour
　　by phone　　 yes　　　　Short answers only

<u>Services available</u>　　　　<u>Limitations</u>
　　copy machine　　yes　　$.10 per sheet or $10 per hour if
　　　　　　　　　　　　　　there are many clips
　　reader/printer
　　reader

<u>Hours of operation</u>　8am-4pm, M-F

<u>Resources</u>
　　clips　　　3,000 files　　　　books　　　240
　　photos　　13,000　　　　　　　pamphlets　 40
　　negs　　　from Apr. 1975　　　maps
　　CPT　　　　　　　　　　　　　　AV

<u>Microform holdings</u>
　　own newspaper　　1881-1886; 1946-present
　　periodicals
　　clippings

<u>Indexes</u>
　　own newspaper
　　other

<u>Special collections</u>

<u>Automation</u>
　Automated files
　　mechanical
　　electronic
　Other automated systems

<u>Products for sale</u>

VIRGINIA Fredericksburg VIRGINIA

The Free Lance-Star

The Free Lance-Star (e) Circulation
P.O. Box 7267 (e) 27,550
Fredericksburg VA 22401
 703/373-5000 x420

 Phyllis Lane, Librarian

Lib. est. 1947 Group Ind. FTE 1

Public access Limitations
 in person yes
 by mail yes
 by phone yes

Services available Limitations
 copy machine yes $.25 for one copy; $.10 each for
 three or more
 reader/printer
 reader yes

Hours of operation 8am-5pm, M-F

Resources
 clips books
 photos pamphlets
 negs maps
 CPT AV

Microform holdings
 own newspaper 1885-present
 periodicals
 clippings

Indexes
 own newspaper
 other

Special collections

Automation
 Automated files
 mechanical
 electronic
 Other automated systems

Products for sale

Daily News-Record (m)
P.O. Box 193
Harrisonburg VA 22801

703/433-2702

Circulation
(m) 28,310

Donna Murphey, Editorial Asst.

Lib. est. c. 1970   Group Ind.   FTE .5

Public access   Limitations
   in person   no   Public referred to public library
   by mail   no
   by phone   no

Services available   Limitations
   copy machine   yes
   reader/printer   yes
   reader

Hours of operation   9am-Midnight, Sun.-F

Resources
   clips   x   books
   photos   pamphlets
   negs   x   maps
   CPT   AV

Microform holdings
   own newspaper
   periodicals
   clippings

Indexes
   own newspaper
   other

Special collections

Automation
  Automated files
    mechanical
    electronic
  Other automated systems

Products for sale

VIRGINIA   Newport News   VIRGINIA

Daily Press (mS)   Circulation
Times Herald (e)   (m) 57,820
7505 Warwick Blvd.   (e) 42,983
Newport News VA 23607   (S) 100,072
                         804/244-8421 x270

           Theresa M. Hammond, Director of Library Services
           Karen R. Booth, Asst. Director of Library Services

Lib. est. 1961   Group Ind.   FTE 7

Public access   Limitations
      in person   yes
      by mail   yes
      by phone   yes

Services available   Limitations
      copy machine   yes
      reader/printer   yes   Limit of two reels of film; charges
                                for copy
      reader   yes

Hours of operation 8am-10pm, M-F

Resources
      clips   215 linear feet   books   1,100
      photos   116 linear feet   pamphlets   10 file drawers
      negs   maps   x
      CPT   15   AV

Microform holdings
      own newspaper   Daily Press 1898-present; Times Herald 1902-
                       present
      periodicals
      clippings

Indexes
      own newspaper   in process
      other   Facts on File 1978-present

Special collections

Automation
  Automated files
    mechanical   Image Systems for microfiche
    electronic   In process; will produce index
  Other automated systems

Products for sale

255

Virginian-Pilot (m)　　　　　　　　　　　　　　　　　Circulation
Ledger-Star (e)　　　　　　　　　　　　　　　　　　　(m) 124,305
Viginian-Pilot/Ledger-Star (S)　　　　　　　　　　　　(e) 96,235
150 West Brambleton Ave.　　　　　　　　　　　　　　 (S) 199,920
Norfolk VA 23510
　　　　　　　　　　804/446-2242

　　　　　　Ann Kinken Johnson, Head Librarian
　　　　　　Clara P. Basnight, Asst. Librarian

Lib. est. 1947　　　Group Landmark Communications Inc.　　FTE 4

Public access　　　　　　　　Limitations
　　in person　　no
　　by mail　　　yes
　　by phone　　 yes　　　　　Ready reference only

Services available　　　　　 Limitations
　　copy machine　　 yes　　 Only for non-local readers
　　reader/printer　 yes　　 No public
　　reader　　　　　 yes　　 No public

Hours of operation 7:30am-10pm, M-F; 7:30am-3pm, Sat.

Resources
　　clips　　x　　　　　　　　books　　　1,000
　　photos　　x　　　　　　　 pamphlets　　100
　　negs　　　　　　　　　　　maps
　　CPT　　 15　　　　　　　　AV

Microform holdings
　　own newspaper　　1865-present
　　periodicals　　　New York Times 1960-present
　　clippings

Indexes
　　own newspaper　　1947-present
　　other　　　　　　New York Times 1913-present

Special collections

Automation
　Automated files
　　mechanical　 Diebold Power Files
　　electronic
　Other automated systems

Products for sale

VIRGINIA   Richmond   VIRGINIA

Richmond Times-Dispatch (mS)   Circulation
The Richmond News Leader (e)   (m) 136,695
333 E. Grace St.   (e) 115,576
Richmond VA 23219   (S) 216,250
                         804/649-6283

            Mary Morris Watt, Librarian
            Gwendolyn C. Wells

Lib. est.   Group Media General Inc.   FTE 7.5

Public access   Limitations
    in person   yes
    by mail   yes
    by phone   yes   Brief questions only

Services available   Limitations
    copy machine   yes $.50 per page in small quantity
    reader/printer
    reader   yes   Staff has preference over public

Hours of operation 9am-5:30pm, M-F

Resources
    clips   x   books   x
    photos   x   pamphlets   x
    negs   maps   x
    CPT   AV

Microform holdings
    own newspaper   1852-present
    periodicals   New York Times 1950-present

Indexes
    own newspaper   Card index of news (including articles from
                      New York Times) 1922-1961
    other

Automation
  Automated files
    mechanical
    electronic
  Other automated systems

Products for sale

VIRGINIA   Roanoke   VIRGINIA

Roanoke Times & World-News

Roanoke Times & World-News (meS) P.O. Box 2491 Roanoke VA 24010	Circulation (m) 66,091 (e) 48,832 (S) 116,010

703/981-3279

Sue Williams, Librarian
Belinda Harris, Asst. Librarian

Lib. est. 1932   Group Landmark Communications Inc.   FTE 4

Public access
     in person   yes
     by mail   yes
     by phone   yes

Limitations

Services available
     copy machine   yes
     reader/printer   yes
     reader

Limitations
$.25 per copy
$1.50 per copy

Hours of operation   8am-5pm, M-F

Resources
     clips   275 drawers   books   2,000
     photos   100 drawers   pamphlets   10 drawers
     negs   maps   2 drawers
     CPT   10   AV

Microform holdings
     own newspaper   1880-present
     periodicals
     clippings

Indexes
     own newspaper   1932-55
     other   New York Times, 1955-72

Automation
   Automated files
     mechanical   Lektriever
     electronic
   Other automated systems

Products for sale

WASHINGTON   Bellevue   WASHINGTON

Daily Journal-American (m)   Circulation
P.O. Box 310   (m) 27,000
Bellevue WA 98009
                         206/453-4260

           Renee Caskey, Librarian
           Judy Lamkin, Librarian

Lib. est. 1976   Group McClelland Newspapers   FTE

Public access   Limitations
    in person   yes   By appointment only
    by mail   yes
    by phone   yes   Dates of articles only

Services available   Limitations
    copy machine   yes $.10 per copy, by appointment
    reader/printer
    reader

Hours of operation   10am-10pm, M-Th; 5pm-10pm, F

Resources
    clips   170,550   books   170
    photos   20,000   pamphlets   200
    negs   maps   15
    CPT   8   AV

Microform holdings
    own newspaper
    periodicals
    clippings

Indexes
    own newspaper   Oct. 77-Sept. 79
    other

Special collections

Automation
  Automated files
    mechanical
    electronic
  Other automated systems

Products for sale

WASHINGTON　　　　　　　　　　Longview　　　　　　　　　　WASHINGTON

Daily News (e)　　　　　　　　　　　　　　　　　　　Circulation
770 11th St.　　　　　　　　　　　　　　　　　　　　(e) 26,443
Longview WA 98632
　　　　　　　　　　206/577-2511

　　　Dorothy Krubeck, Librarian
　　　Judy Wornick, Asst.

Lib. est. 1954　　　　　Group McClelland Newspapers　　FTE 2

Public access　　　　　　　　Limitations
　　in person　　yes
　　by mail　　　yes
　　by phone　　 yes

Services available　　　　　Limitations
　　copy machine　　yes　　$.20 per copy
　　reader/printer
　　reader　　　　　yes

Hours of operation 8am-5pm, M-F

Resources
　　clips　　　x　　　　　　　　　　books　　　　x
　　photos　　 34 file cabinets　　pamphlets　 1 file cabinet
　　negs　　　 x　　　　　　　　　　maps　　　　 x
　　CPT　　　 10　　　　　　　　　　AV

Microform holdings
　　own newspaper　　1923-present
　　periodicals
　　clippings

Indexes
　　own newspaper
　　other

Special collections

Automation
　Automated files
　　mechanical
　　electronic
　Other automated systems

Products for sale

260

Seattle Post-Intelligencer (mS)
6th and Wall St.
Seattle WA 98121
206/628-8357

Circulation
(m) 167,177
(S) 231,367

Florence Frye, Librarian
L. Smith, Asst. Librarian

Lib. est. 1925   Group   Hearst Corp.   FTE   5

Public access   Limitations
   in person   no
   by mail   yes
   by phone   no

Services available   Limitations
   copy machine
   reader/printer yes   Staff only
   reader

Hours of operation   9am-8:30, M-F; Noon-8pm, Sat.; 12:30pm-8:30pm, Sun.

Resources
   clips   x   books   103
   photos   x   pamphlets   67
   negs   maps   200
   CPT   AV

Microform holdings
   own newspaper   x
   periodicals
   clippings

Indexes
   own newspaper   1925-79
   other

Special collections

Automation
  Automated files
    mechanical
    electronic
  Other automated systems   New York Times Information Bank

Products for sale

Seattle Times (eS)
P.O. Box 70
Seattle WA 98111
　　　　　　　　　206/464-2311

Circulation
(e) 257,383
(S) 348,333

　　Beverly Russell, Chief Librarian
　　Sandra Freeman, Asst. Librarian
　　D. Ann Carver, Asst. Librarian

<u>Lib. est.</u> 1900　　　　　<u>Group</u> Ind.　　　　　FTE 20

<u>Public access</u>		<u>Limitations</u>
in person	no	Exceptions with permission
by mail	yes	Decided by Chief Librarian; fee charged
by phone	yes	Date of recent articles only

<u>Services available</u>		<u>Limitations</u>
copy machine	yes	Staff only
reader/printer	yes	Staff only
reader	yes	Staff only

<u>Hours of operation</u>   7am-1am, Sun.-Thurs.; 7am-2am, F; 9am-2am, Sat.

<u>Resources</u>
　　clips　　　13,000,000　　　　books　　　6,000
　　photos　　　2,000,000　　　　pamphlets　5,000
　　negs　　　　　　　　　　　　　maps　　　　3,000
　　CPT　　　　　　40　　　　　　AV

<u>Microform holdings</u>
　　own newspaper　　May 1886-present
　　periodicals
　　clippings

<u>Indexes</u>
　　own newspaper　　none
　　other

<u>Automation</u>
　Automated files
　　mechanical　　Sperry Rand Lektrievers
　　electronic
　Other automated systems　　New York Times Information Bank; DIALOG;
　　　　　　　　　　　　　　　　AP Political Databank; ORBIT

<u>Products for sale</u>

WASHINGTON Spokane WASHINGTON

Spokesman-Review (mS)
Spokane Daily Chronicle (e)
508 Chronicle Building
Spokane WA 99210

509/455-6891

Circulation
(m) 71,895
(e) 60,930
(S) 120,492

Robert A. Neswick, Library Manager

Lib. est. 1928   Group Ind.   FTE 8

Public access   Limitations
   in person   yes   By appointment; 8am-5pm
   by mail   yes   No extensive research or school work
   by phone   yes   No extensive research or school work

Services available   Limitations
   copy machine   yes $.50 per copy; $.75 per copy if mailed
   reader/printer yes $.50 per copy; $.75 per copy if mailed
   reader

Hours of operation 8am-11pm

Resources
   clips   180 drawers   books   3,000
   photos   250,000   pamphlets   18 drawers
   negs   6 drawers   maps   x
   CPT   20   AV

Microform holdings
   own newspaper   1881-present
   periodicals
   clippings

Indexes
   own newspaper   1887-1928 Spokesman-Review
   other   1923-present New York Times

Special collections

Automation
  Automated files
    mechanical
     electronic
  Other automated systems

Products for sale

Tacoma News Tribune (eS)
950 S. State St.
Tacoma WA 98411
206/597-8626 or 8629

Circulation
(e) (101,572)
(S) (105,418)

N. L. Kirkland, Librarian

Lib. est. 1955   Group Ind.   FTE 4

Public access   Limitations
   in person   no
   by mail   yes $15.00 per hour
   by phone   yes

Services available   Limitations
   copy machine   yes
   reader/printer   yes
   reader

Hours of operation   6:30am-11pm, M-Sat.

Resources
   clips   x   books   x
   photos   x   pamphlets   x
   negs   x   maps   x
   CPT   x   AV

Microform holdings
   own newspaper   1909-present
   periodicals

Indexes
   own newspaper   1975-present
   other

Special collections

Automation
  Automated files
    mechanical
    electronic   On-line index of newspaper, using PDP-11 and in-house created software
  Other automated systems

Products for sale   Newspaper index, 1975-79

WASHINGTON Vancouver WASHINGTON

The COLUMBIAN

Columbian (eS)
P.O. Box 180
Vancouver WA 98666

Circulation
(e) 44,938
(S) 46,917

206/694-3391 x252

Konnie J. O'Hearn, Head Librarian
Sheila Boyle, Asst. Librarian

Lib. est.   Group Ind.   FTE 2

Public access   Limitations
    in person   yes   First-come, first-served basis
    by mail   yes
    by phone   yes

Services available   Limitations
    copy machine   yes $.10 per copy
    reader/printer   yes $.50 per copy
    reader

Hours of operation 8am-5pm, M-F

Resources
    clips   96 drawers   books   300
    photos 40 drawers   pamphlets 250
    negs   32 drawers   maps   x
    CPT   AV

Microform holdings
    own newspaper   1890-present
    periodicals
    clippings

Indexes
    own newspaper
    other

Special collections

Automation
  Automated files
    mechanical
    electronic
  Other automated systems

Products for sale

WASHINGTON　　　　　　　　　　Yakima　　　　　　　　　　　　WASHINGTON

Yakima Herald Republic (all day & S)　　　　　Circulation
114 N. 4th St.　　　　　　　　　　　　　　　　　(all day)
Yakima   WA 98907　　　　　　　　　　　　　　　　29,353
　　　　　　　　　　　　　　　　　　　　　　　(S) 43,522
　　　　　　　　509/248-1251   x70

　　　　　　Phyllis M. Jones, Librarian

<u>Lib. est.</u> 1903　　　<u>Group</u> Harte Hanks Communications Inc.   <u>FTE</u> 1

<u>Public access</u>　　　　　　　<u>Limitations</u>
　　in person　　yes　　　Use of News Index only
　　by mail　　　yes
　　by phone　　 yes

<u>Services available</u>　　　<u>Limitations</u>
　　copy machine　　yes　　Staff only
　　reader/printer　yes　　Staff only
　　reader

<u>Hours of operation</u>   8am-5pm, M-F

<u>Resources</u>
　　clips　　x　　　　　　　books　　　x
　　photos　 x　　　　　　　pamphlets　x
　　negs　　 x　　　　　　　maps　　　 x
　　CPT　　　x　　　　　　　AV

<u>Microform holdings</u>
　　own newspaper　　1889-present
　　periodicals
　　clippings

<u>Indexes</u>
　　own newspaper　　1959-present
　　other

<u>Special collections</u>

<u>Automation</u>
　Automated files
　　mechanical
　　electronic   Index with text; Digital PDP 8/E
　Other automated systems

<u>Products for sale</u>

266

WEST VIRGINIA   Bluefield   WEST VIRGINIA

Bluefield Daily Telegraph (mS)   Circulation
P.O. Box 208   (m) 29,254
Bluefield WV 24701   (S) 36,595
                            304/327-6171 x234

              Karen Kaplan, Librarian

Lib. est. 1930   Group Ind.   FTE 1

Public access   Limitations
     in person   yes
     by mail   yes
     by phone   yes

Services available   Limitations
     copy machine
     reader/printer
     reader   yes

Hours of operation 10am-6:30pm, M-F

Resources
     clips   5,000+   books   x
     photos   2,500+   pamphlets   5,000+
     negs   10,000+   maps   x
     CPT   x   AV

Microform holdings
     own newspaper   1893-present
     periodicals
     clippings

Indexes
     own newspaper   Currently being indexed; 1973-78 to be complete
                      by June 1980
     other

Special collections Great deal of material about coal and coal
                     mining
Automation
   Automated files
     mechanical
     electronic
   Other automated systems

Products for sale

267

WEST VIRGINIA   Huntington   WEST VIRGINIA

The Herald-Dispatch

Herald-Dispatch (mS)
946 5th Ave.
Huntington WV 25701

304/696-5627

Circulation
(m) 42,993
(S) 50,528

Patty Clay, Library Asst.

Lib. est. ?   Group Gannett Newspapers   FTE 1

Public access   Limitations
    in person   yes
    by mail   yes
    by phone   yes

Services available   Limitations
    copy machine   yes $.50 per page
    reader/printer   yes $3.50 per page
    reader   yes
    other   yes   Photo reprints $4.00-$5.00

Hours of operation   9am-6pm, M-F

Resources
    clips   900,000   books   x
    photos   3,000   pamphlets
    negs   maps
    CPT   AV

Microform holdings
    own newspaper   1896-present
    periodicals
    clippings

Indexes
    own newspaper   none
    other

Automation
  Automated files
    mechanical
    electronic
  Other automated systems

Products for sale

WISCONSIN   La Crosse   WISCONSIN

La Crosse Tribune (eS)
401 N. 3rd. St.
La Crosse WI 54601
          608/782-9710 x232

Circulation
  (e) 35,015
  (S) 35,100

Marilyn R. Wolden, Librarian

Lib. est. 1947   Group Lee Newspapers   FTE

Public access   Limitations
- in person   yes
- by mail   yes
- by phone   yes

Services available   Limitations
- copy machine   yes $.25 per page
- reader/printer   yes   Staff only
- reader

Hours of operation   7:30am-4:00pm, M-F

Resources
- clips   x   books   120
- photos   x   pamphlets
- negs   maps   15
- CPT   AV

Microform holdings
- own newspaper   1904-present
- periodicals
- clippings

Indexes
- own newspaper
- other

Special collections

Automation
   Automated files
- mechanical
- electronic

   Other automated systems

Products for sale

WISCONSIN　　　　　　　　　Madison　　　　　　　　　WISCONSIN

Capitol Times (e)　　　　　　　　　　　　　　　　Circulation
1901 Fish Hatchery Rd.　　　　　　　　　　　　　(e) 36,500
Madison WI 53708
　　　　　　　　　608/252-6412

　　　　Jan Sullivan, Librarian
　　　　Ann Lund, Library Asst.

Lib. est. ?　　　　　　　Group Ind.　　　　　　FTE 1.75

Public access　　　　　　Limitations
　　in person　　yes　　　8am-Noon, M-F
　　by mail　　　yes
　　by phone　　 yes　　　8am-3pm, M-F

Services available　　　 Limitations
　　copy machine　　yes　 $.25 per page
　　reader/printer　　　 Access to printer, $.25 per page
　　reader　　　　　yes

Hours of operation   7:30am-3:30pm, M-F

Resources
　　clips　　x　　　　　　　　books　　　x
　　photos　 x　　　　　　　　pamphlets
　　negs　　　　　　　　　　　maps
　　CPT　　　　　　　　　　　 AV

Microform holdings
　　own newspaper　　1917-present
　　periodicals
　　clippings

Indexes
　　own newspaper
　　other

Special collections   Frank Lloyd Wright

Automation
　Automated files
　　mechanical
　　electronic
　Other automated systems

Products for sale

WISCONSIN   Madison   WISCONSIN

Wisconsin State Journal

Wisconsin State Journal (mS)
1901 Fish Hatchery Rd.
Madison WI 53708
                      608/252-6112

Circulation
(m) (72,000)
(S) (130,000)

Ron Larson, Librarian

Lib. est. 1930   Group Lee Newspapers   FTE 1

Public access   Limitations
- in person   yes   10am-Noon, M-F; no extensive research
- by mail   yes
- by phone   yes   10am-Noon, M-F; no extensive research

Services available   Limitations
- copy machine yes   10 page limit; $.25 per page
- reader/printer yes   10 page limit; $.25 per page
- reader

Hours of operation   10am-8pm, M-F; 10am-4:30pm, Sat.

Resources
- clips   25 drawers   books   60
- photos   15 drawers   pamphlets 1 drawer
- negs   Oct. 1978-present maps   x
- CPT   AV

Microform holdings
- own newspaper   Sept. 1852-present
- periodicals
- clippings

Indexes
- own newspaper
- other

Special collections   University of Wisconsin-Madison anti-war photos and clippings; Joseph McCarthy clippings

Automation
Automated files
- mechanical
- electronic

Other automated systems

Products for sale

Milwaukee Sentinel (m)
Milwaukee Journal (eS)
P.O. Box 661 (Journal)
P.O. Box 371 (Sentinel)
Milwaukee WI 53201

Circulation
(m) 161,641
(e) 329,638
(S) 532,638

414/224-2376

Jo Reitman, Chief Librarian
Joy Sanasarian, Asst. Librarian

Lib. est. 1924   Group Ind.   FTE 23

Public access   Limitations
    in person   yes   No extensive, general research;
    by mail   yes   10am-4pm, M-Sat.
    by phone   yes

Services available   Limitations
    copy machine   yes $.50 per page
    reader/printer   yes   Staff only
    reader   yes   Staff only

Hours of operation   5am-Midnight, Sun.-Sat.

Resources
    clips   2,500,000+   books   3,500
    photos   2,000,000   pamphlets   3,500+
    negs   maps   2,000
    CPT   155   AV

Microform holdings
    own newspaper   x
    periodicals

Indexes
    own newspaper   x
    other   New York Times 1913-present

Special collections

Automation
  Automated files
    mechanical   Lektriever 200
    electronic
  Other automated systems

Products for sale

WISCONSIN   Oshkosh   WISCONSIN

Oshkosh Northwestern (e)   Circulation
224 State St.   (e) 29,245
Oshkosh WI 54901
                              414/235-7700

                    Betty Gibson, Clerk

Lib. est. ?   Group Ind.   FTE

Public access   Limitations
    in person   yes
    by mail   yes
    by phone   yes

Services available   Limitations
    copy machine
    reader/printer
    reader   yes

Hours of operation   8am-4pm, M-F

Resources
    clips   books
    photos   pamphlets
    negs   maps
    CPT   AV

Microform holdings
    own newspaper   1875-present
    periodicals
    clippings

Indexes
    own newspaper
    other

Special collections

Automation
  Automated files
    mechanical
    electronic
  Other automated systems

Products for sale

WISCONSIN   Racine   WISCONSIN

Journal Times (eS)   Circulation
212 Fourth St.   (e) 39,169
Racine WI 53403   (S) 40,461
                         414/634-3322

              Karolyn Cotton, Library Clerk

Lib. est. 1949   Group   Lee Newspapers   FTE   1

Public access   Limitations
    in person   yes   With Managing Editor's permission
    by mail   no
    by phone   no

Services available   Limitations
    copy machine
    reader/printer
    reader   yes

Hours of operation   7:30am-3:30pm, M-F

Resources
    clips   books
    photos   pamphlets
    negs   maps
    CPT   AV

Microform holdings
    own newspaper
    periodicals
    clippings

Indexes
    own newspaper
    other

Special collections

Automation
  Automated files
    mechanical
    electronic
  Other automated systems

Products for sale

274

The Sheboygan Press

Sheboygan Press (e)
632 Center Ave.
Sheboygan WI 53081

414/457-7711 x147

Janice Hildebrand, Librarian

Circulation
(e) 32,324

Lib. est. 1907   Group Ind.   FTE 1

Public access   Limitations
   in person   yes   7:30am-4:30pm, M-F
   by mail   yes
   by phone   yes

Services available   Limitations
   copy machine   yes $.10 per page
   reader/printer
   reader   yes

Hours of operation   7:30am-4:30pm, M-F

Resources
   clips   x   books   x
   photos   x   pamphlets   x
   negs   x   maps   x
   CPT   AV

Microform holdings
   own newspaper   1907-present
   periodicals
   clippings

Indexes
   own newspaper   Dec. 1907-present
   other

Special collections   Historical Sheboygan, obituaries 1968-present

Automation
  Automated files
   mechanical
   electronic
  Other automated systems

Products for sale

WISCONSIN   Waukesha   WISCONSIN

Waukesha Freeman (e)   Circulation
200 Park Place   (e) 26,000
Waukesha WI 53187
                          415/542-2501 x31

          Lorrayne Mathews, Librarian

Lib. est. 1965   Group Ind.   FTE 1

Public access   Limitations
    in person   yes   Look at files and papers but no research
    by mail   yes   provided
    by phone   yes

Services available   Limitations
    copy machine   yes
    reader/printer
    reader

Hours of operation M-F

Resources
    clips   4 cabinets   books   x
    photos   x   pamphlets   2 drawers
    negs   2 years   maps   x
    CPT   AV

Microform holdings
    own newspaper   1859-present
    periodicals
    clippings

Indexes
    own newspaper
    other

Special collections

Automation
  Automated files
    mechanical
    electronic
  Other automated systems

Products for sale

ALBERTA — Calgary — ALBERTA

Albertan (mS)
830-10th Ave. S.W.
Calgary AB T2R 0B1
403/263-7730

Circulation
(m) 41,994
(S) 53,058

Marilyn Wood, Librarian
Laurie Fitzgerald, Asst. Librarian

Lib. est. c. 1956   Group F.P. Publications   FTE 2

Public access
   in person   yes
   by mail   yes
   by phone   yes

Limitations
At Librarian's discretion

Services available
   copy machine   yes
   reader/printer
   reader   yes

Limitations
$.10 per page

Hours of operation   9am-5pm, M-F

Resources
clips	x	books	x
photos	x	pamphlets	x
negs	x	maps	x
CPT	x	AV	

Microform holdings
   own newspaper   1897-present
   periodicals
   clippings

Indexes
   own newspaper
   other

Special collections   Stampede picture collection; local historical picture collection

Automation
  Automated files
    mechanical
    electronic
  Other automated systems

Products for sale

ALBERTA — Calgary — ALBERTA

The Calgary Herald

Calgary Herald (e)
206-7th Ave. S.W.
Calgary AB T2P 0W8
                403/269-6361

Circulation
(e) 127,248

Margaret Hogan, Librarian
Karen Crosby, Asst. Librarian

<u>Lib. est.</u> 1949   <u>Group</u> Southam Newspapers   <u>FTE</u> 6

<u>Public access</u>
- in person   yes
- by mail   yes
- by phone   yes

<u>Limitations</u>
Not open to students

<u>Services available</u>
- copy machine   yes
- reader/printer   yes
- reader   yes

<u>Limitations</u>
$.25 per copy up to ten, $.10 per copy after ten

<u>Hours of operation</u>   9am-5pm, M-F; 9am-1pm, Sat.

<u>Resources</u>

clips	8,000,000	books	350
photos	30,000	pamphlets	150
negs		maps	x
CPT	10	AV	

<u>Microform holdings</u>
- own newspaper   1883-present
- periodicals
- clippings   1,215,000 rolls

<u>Indexes</u>
- own newspaper   Approximately 35 years
- other

<u>Special collections</u>

<u>Automation</u>
  Automated files
    mechanical
    electronic
  Other automated systems

<u>Products for sale</u>

ALBERTA   Lethbridge   ALBERTA

The Lethbridge Herald

Lethbridge Herald (e)
P.O. Box 670
Lethbridge AB T1J 3Z7

403/328-4411

Circulation
(e) 27,752

Bernice Duquay, Librarian
Cheryl Rohovie, Asst. Librarian

Lib. est. 1958   Group   F.P. Publications   FTE   2

Public access   **Limitations**
- in person   yes
- by mail   yes
- by phone   yes

Services available   **Limitations**
- copy machine   yes   5 copies free; $.25 for each additional
- reader/printer   copy
- reader   yes

Hours of operation   8am-4pm, M-F

Resources
- clips   5 years   books   1,000
- photos   9 drawers   pamphlets
- negs   5 years   maps   20
- CPT   5   AV

Microform holdings
- own newspaper   1905-present
- periodicals
- clippings

Indexes
- own newspaper   1958-present
- other

Special collections

Automation
   Automated files
     mechanical
     electronic
   Other automated systems

Products for sale

BRITISH COLUMBIA — Vancouver — BRITISH COLUMBIA

the province

Province (m)
2250 Granville St.
Vancouver   BC   V6H 3G2
      604/732-2605; 732-2519 (office)

Circulation
(m) 133,292

Shirley E. Mooney, Library Manager
Barbara Valle, Asst. Manager

Lib. est. c. 1940   Group Southam Newspapers   FTE 18

Public access
- in person   no
- by mail   yes
- by phone   yes

Limitations
Research for fee, copying, interlibrary loan for books
Dates, copying
Dates

Services available
- copy machine   yes
- reader/printer   yes
- reader   yes

Limitations

Hours of operation   5:30am-2am, Sat.-Sun.

Resources
clips	3,000,000	books	3,200
photos	5,500	pamphlets	48 drawers
negs		maps	10 drawers
CPT	75	AV	

Microform holdings
- own newspaper   1894-present
- periodicals
- clippings

Indexes
- own newspaper
- other   British Columbia Provincial Index   1900-1969

Special collections

Automation
  Automated files
    mechanical
    electronic   Computerized thesaurus of subject headings
  Other automated systems

Products for sale

BRITISH COLUMBIA   Vancouver   BRITISH COLUMBIA

The Vancouver Sun

Vancouver Sun (e)
2250 Granville St.
Vancouver BC V6H 3G2
    604/732-2605; 732-2519 (office)

Circulation
(e) 249,712

Shirley E. Mooney, Library Manager
Barbara Valle, Asst. Manager

<u>Lib. est.</u> c. 1930   <u>Group</u> F.P. Publications   <u>FTE</u> 18

<u>Public access</u>
    in person   no
    by mail   yes
    by phone   yes

<u>Limitations</u>
No in-depth research, photocopies, interlibrary loan for books

<u>Services available</u>
    copy machine   yes
    reader/printer yes
    reader   yes

<u>Limitations</u>

<u>Hours of operation</u> 5:30am-2am, Sun.-Sat.

<u>Resources</u>
    clips   8,000,000   books   3,200
    photos   80,000   pamphlets 48 drawers
    negs   maps   10 drawers
    CPT   75   AV

<u>Microform holdings</u>
    own newspaper   1886-present
    periodicals
    clippings

<u>Indexes</u>
    own newspaper
    other   British Columbia Provincial Index 1900-1969

<u>Special collections</u> British Columbia, Canadian government documents

<u>Automation</u>
  Automated files
    mechanical
    electronic   Computerized thesaurus of subject headings
  Other automated systems

<u>Products for sale</u>

Winnipeg Free Press (e)　　　　　　　　　　　　　Circulation
300 Carleton St.　　　　　　　　　　　　　　　　　(e) 138,770
Winnipeg MB R3C 3C1
　　　　　　　　　204/943-9331 x263

　　　　Esme Langer, Librarian
　　　　Marcia Stephenson, Asst. Librarian

Lib. est. 1930's　　　　　Group F.P. Publications　　　FTE 7

Public access　　　　　　　Limitations
　　in person　　no
　　by mail　　　yes
　　by phone　　 yes

Services available　　　　 Limitations
　　copy machine　　yes　　$.25 per copy
　　reader/printer
　　reader　　　　 yes

Hours of operation 7:30am-4:30pm, M-F

Resources
　　clips　　2,000,000　　　　books　　　　500
　　photos　 1,200,000　　　　pamphlets　 15,000
　　negs　　　　　　　　　　　maps　　　　 700
　　CPT　　　　　　　　　　　 AV

Microform holdings
　　own newspaper　　1874-present
　　periodicals
　　clippings

Indexes
　　own newspaper
　　other　　　　　　New York Times

Special collections

Automation
　Automated files
　　mechanical
　　electronic
　Other automated systems

Products for sale

MANITOBA   Winnipeg   MANITOBA

The Winnipeg Tribune

Winnipeg Tribune (e)   **Circulation**
P.O. Box 7000   (e) 106,463
Winnipeg MB R3C 3B2
                        204/985-4600

            Karen Liddiard, Chief Librarian
            Peggy Roberts, Asst. Librarian

Lib. est. c. 1930   Group Southam Newspapers   FTE 4

Public access   Limitations
    in person   no   With Managing Editor's approval
    by mail   no
    by phone   yes   Dates given if information not available
                             elsewhere

Services available   Limitations
    copy machine
    reader/printer
    reader   yes   Staff only

Hours of operation   7am-5:30pm, M-F

Resources
    clips   25 filing cabinets   books   450
    photos   pamphlets
    negs   maps
    CPT   25   AV

Microform holdings
    own newspaper   1890-present
    periodicals
    clippings

Indexes
    own newspaper
    other

Special collections

Automation
  Automated files
    mechanical   3 Sperry Remington Lektrievers #110
    electronic
  Other automated systems

Products for sale

283

Spectator (e)
44 Frid St.
Hamilton ON L8N 3G3
416/526-3315

Circulation
(e) 145,308

Jean M. Tebbutt, Chief Librarian
Heather Hopgood, Asst. Librarian

Lib. est. 1925   Group Southam Newspapers   FTE 4

Public access   Limitations
- in person   yes
- by mail   yes
- by phone   yes

Services available   Limitations
- copy machine
- reader/printer   yes
- reader   yes

Hours of operation   9am-4:30pm, 6 days

Resources
clips	15,000 titles	books	3,500
photos	20,000	pamphlets	
ncgs		maps	200
CPT		AV	

Microform holdings
- own newspaper   1846-present
- periodicals
- clippings

Indexes
- own newspaper
- other

Special collections   400 volume collection of American, Canadian, and British journalism

Automation
- Automated files
  - mechanical   Lektrievers
  - electronic
- Other automated systems

Products for sale

Kitchener-Waterloo Record (e) Circulation
225 Fairway Rd. S. (e) 68,391
Kitchener ON N2G 4E5
                519/579-2231 x295

    Penny Coates, Chief Librarian
    Clifford Cunningham, Asst. Librarian

<u>Lib. est.</u> 1972   <u>Group</u> Ind.   <u>FTE</u> 2

<u>Public access</u>   <u>Limitations</u>
    in person yes   By appointment
    by mail   yes
    by phone   yes

<u>Services available</u>   <u>Limitations</u>
    copy machine yes $.10 per page
    reader/printer yes   Staff only
    reader

<u>Hours of operation</u> 7:30am-8:30pm, M-F

<u>Resources</u>
    clips   4,400+   books   250
    photos   10,000   pamphlets
    negs   maps   150
    CPT   20   AV

<u>Microform holdings</u>
    own newspaper   1893-present (1858-1892 incomplete)
    periodicals
    clippings

<u>Indexes</u>
    own newspaper
    other

<u>Special collections</u>

<u>Automation</u>
  Automated files
    mechanical   Lektriever
    electronic
  Other automated systems

<u>Products for sale</u>

London Free Press (me)　　　　　　　　　　　　　　　　　Circulation
P.O. Box 2280　　　　　　　　　　　　　　　　　　　　　　(m) 85,710
London　ON　N6A 4G1　　　　　　　　　　　　　　　　　　(e) 45,843
　　　　　　　　　　　519/679-1111 x257

　　　　　　　Edythe Cusack, Librarian

Lib. est. 1950's　　　　　　　Group Ind.　　　　　　　FTE 4

Public access　　　　　　　　　Limitations
　　in person　　yes　　　　　By appointment
　　by mail　　　yes
　　by phone　　 yes

Services available　　　　　　Limitations
　　copy machine　　yes　　　 $.50 per page, limited use
　　reader/printer　yes　　　 $.50 per page, limited use
　　reader　　　　　yes

Hours of operation 7:30am-Midnight, M-F; 8am-Midnight, Sat.
　　　　　　　　　　6pm-Midnight, Sun.
Resources
　　clips　　　125,000　　　　　　　books　　　　500
　　photos　　 100,000　　　　　　　pamphlets　　100
　　negs　　　　　　　　　　　　　　maps　　　　　70
　　CPT　　　　　　50　　　　　　　 AV

Microform holdings
　　own newspaper　　　　1874-present
　　periodicals
　　clippings

Indexes
　　own newspaper　　　None
　　other

Special collections

Automation
　Automated files
　　mechanical　　　3 Lektrievers
　　electronic
　Other automated systems

Products for sale

Citizen (e)
1101 Baxter Rd.
Ottawa ON K2C 3M4

613/829-9100 x317

Circulation
(e) 120,544

Steven Proulx, Chief Librarian
Ronald P. Tysick, Librarian

| Lib. est. | | | Group Southam Newspapers | FTE 3 |

Public access
    in person   yes
    by mail   yes
    by phone   yes

Limitations
No photocopying facilities

Services available
    copy machine
    reader/printer   yes
    reader

Limitations

Staff only

Hours of operation   6am-4pm, M-F; 6:30pm-Midnight, M-Thurs.

Resources
    clips   450,000   books   200
    photos   10,000   pamphlets
    negs   maps   250
    CPT   6   AV

Microform holdings
    own newspaper   x
    periodicals
    clippings

Indexes
    own newspaper   1970-present
    other

Special collections

Automation
  Automated files
    mechanical   Lektriever 200
    electronic
  Other automated systems

Products for sale

THE OTTAWA Journal

Ottawa Journal (e)　　　　　　　　　　　　　Circulation
365 Laurier Ave. W.　　　　　　　　　　　　(e) 82,826
Ottawa ON K1G 3K6
　　　　　　　　　613/563-3757

　　　Marion R. Barron, Librarian
　　　Lynda Martin, Library Technician
　　　Andrea Gillespie, Library Clerk

Lib. est. 1960　　　　Group F.P. Publications　　　FTE 3

Public access　　　　　　　Limitations
　　in person　no
　　by mail　　no
　　by phone　 no

Services available　　　　Limitations
　　copy machine
　　reader/printer
　　reader

Hours of operation　9am-2am, M-F; 6pm-Midnight, Sun.

Resources
　　clips　　2,000,000　　　　books　　　3,500
　　photos　　500,000　　　　pamphlets　2,500
　　negs　　　　　　　　　　　maps　　　　100
　　CPT　　　　　　　　　　　 AV

Microform holdings
　　own newspaper　　1885-present
　　periodicals
　　clippings

Indexes
　　own newspaper　　July 1, 1979-present
　　other

Special collections

Automation
　Automated files
　　mechanical
　　electronic
　Other automated systems　INFO GLOBE

Products for sale　Ottawa Journal Index July 1, 1979-present

ONTARIO — Toronto — ONTARIO

Globe and Mail (m)
444 Front St. W.
Toronto ON M5V 2S9

416/361-5075

Circulation
(m) 275,812

Amanda Valpy, Chief Librarian

Lib. est. 1938   Group F.P. Publications   FTE

Public access
   in person   no
   by mail   no
   by phone   no

Limitations

Services available
   copy machine   yes
   reader/printer yes
   reader   yes

Limitations
Staff only

Hours of operation 8:30am-2am, M-F; Noon-8pm, Sat.; Noon-2am, Sun.

Resources
   clips   6,500,000   books   7,000
   photos   1,000,000   pamphlets
   negs   250,000   maps
   CPT   AV

Microform holdings
   own newspaper   1849-present
   periodicals
   clippings   40,000 microfiche

Indexes
   own newspaper
   other

Special collections

Automation
  Automated files
    mechanical   6 Diebold Power Files
    electronic   INFO GLOBE: full text, on-line system
  Other automated systems

Products for sale

Toronto Star (eS)
One Yonge St.
Toronto ON M5E 1E6
                        416/367-2422

Circulation
  (e) 489,246
  (S) 310,536

Carol Lindsay, Chief Librarian
Donald Swoger, Librarian

Lib. est. 1923   Group Ind.   FTE 14

Public access
   in person   no
   by mail   no
   by phone   no

Limitations

Services available   Limitations
   copy machine   yes   Staff only
   reader/printer yes
   reader   yes

Hours of operation   Sun. Midnight-F Midnight; 5pm-Midnight, Sat.

Resources
   clips   340,000   books   4,000
   photos   500,000   pamphlets   x
   negs   x   maps   x
   CPT   40   AV

Microform holdings
   own newspaper   1894-present
   periodicals
   clippings

Indexes
   own newspaper   Star indexed in Canadian Newspaper Index since Jan. 1977

Special collections

Automation
  Automated files
    mechanical
    electronic
  Other automated systems   New York Times Information Bank; INFOMART (ORBIT data base)

Products for sale

Toronto Sun (mS)
333 King St. East
Toronto ON M5A 3X5
      416/868-2257

<u>Circulation</u>
 (m) 205,651
 (S) 337,054

  Shirley Goodhand, Department Head

<u>Lib. est.</u> c. 1920   <u>Group</u> Ind.   <u>FTE</u> 7

<u>Public access</u>   <u>Limitations</u>
 in person   no   Exceptions by permission
 by mail   no
 by phone   no

<u>Services available</u>   <u>Limitations</u>
 copy machine   yes   Staff only
 reader/printer   yes   Staff only
 reader   yes   Staff only

<u>Hours of operation</u>   9am-11pm, M-Sun. (9am-4pm, F)

<u>Resources</u>
 clips   100,000   books   100
 photos   50,000   pamphlets   300
 negs   maps   20
 CPT   5   AV

<u>Microform holdings</u>
 own newspaper   x
 periodicals
 clippings

<u>Indexes</u>
 own newspaper
 other

<u>Special collections</u>

<u>Automation</u>
  Automated files
 mechanical   Diebold Power files
 electronic
  Other automated systems

<u>Products for sale</u>

ONTARIO Windsor ONTARIO

Windsor Star (e) **Circulation**
167 Ferry St. (e) 89,468
Windsor ON N9A 4M5
                519/255-5672

        Frances Curry, Librarian

<u>Lib. est.</u> 1946   <u>Group</u> Southam Newspapers   <u>FTE</u>

<u>Public access</u>   <u>Limitations</u>
   in person   yes   Patron does own research
   by mail   yes
   by phone   yes

<u>Services available</u>   <u>Limitations</u>
   copy machine   yes
   reader/printer
   reader   yes

<u>Hours of operation</u> 8:30am-5pm, M-F; 8:30am-Noon, Sat.

<u>Resources</u>
   clips   10,000   books   x
   photos   50,000   pamphlets 5 drawers
   negs   maps   3 drawers
   CPT   AV

<u>Microform holdings</u>
   own newspaper   1893-present
   periodicals
   clippings

<u>Indexes</u>
   own newspaper   none
   other

<u>Special collections</u>

<u>Automation</u>
  Automated files
    mechanical
    electronic
  Other automated systems

<u>Products for sale</u>

Le Devoir (m-French)　　　　　　　　　　　　　　　　Circulation
211 Rue St.-Sacrement　　　　　　　　　　　　　　　　(m) 44,000
Montreal　PQ　H2Y 1X1
　　　　　　　　　　514/844-3361 x215

　　　　　Gilles Pare, Responsable

Lib. est. 1972　　　　　　　Group　Ind.　　　　　　FTE　3

Public access　　　　　　　　Limitations
　　in person　　no
　　by mail　　　no
　　by phone　　 no

Services available　　　　　Limitations
　　copy machine　　yes　　Staff only
　　reader/printer　yes　　Staff only
　　reader

Hours of operation　9am-7pm, M-F

Resources
　　clips　　200,000　　　　books　　　6,000
　　photos　　25,000　　　　pamphlets
　　negs　　　　　　　　　　maps
　　CPT　　　　 100　　　　 AV

Microform holdings
　　own newspaper　　1910-present
　　periodicals
　　clippings

Indexes
　　own newspaper
　　other

Special collections

Automation
　Automated files
　　mechanical
　　electronic
　Other automated systems

Products for sale

Gazette (m)
1000 St.-Antoine West
Montreal PQ H3C 3E2

514/861-1111

Circulation
(m) 187,137

A. McFarlane, Head Librarian
M.R. Coonan, Asst. Librarian

Lib. est. 1950   Group Southam Newspapers   FTE 8

Public access
- in person   yes
- by mail   yes
- by phone   no

Limitations
By appointment; Research fee $20

Services available
- copy machine   yes
- reader/printer yes
- reader   yes

Limitations

Hours of operation 9:30am-12:30am, M-F; Noon-12:30am, Sun.

Resources
clips	2,000,000	books	5,000
photos	40,000	pamphlets	12 drawers
negs		maps	1 drawer
CPT	50	AV	

Microform holdings
- own newspaper   1778-present
- periodicals
- clippings

Indexes
- own newspaper   1950-present
- other   New York Times Index

Special collections

Automation
  Automated files
    mechanical
    electronic
  Other automated systems

Products for sale

QUEBEC   Montreal   QUEBEC

La Presse (e-French)   Circulation
7 St.-Jacques St., West   (e) 167,769
Montreal PQ H2Y 1K9
                              514/282-7007

           Fernand Drouin, Director
           Gerard Monette, Asst. to Director
           Louise Audet, Asst. to Director

Lib. est. 1965   Group Trans-Canada   FTE 15

Public access   Limitations
     in person   no
     by mail   yes
     by phone   no

Services available   Limitations
     copy machine   yes
     reader/printer yes
     reader

Hours of operation

Resources
     clips   15,000 subjects   books   5,000
     photos   1,000,000   pamphlets
     negs   maps   500
     CPT   AV

Microform holdings
     own newspaper   1884-present
     periodicals
     clippings

Special collections La Patrie on microfilm 1879-present; Le Nouveau
                     Journal on microfilm 1971 and 1972, complete

Automation
   Automated files
     mechanical
     electronic
   Other automated systems

Products for sale   Pamphlets of different articles in our newspaper

Le Soleil (e-French)
390 St.-Vallier est
Quebec PQ G1K 7J6
                    418/647-3369

Circulation
(e) 128,977

Pierre Mathieu, Directeur

Lib. est. 1967   Group UniMedia Inc.   FTE 11

Public access   Limitations
- in person   yes
- by mail   yes
- by phone   yes

Services available   Limitations
- copy machine   yes
- reader/printer   yes
- reader

Hours of operation   7 days a week

Resources
- clips   65 files   books   5,000
- photos   19 files   pamphlets
- negs   maps
- CPT   65   AV

Microform holdings
- own newspaper   1896-present
- periodicals
- clippings

Indexes
- own newspaper   1973-present
- other

Special collections

Automation
- Automated files
  - mechanical
  - electronic
- Other automated systems

Products for sale   Pamphlets of newspaper articles

SASKATCHEWAN　　　　　　　　　Saskatoon　　　　　　　　　SASKATCHEWAN

StarPhoenix

Star-Phoenix (e)
204-5 Ave. North
Saskatoon SK S7K 2P1

306/664-8223

Don Perkins, Librarian

Circulation
(e) 53,477

Lib. est.　　　　　　　　　Group Armadale　　　　　　FTE 1.5

Public access　　　　　　　Limitations
   in person yes   As staff time is available
   by mail   yes
   by phone   yes

Services available　　　　　Limitations
   copy machine yes $.25 per page
   reader/printer
   reader   yes

Hours of operation   8am-4:30pm, M-F

Resources
   clips   40+ drawers   books   700
   photos   pamphlets
   negs   maps
   CPT   AV

Microform holdings
   own newspaper   1902-present
   periodicals
   clippings

Indexes
   own newspaper   none
   other

Special collections

Automation
  Automated files
    mechanical
    electronic
  Other automated systems

Products for sale

WASHINGTON DC BUREAU LIBRARIES

American Newspaper Publishers Association
Newspaper Center
P.O. Box 17407
Dulles International Airport
Washington DC 20041

703/620-4500
Librarian: Yvonne Egertson

Baltimore Sun
1214 National Press Building
Washington DC 20045

202/347-8250
Librarian: Tim Berlett

Chicago Sun-Times
708 National Press Building
Washington DC 20045

202/785-8200
Librarian: Virginia Martino

Chicago Tribune
1707 H St. NW
Washington DC 20006

202/785-9430
Librarian: Carolyn Hardnett

Cox Newspapers
1901 Pennsylvania Ave. NW
Washington DC 20006

202/331-0900

Gannett News Service
1627 K St. NW
Washington DC 20006

202/862-4900

Knight-Ridder Newspapers
1195 National Press Building
Washington DC 20045

202/637-3610
Librarian: Jo Kirks

Los Angeles Times
1700 Pennsylvania Ave. NW
Washington DC 20006

202/393-2424
Librarians: Gloria Doyle
           Diana Moore

New York Daily News
2101 L St. NW
Washington DC 20037

202/467-6670
Librarian: Robert Gearty

New York Times
1000 Connecticut Ave. NW
Washington DC 20036

202/862-0333
Librarian: Sunday Orme

Newsday
1750 Pennsylvania Ave. NW
Washington DC 20006

202/393-5630
Librarian: Cathy Wood

Newhouse News Service
1750 Pennsylvania Ave. NW
Washington DC 20006

202/383-7800
Librarian: Grace Gerino

UNITED STATES CITY INDEX

Akron OH (Beacon Journal) 190
Albuquerque NM (Journal) 164
Allentown PA (Call-Chronicle) 209
Amarillo TX (News-Globe) 239
Anchorage AK (Times) 4
Asbury Park NJ (Press) 150
Atlanta GA (Journal & Constitution) 70
Atlantic City NJ (Press) 151
Augusta GA (Chronicle-Herald) 71
Austin TX (American Statesman) 240

Baltimore MD (News-American) 109
             (The Sun) 110
Bangor ME (Daily News) 108
Baton Rouge LA (Advocate & State-Times) 105
Beaver PA (Beaver County Times) 210
Bellevue WA (Daily Journal-American) 259
Biloxi MS (Sun Herald) 137
Binghamton NY (Sun Bulletin & Press) 165
Birmingham AL (News) 1
             (Post Herald) 2
Bismark ND (Tribune) 188
Bloomington IL (Daily Pantagraph) 75
Bluefield WV (Daily Telegraph) 267
Boise ID (Idaho Statesman) 74
Boston MA (Globe) 111
       (Herald American) 112
       (Christian Science Monitor) 113
Boulder CO (Daily Camera) 37
Bradenton FL (Herald) 55
Bridgewater NJ (Courier-News) 152
Brockton MA (Enterprise) 114
Buffalo NY (Courier-Express) 166
      (Evening News) 167
Burlington VT (Free Press) 252

Camden NJ (Courier Post) 153
Cedar Rapids IA (Gazette) 95
Champaign IL (Champaign-Urbana News-Gazette) 76
Charleston SC (News and Courier/Evening Post) 227
Charlotte NC (Observer & News) 182
Chattanooga TN (Times) 230
Chicago IL (Sun-Times) 77
      (Tribune) 78
Chico CA (Enterprise-Record) 11
Cincinnati OH (Enquirer) 191
       (Post) 192
Cleveland OH (Press) 194
      (Plain Dealer) 193
Colorado Springs CO (Gazette Telegraph) 38
            (Sun) 39

Columbia SC (Record) 228
Columbus GA (Ledger-Enquirer) 72
Columbus OH (Citizen-Journal) 195
Corpus Christi TX (Caller-Times) 241
Covington KY (Post) 101

Dallas TX (Morning News) 242
        (Times Herald) 243
Danbury CT (News-Times) 44
Davenport IA (Quad-City Times) 96
Dayton OH (Journal Herald and Daily News) 197
Daytona Beach FL (News-Journal) 56
Decatur IL (Herald & Review) 79
Denver CO (Post) 40
        (Rocky Mountain News) 41
Des Moines IA (Register and Tribune) 97
Detroit MI (Free Press) 122
        (News) 123
Dover DE (Delaware State News and Maryland State News) 51
Dubuque IA (Telegraph Herald) 98
Duluth MN (News-Tribune and Herald) 132
Durham NC (Morning Herald and Sun) 183

Easton PA (The Express) 211
Elizabeth NJ (The Daily Journal) 154
Elmira NY (Star Gazette) 168
Elyria OH (Chronicle Telegram) 198
Eugene OR (Register-Guard) 207
Evansville IN (Courier & Press) 88

Fargo ND (The Forum) 189
Fayetteville NC (Observer-Times) 184
Flint MI (Journal) 124
Fort Lauderdale FL (News and Sun Sentinel) 57
Fort Myers FL (News-Press) 58
Fort Wayne IN (Journal-Gazette) 89
Fort Worth TX (Star-Telegram) 244
Framingham MA (South Middlesex News) 115
Fredericksburg VA (The Free Lance-Star) 253

Gainesville FL (Sun) 59
Gary IN (Post-Tribune) 98
Grand Junction CO (Daily Sentinel) 42
Grand Rapids MI (Press) 125
Greensboro NC (Daily News and Record) 185
Greensburg PA (Tribune Review) 212
Greenville SC (News-Piedmont) 229

Hackensack NJ (Record) 155
Harrisonburg VA (Daily News-Record) 254

Hartford CT (Courant) 45
Hollywood FL (Sun-Tattler) 60
Holyoke MA (Transcript Telegram) 116
Honolulu HI (Star Bulletin & Advertiser) 73
Houston TX (Chronicle) 245
       (Post) 246
Huntington WV (Herald-Dispatch) 268
Huntsville AL (Times) 3

Indianapolis IN (Star & News) 91

Jackson MS (Clarion-Ledger and News) 138
Jackson MI (Citizen Patriot) 126
Jackson TN (Sun) 231
Jacksonville FL (Florida Times-Union and Journal) 61
Jamestown NY (Post-Journal) 169
Johnson City TN (Press-Chronicle) 232
Joliet IL (Herald-News) 80
Joplin MO (Globe) 139

Kankakee IL (Journal) 81
Kansas City MO (Star Times) 140
Kent OH (Record Enquirer) 199
Knoxville TN (Journal) 233
       (News-Sentinel) 234
Kokomo IN (Tribune) 92

La Crosse WI (Tribune) 269
Lake Charles LA (American Press) 106
Lakeland FL (The Ledger) 62
Lancaster PA (Intelligencer Journal and New Era and News) 213
Lansing MI (The State Journal) 127
Las Vegas NV (Review-Journal) 147
Lawrence MA (Eagle-Tribune) 117
Levittown PA (Bucks County Courier Times) 214
Lexington KY (Herald and Leader) 102
Lima OH (News) 200
Lincoln NE (Journal-Star) 145
Little Rock AR (Arkansas Democrat) 9
       (Arkansas Gazette) 10
Long Beach CA (Independent Press-Telegram) 12
Longview WA (Daily News) 260
Los Angeles CA (Herald Examiner) 13
       (Times) 14
Louisville KY (Courier-Journal and Times) 103
Lynn MA (Daily Evening Item) 118

Madison WI (Capitol Times) 270
       (Wisconsin State Journal) 271
Manchester CT (Journal Enquirer) 46
Manchester NH (Union Leader and News) 149

Mankato MN (Free Press) 133
Mansfield OH (News Journal) 170
Mellville, Long Island NY (Newsday) 170
Memphis TN (Commercial Appeal) 235
        (Press-Scimitar) 236
Mesa AZ (Tribune) 5
Miami FL (Herald) 63
      (News) 64
Midwest City OK (The Journal) 204
Milwaukee WI (Sentinel and Journal) 272
Minneapolis MN (Tribune and Star) 134
Modesto CA (Bee) 15
Moline IL (The Daily Dispatch) 82
Monroe MI (Evening News) 128
Monterey CA (Peninsula Herald) 16
Muncie IN (Star and Evening Press) 93
Muskegon MI (Chronicle) 129

Nashville TN (Banner) 237
      (The Tennessean) 238
New Brunswick NJ (Home News) 156
New Haven CT (Journal-Courier and Register) 47
New London CT (The Day) 48
New York NY (Daily World) 171
      (Daily News) 172
      (Post) 173
      (Times) 174
      (Wall Street Journal) 175
Newark NJ (Star-Ledger) 157
Newport News VA (Daily Press and Times Herald) 255
Niagara Falls NY (Niagara Gazette) 176
Norfolk VA (Virginian-Pilot and Ledger-Star) 256

Oakland CA (Eastbay Today and Tribune) 17
Oklahoma City OK (Daily Oklahoman and Times) 205
Omaha NE (World-Herald) 146
Orlando FL (Sentinel Star) 65
Oshkosh WI (Northwestern) 273
Owensboro KY (Messenger-Inquirer) 104

Palo Alto CA (Peninsula Times-Tribune) 18
Parsippany NJ (Daily Record) 158
Passaic NJ (Herald News) 159
Paterson NJ (News) 160
Pawtucket RI (Evening Times) 225
Peoria IL (Journal Star) 83
Philadelphia PA (The Bulletin) 215
        (Inquirer and Daily News) 216
Phoenix AZ (Arizona Republic) 6
Pittsburgh PA (Post-Gazette) 217
      (Press) 218

Pittsfield MA (Berkshire Eagle) 119
Port Huron MI (The Times Herald) 130
Portland OR (The Oregonian and Oregon Journal) 208
Primos PA (Delaware County Daily Times) 219
Providence RI (Journal and Evening Bulletin) 226
Pueblo CO (Star Journal & Chieftain) 43

Quincy IL (Herald-Whig) 84

Racine WI (Journal Times) 274
Raleigh NC (News and Observer and Times) 186
Reading PA (Times and Eagle) 220
Redding CA (Record Searchlight) 19
Reno NV (Nevada State Journal and Evening Gazette) 148
Richmond VA (Times-Dispatch and News Leader) 257
Riverside CA (The Press Enterprise) 20
Roanoke VA (Times & World-News) 258
Rochester MN (Post-Bulletin) 135
Rochester NY (Times Union) 177
Rockford IL (Register Star) 85

Sacramento CA (Bee) 21
            (Union) 22
Saginaw MI (News) 131
St. Joseph MO (Gazette and News-Press) 141
St. Louis MO (Globe-Democrat) 142
            (Post-Dispatch) 143
St. Paul MN (Pioneer Press and Dispatch) 136
St. Petersburg FL (Times and Evening Independent) 66
Salt Lake City UT (Deseret News) 250
                  (Tribune) 251
San Angelo TX (Standard Times) 247
San Antonio TX (Express-News) 248
            (Light) 249
San Bernardino CA (Sun) 23
San Diego CA (Union and Evening Tribune) 24
San Francisco CA (Chronicle) 25
                 (Examiner) 26
San Jose CA (Mercury News) 27
San Mateo CA (The Times) 28
Sandusky OH (Register) 202
Santa Ana CA (Register) 29
Santa Barbara CA (News-Press) 30
Santa Rosa CA (Press Democrat) 31
Sarasota FL (Herald-Tribune and Journal) 67
Schenectady NY (Gazette) 178
Scranton PA (Times) 221
            (Tribune and Scrantonian) 222
Seattle WA (Post-Intelligencer) 261
           (Times) 262
Sheboygan WI (Press) 275

Shreveport LA (Times) 107
Shrewsbury NJ (Daily Register) 94
South Bend IN (Tribune) 94
Spokane WA (Spokesman Review and Daily Chronicle) 263
Springfield IL (State Journal & Register) 86
Springfield MA (Morning Union and Daily News) 120
Springfield MO (Daily News and Leader & Press) 144
Stamford CT (The Advocate) 49
Stockton CA (Record) 32
Sunbury PA (The Daily Item) 223

Tacoma WA (News Tribune) 264
Tampa FL (Tribune & Times) 68
Tarentum PA (Valley News Dispatch) 224
Toledo OH (Blade) 203
Topeka KS (Capital and State Journal) 100
Torrance CA (Daily Breeze) 33
Trenton NJ (Times Advertiser) 162
Troy NY (Times Record) 179
Tucson AZ (Arizona Daily Star) 7
         (Citizen) 8
Tulsa OK (Daily World and Tribune) 206

Van Nuys CA (Valley News) 34
Vancouver WA (Columbian) 265
Ventura CA (Ventura County Star-Free Press) 35

Walnut Creek CA (Contra Costa Times) 36
Washington DC (Post) 53
              (Star) 54
Waterbury CT (Republican and American) 50
Waterloo IA (Courier) 99
Watertown NY (Daily Times) 180
Waukegan IL (News-Sun) 87
Waukesha WI (Freeman) 276
West Palm Beach (Palm Beach Post-Times) 69
White Plains NY (The Reporter Dispatch) 181
Wilmington DE (Morning News and Evening Journal) 52
Winston-Salem NC (Journal and Sentinel) 187
Woodbridge NJ (News Tribune) 163
Worcester MA (Telegram and Evening Gazette) 121

Yakima WA (Herald Republic) 266

CANADIAN CITY INDEX

Calgary AB (Albertan) 277
        (Herald) 278

Hamilton ON (Spectator) 284

Kitchner ON (Kitchner-Waterloo Record) 285

Lethbridge AB (Herald) 279
London ON (Free Press) 286

Montreal PQ (Le Devoir) 293
        (Gazette) 294
        (La Presse) 295

Ottawa ON (Citizen) 287
       (Journal) 288

Quebec PQ (Le Soleil) 296

Saskatoon SK (Star-Phoenix) 297

Toronto ON (Globe and Mail) 289
       (Star) 290
       (Sun) 291

Vancouver BC (Province) 280
         (Sun) 281

Windsor ON (Star) 292
Winnipeg MB (Free Press) 282
        (Tribune) 283

UNITED STATES NEWSPAPER GROUP INDEX

Allbritton Newspapers
    The Paterson (NJ) News   160

Block Newspapers
    Daily Register (Shrewsbury NJ)   161
    Blade (Toledo OH)   203
    Pittsburgh (PA) Post-Gazette   217

Booth Newspapers
    Grand Rapids (MI) Press   125
    Jackson City (MI) Citizen Patriot   126
    The Saginaw (MI) News   131

Calkins Newspapers
    Beaver County Times (Beaver PA)   210
    Bucks County Courier Times (Levittown PA)   214

Capital Cities Communications Inc.
    Kansas City (MO) Star Times   140
    Fort Worth (TX) Star Telegram   244

Central Newspapers
    Indianapolis (IN) Star and News   91

Combined Communications Corp.
    Cincinnati (OH) Enquirer   191

Copley Newspapers
    Daily Breeze (Torrance CA)   33
    San Diego (CA) Union   24
    Herald-News (Joliet IL)   80
    State Journal & Register (Springfield IL)   86

Cowles Newspapers
    Minneapolis (MN) Tribune and Star   134

Cox Enterprises
    Miami (FL) News   64
    Palm Beach Post-Times (West Palm Beach FL)   69
    Atlanta (GA) Journal and Constitution   70
    Journal Herald and Dayton Daily News (OH)   197
    Austin (TX) American Statesman   240

Des Moines Register & Tribune Co.
    Jackson (TN) Sun   231

Donrey Media
    Las Vegas (NV) Review-Journal   147

Drukker Communications Inc.
    Herald News (Passaic NJ)   159

Freedom Newspapers Inc.
    Register (Santa Ana CA) 29
    Colorado Springs (CO) Gazette Telegraph 38
    The Lima (OH) News 200

Gannett Newspapers
    Tucson (AZ) Citizen 8
    Eastbay Today (Oakland CA) 17
    Stockton (CA) Record 32
    Sun (San Bernardino CA) 23
    News-Journal (Wilmington DE) 52
    Fort Myers (FL) News-Press 58
    Idaho Statesman (Boise) 74
    Rockford (IL) Register Star 85
    The State Journal (Lansing MI) 127
    The Times Herald (Port Huron MI) 130
    Springfield (MO) Daily News and Leader & Press 144
    Nevada State Journal and Reno Evening Gazette 148
    Courier-News (Bridgewater NJ) 152
    Courier-Post (Camden NJ) 153
    Evening Press and Sun Bulletin (Binghamton NY) 165
    Niagara Gazette (Niagara Falls NY) 176
    The Reporter-Dispatch (White Plains NY) 181
    Star Gazette and Sunday Telegram (Elmira NY) 168
    Times Union and Democrat & Republican (Rochester NY) 177
    Valley News Dispatch (Tarentum PA) 224
    Nashville (TN) Banner 237
    The Tennessean (Nashville TN) 238
    The Burlington (VT) Free Press 252
    Herald-Dispatch (Huntington WV) 268

Gannett Pacific Corp.
    Honolulu (HI) Star-Bulletin 73

Hagadone Newspapers
    The Daily Journal (Elizabeth NJ) 154

Harte-Hanks Communications Inc.
    South Middlesex News (Framingham MA) 115
    Corpus Christi (TX) Caller-Times 241
    Standard Times (San Angelo TX) 247
    Yakima (WA) Herald Republic 266

Hearst Newspapers
    Los Angeles (CA) Herald Examiner 13
    San Francisco (CA) Examiner 26
    News-American (Baltimore MD) 109
    Boston (MA) Herald American 112
    San Antonio (TX) Light 249
    Seattle (WA) Post-Intelligencer 261

Horvitz Newspapers
    Times Record (Troy NY) 179
    News Journal (Mansfield OH) 201

Independent Newspapers Inc.
    Delaware State News and Maryland State News (Dover DE) 51

Ingersoll Publications Inc.
    Delaware County Daily Times (Primos PA) 219

John P. Scripps Newspaper Group
    Record Searchlight (Redding CA) 19
    Ventura County Star-Free Press (Ventura CA) 35

Keystone-Printing Service Inc.
    News-Sun (Waukegan IL) 87

Knight-Ridder Newspapers
    Independent Press-Telegram (Long Beach CA) 12
    San Jose (CA) Mercury-News 27
    Daily Camera (Boulder CO) 37
    The Bradenton (FL) Herald 55
    Miami (FL) Herald 63
    The Columbus (GA) Enquirer-Ledger 72
    Post-Tribune (Gary IN) 98
    Lexington (KY) Herald and Leader 102
    Detroit (MI) Free Press 122
    Duluth (MN) News-Tribune and Herald 132
    St. Paul (MN) Pioneer Press and Dispatch 136
    Charlotte (NC) Observer and News 182
    Akron (OH) Beacon Journal 190
    Philadelphia (PA) Inquirer and Daily News 216

Landmark Communications Inc.
    Greensboro (NC) Daily News and Record 185
    Roanoke (VA) Times and World-News 258
    Virginian-Pilot and Ledger-Star (Norfolk VA) 256

Lee Newspapers
    Lincoln (NE) Star 145
    The Bismarck (ND) Tribune 188
    Journal Times (Racine WI) 274
    La Crosse (WI) Tribune 269
    Wisconsin State Journal (Madison WI) 271

Lindsay-Schaub Newspapers
    Decatur (IL) Herald and Review 79

Lorain County Printing and Publishing Co.
    The Chronicle Telegram (Elyria OH) 198

McClatchy Newspapers
- Modesto (CA) Bee 15
- Sacramento (CA) Bee 21

McClelland Newspapers
- Daily Journal-American (Bellevue WA) 259
- Daily News (Longview WA) 260

Media General Inc.
- Tampa (FL) Tribune and Times 68
- Winston-Salem (NC) Journal and Sentinel 187
- Richmond (VA) Times-Dispatch and News Leader 257

Morris Communications Corp.
- Amarillo (TX) Daily News and Globe-Times 239

Multimedia Newspapers
- Greenville (SC) News-Piedmont 229

New York Times Co.
- Gainesville (FL) Sun 59
- The Ledger (Lakeland FL) 62
- New York (NY) Times 174

Newhouse Newspapers
- Birmingham (AL) News 1
- Huntsville (AL) Times 3
- The Morning Union and Daily News (Springfield MA) 120
- Flint (MI) Journal 124
- Muskegon (MI) Chronicle 129
- St. Louis (MO) Globe-Democrat 142
- Star-Ledger (Newark NJ) 157
- The Plain Dealer (Cleveland OH) 193
- The Oregonian (Portland) 208

News America Publishing Co.
- San Antonio (TX) Express-News 248

Newspapers of New England
- Transcript-Telegram (Holyoke MA) 116

Ogden Newspapers
- Post-Journal (Jamestown NY) 169

Ottaway Newspapers
- The News-Times (Danbury CT) 44
- Free Press (Mankato MN) 133
- Joplin (MO) Globe 139
- The Daily Item (Sunbury PA) 223

Pulitzer Publishing Co.
    Arizona Daily Star (Tucson) 7
    St. Louis (MO) Post-Dispatch 143

Scripps-Howard Newspapers
    Post-Herald (Birmingham AL) 2
    Rocky Mountain News (Denver CO) 41
    Hollywood (FL) Sun-Tattler 60
    Kentucky Post (Covington) 101
    The Cincinnati (OH) Post 192
    Cleveland (OH) Press 194
    The Pittsburgh (PA) Press 218
    Commercial Appeal (Memphis TN) 235
    Knoxville (TN) News-Sentinel 234
    Memphis (TN) Press-Scimitar 236

Shearman Newspapers
    Lake Charles (LA) American Press 106

Sierra Publishing Co.
    Sacramento (CA) Union 22

Small Newspapers
    The Daily Dispatch (Moline IL) 82
    Journal (Kankakee IL) 81
    Rochester (MN) Post-Bulletin 135

Southeastern Newspapers Corp.
    Augusta (GA) Herald and Chonicle 71

Stauffer Communications Inc.
    Capital Journal (Topeka KS) 100

Time Inc.
    Washington (DC) Star 54

Times Mirror Co.
    Los Angeles (CA) Times 14
    The Advocate (Stamford CT) 49
    Newsday (Melville, Long Island NY) 170
    Dallas (TX) Times Herald 243

Tribune Co.
    Peninsula Times-Tribune (Palo Alto CA) 18
    Valley News (Van Nuys CA) 34
    News and Sun Sentinel (Fort Lauderdale FL) 57
    Sentinel Star (Orlando FL) 65
    New York (NY) Daily News 172

Washington Post Co.
    Washington (DC) Post 53
    Trenton (NJ) Times and Advertiser 162

CANADIAN NEWSPAPER GROUP INDEX

Armadale
    Star-Phoenix (Saskatoon SK) 297

F.P. Publications
    Albertan (Calgary AB) 277
    Lethbridge (AB) Herald 279
    Vancouver (BC) Sun 281
    Winnipeg (MB) Free Press 282
    Globe and Mail (Toronto ON) 289
    Ottawa (ON) Journal 288

Southam Newspapers
    Calgary (AB) Herald 278
    Province (Vancouver BC) 280
    Winnipeg (MB) Tribune 283
    Citizen (Ottawa ON) 287
    Spectator (Hamilton ON) 284
    Windsor (ON) Star 292
    Gazette (Montreal PQ) 294

Trans-Canada
    La Presse (Montreal PQ) 295

UniMedia Inc.
    Le Soleil (Quebec PQ) 296

PERSONNEL INDEX

Ahearn, Judith 131
Alonso, Willie 249
America, Mildred 57
Anderson, Elizabeth 246
Anderson, Karen 240
Andrews, Dobie 49
Apple, Barbara 87
Arleth, Hettie 244
Arnold, Eugene R. 220
Audet, Louise 295
Austin, Valerie 230

Badgley, Mary R. 164
Bagley, Marcy 6
Barager, Wendy A. 65
Barensfeld, Thomas 194
Barker, Elaine 202
Barron, Marion R. 288
Basar, Dorothy L. 210
Basnight, Clara P. 256
Batliner, Doris 103
Beatty, Victoria 202
Beck, Michelle 100
Belchen, Dona 180
Belletete, Kathleen 80
Bergan, Ruth 9
Betker, Edward C. 123
Bierek, Nellie 198
Biggs, Robert 28
Blair, David 139
Blanchard, Carol 38
Boeckel, Olga 161
Booth, Karen R. 255
Borgman, Beverly 36
Boyle, Sheila 265
Boyles, Lorraine 50
Brady, Eugene G. (Jr.) 235
Bridger, Edith 232
Bril, Margie 58
Brown, Dorothy 52
Brown, Emily 16
Brown, Gerald R. 143
Brown, Jerry W. 71
Brown, Katherine 51
Brown, Lynn 137
Brown, Nancy M. 2
Budro, Janet 33
Bueno, Luis 63
Bullock, Jessie M. 213
Burford, Susan 107
Burk, Jaqueline 153

Campbell, Nancy 104
Campo, Charles A. 108
Cannon, Sharon 51
Cant, Elaine Barnard 31
Carey, Cathy 119
Carlson, Norma 169
Carnes, Betty M. 43
Caron, Pauline R. 149
Carrigan, Pat 250
Carter, Sharon C. 121
Carter, Shirley 234
Carver, D. Ann 262
Caskey, Renee 259
Casten, Suzanne 25
Chance, Peggy J. 219
Chanslor, Elayne 16
Chao, Jennifer 111
Chisolm, Carol 90
Christensen, Connie 250
Chysh, Zola Mae 210
Clay, Patty 268
Coates, Penny 285
Connery, Susan 162
Conroy, Mary 158
Coonan, M. R. 294
Corby, Katherine 201
Costello, Beryl 114
Cotton, Karolyn 274
Crespo, Lucille 21
Cronin, John R. 112
Crosby, Karen 278
Crotts, Martin L. 61
Crow, Linda H. 152
Cunningham, Charles 206
Cunningham, Clifford 285
Cupp, Kay 2
Curry, Frances 292
Cusack, Edythe 286
Czlonka, Alison 125

Daniels, Flo 60
Davis, Betty 157
Davis, Eric 192
Davis, Mary Ellen 142
Daze, Colleen J. 178
Deamer, Debra 162
DeLancett, Jeannine 65
Dellapa, June 25
DiMarino, Joseph D. (Jr.) 216
Ditterlines, Sue 214
Dobrowolski, Joan 156

Doncevic, Lois A. 209
Dougherty, Linda 38
Douglas, Esther 11
Drouin, Fernand 295
Duquay, Bernice 279
Duren, Doris E. 195
Dye, Mary 4

Eckerle, Lisa 101
Eisberg, Shirla 89
Eliason, Mary 122
Ellingsen, Barbara 132
Ellwood, Georgette 144
Epstein, Judith 120
Everts, Helen L. 213

Farrar, Florence E. 126
Fingland, Geoffrey 113
Finster, Eileen 218
Fitzgerald, Laurie 277
Fitzgerald, Sandra 91
Foley, Kathy 246
Follett, Lelia 179
Fortenberry, Bobbie 239
Fox, Frank 221
Frankhouse, Dorothy M. 32
Freeman, Sandra 262
Fritz, A.M. 74
Frye, Florence 261

Galbreath, Tomie 158
Gammon, Claudette A. 149
Geers, Elmer L. 192
Geiger, Richard 27
Gentry, Christie 233
Gerritts, Judy 26
Gess, Catherine 68
Gibson, Betty 273
Gillespie, Andria 288
Ginter, Kathy 94
Golembiewski, Terri M. 77
Goodhand, Shirley 291
Gravel, Mrs. Ralph 94
Graziano, Patti 193
Greenfeder, Paul 174
Greer, Janis W. 107
Gretz, Dolores 80
Guleke, Kay Smith 240

Halgrimson, Andrea H. 189
Hall, Sandy 7

Hammond, Theresa M. 255
Hampton, Judy 204
Hannan, Mark 53
Hardy, Patricia F. 72
Harmon, Marvin 191
Harris, Belinda 258
Harris, Dorothy 106
Harris, Glenda 147
Harrison, Marilyn L. 40
Hastings, Mrs. Peter 150
Havlena, Betty W. 123
Hayes, Cynthia 166
Hayes, Mary 86
Heard, Emily 113
Hearn, Doris 225
Hearn, Geraldine 79
Heckman, Karen L. 19
Hendricks, Cheri 133
Herman, Kelli 188
Hertzel, Laurie 132
Hifner, William 53
Hildebrand, Janice 275
Hill, Joy 177
Hodge, Connie 80
Hoffman, Dave 170
Hoffman, Donna 188
Hogan, Margaret 278
Homcha, George 220
Hopgood, Heather 284
Houk, Vickie J. 52
Howard, Judy A. 83
Hudock, Anne McRae 49
Huff, Betty 1
Hughes, Rebecca 106
Hulbert, Joan 56
Hunter, James 196
Huschen, Mary 78

Ickes, Clark 109
Ippolito, Andrew 170
Irons, Lynda 74
Isaacs, Bobby D. 185
Ivey, Robert 59
Iwamoto, Margaret 73

James, Linda 241
James, Naomi 247
Jansen, Robert H. 134
January, Leo F. 142
Janus, Bridget 95
Jennings, David 111

Jett, Jeannie 8
Johnson, Ann Kinken 256
Johnson, Carl H. 67
Johnson, Sandy 5
Johnston, Patricia 100
Joiner, Gerald 70
Jones, Phyllis M. 266

Kamber, Clarence 85
Kane, Angelika 217
Kapecky, Michele Ann 122
Kaplan, Karen 267
Katzung, Judith 136
Kaya, Beatrice 73
Keenan, Gloria E. 165
Kehler, Carol 223
Kelso, Elizabeth D. 185
Kendall, Vonnie 31
Kirby, Mary 114
Kirchner, Adelaide 155
Kirkland, N. L. 264
Knipp, Beverly 99
Kowitz, Carol L. 211
Krubeck, Dorothy 260
Kuschube, Anita 23

Lamkin, Judy 259
Lane, Jean 138
Lane, Phyllis 253
Lang, Audrey H. 224
Langer, Esme 282
Larson, Ron 271
Larzelere, David W. 124
Lasher, Teresa 176
Laukaitis, Clarissa D. 50
Legett, Anne 105
Legette, Louise 68
Lewis, Blanche 23
Lewis, Hal 222
Liddiard, Karen 283
Lindberg, Lottie 175
Linders, Larry 46
Lindsay, Carol 290
Loewenkamp, Lucille 88
Logan, Henrietta 151
Loos, Pat 145
Lopez, Robert A. 134
Lowery, Lorie 93
Lund, Ann 270
Lynch, Cheryl 117
Lynch, Kay 116

Lyon, Virginia 69

McBee, Marge 128
McCarthy, Joe 172
McCurry, L. Dee 228
McDermott, Dorothy 64
McFarlane, A. 294
McKula, Kathleen 45
McLeod, Trina 230
McMahon, Trudy 108
Macomber, Sandra 208
Macpherson, Sarah 200
McVicker, Alice 141
Madsen, Flora 163
Maley, Grayce O. 211
Malkemus, June C. 28
Mallory, Sandra 56
Manke, Dorthea 15
Maples, Avita 237
Marino, Carol 161
Martin, Homer E. (Jr.) 155
Martin, Lynda 288
Martino, Bernice 159
Mathews, Lorrayne 276
Mathieu, Pierre 296
Maxwell, Daisy Dockery 184
Maxwell, Joann 130
May, Barbara C. 242
Mazalewski, Florence 148
Mazeika, Denise 214
Mazorol, Louise N. 227
Mecca, Raymond G. 215
Medley, Nora 63
Mehr, Joseph O. 226
Meredith, Jeanne 198
Merrill, Andrew 34
Mesing, Wilbur 47
Matcalf, Judy 242
Michael, Anna M. 21
Middleton, Carolyn 156
Milizia, Jane 252
Miller, Diane 75
Miller, Elizabeth R. 18
Milstead, Helen J. 55
Miner, Elizabeth 7
Minesinger, Joan 20
Mitchell, Edward S. (Jr.) 71
Molt, Lucille 76
Mondschein, Henri 34
Monette, Gerard 295
Moon, Gerald 221

Mooney, Shirley E. 280, 281
Moore, Diane 3
Moran, Sally 237
Morgener, Fred E. 191
Morris, Meg 18
Mosher, Kathleen 199
Murphey, Donna 254

Nelson, (Jewell) Monteray 205
Neswick, Robert A. 263
Newcombe, Barbara 78
North, Dawn L. 92
Noyes, Robert E. 194
Nusser, Charlotte 8

O'Donnell, Angelina 54
Ogden, Hub 146
O'Hearn, Konnie J. 265
Olshan, Irving 57
Osborne, Cecil 43

Paine, Ruth C. 98
Parch, Grace D. 193
Pare, Gilles 293
Parr, Sammie 239
Peacock, Jan 95
Peckham, Clare 48
Peluso, Kathy 32
Perez, Ernest 77
Perkins, Don 297
Perry, Ruth 87
Phillips, Violet R. 12
Piercy, Edith 85
Pirkowski, Theresa 154
Ploch, Richard 69
Pomeroy, Leslie 238
Post, James 91
Powers, Cynthia 109
Pretzer, Jean 115
Proulx, Steven 287
Pustay, Marilyn 137

Raines, Elaine 7
Ray, Sherry 245
Reeves, Sharon Stewart 24
Reidy, Robin 22
Reinold, Linda 84
Reitman, Jo 272
Richards, Dargan A. 228
Richardson, Emily 58
Rickman, Delores J. 55

Riley, Sara J. 35
Ritter, Linda F. 24
Roberts, Peggy 283
Roberts, Sandra 238
Robinson, James A. 121
Robinson, Judy 248
Rogers, Nancy Ann 118
Rohouie, Cheryl 279
Rollins, Marilyn H. 187
Rose, Janice 29
Rose, Leslie 189
Rosenthal, Faigi 173
Ross, Doris 89
Rouse, Joan 1
Rubaloff, Marijoy 207
Russell, Beverly 262

Sabino, Nancy 160
St. John, Patsy 39
Sanasarian, Joy 272
Sandoval, Gladys 72
Saplee, Elizabeth 153
Sauer, Pauline 61
Saunders, Margo 164
Sausedo, Ann E. 13
Sawyer, Marcy 135
Schaeffer, Rex 177
Schartel, Frank 220
Schlaerth, Sally 167
Schmitt, Helene 44
Schulman, Saul 171
Schultz, Mary A. 110
Schwellenbach, Susan 41
Scofield, James S. 66
Seager, Betty 9
Seebers, Barbara 245
Seldon, Norma 181
Semo, Kathy 165
Semonche, Barbara P. 183
Shabkie, Susan 229
Sharke, Ingrid 179
Sharp, Gail 62
Sharp, Jeanne 5
Sherr, Merrill F. 173
Shinomiya, Yae 17
Shonkwiler, Paula 41
Shrader, Bette 146
Simpson, Seth 17
Smith, Doris N. 208
Smith, L. 261
Smith, Linda L. 102

Smith, Patricia (CA) 32
Smith, Patricia (MO) 140
Sowby, Laurene 251
Spencer, Faye 79
Spina, Nan 148
Spinelli, Margo 60
Splinter, Letha 98
Springer, John 140
Spruill, Betty 89
Staggs, Sherry L. 42
Stephenson, Marcia 282
Stevens, Karen 207
Stier, Rosalina 89
Stoddard, Nancy Williams 143
Strong, Jean 168
Sullivan, Debra 145
Sullivan, Gina 248
Sullivan, Jan 270
Sullivan, Sandra 46
Surace, Cecily 14
Swaney, Chriss 212
Sweeney, Kathryn D. 40
Swoger, Donald 290

Tankerly, David 236
Tebbutt, Jean M. 284
Tedards, Helen B. 229
Terry, Gladys 6
Tew, Murlene 184
Tharp, Leonard 103
Thomas, Alfred M. 10
Thomas, Lou 105
Thompson, Linda 129
Thrower, Marie 183
Tierney, Catherine M. 190
Tomiyami, Alan 22
Towry, Lucy 206
Trimble, Kathleen 203
Trivedi, Harish 197
Tucker, Louise 90
Turner, Betty A. 10
Tysick, Ronald P. 287

Uhrmann, Linda J. 151

Valle, Barbara 280, 281
Valpy, Amanda 289
Van Dinter, Nancy 74
Van Lauwe, Elizabeth 96
Vance, Julia M. 70
Vance, Sally 75

Vance, Sandra 86
Vera, Dorothy 175
Victoria, Vicki 190
Vitek, Clement G. 110
Voigt, Deborah 76
Von Bruns, Barbara R. 252

Walden, Elaine 243
Walker, Danny 231
Walker, Joy 182
Wall, Celia 186
Waterman, Glenn 46
Watrous, Leland R. 131
Watt, Mary Morris 257
Webb, Barbara 102
Wells, Christine 127
Wells, Gwendolyn C. 257
Wendt, Lillian J. 15
Wheeler, Diane 125
White, Mary Lou 54
Wiggs, Susan 241
Wiklund, Joanne 82
Williams, Sue 258
Wilson, Carol 30
Winchell, Linda L. 126
Winter, Madeline F. 119
Wolden, Marilyn R. 269
Wolfe, Phyllis 97
Wood, Edith 37
Wood, Ellen D. 36
Wood, Marilyn 277
Workman, Wilda 99
Wornick, Judy 260
Wright, Joseph 64
Wyman, Judith 33
Wysong, Breena 93

Youngclaus, Regina 117
Youngdoff, Naomi 28

Zwick, Raymond 191

REF Z 675 .N4 S63 1980